# Kellogg
## on
# Advertising
# & Media

## THE KELLOGG SCHOOL OF MANAGEMENT

EDITED BY

## Bobby J. Calder

**WILEY**

John Wiley & Sons, Inc.

For general information on our other products and services or for technical support, please contact our Customer Care Department within the United States at (800) 762-2974, outside the United States at (317) 572-3993 or fax (317) 572-4002.

Wiley also publishes its books in a variety of electronic formats. Some content that appears in print may not be available in electronic books. For more information about Wiley products, visit our web site at www.wiley.com.

*Library of Congress Cataloging-in-Publication Data:*

Kellogg on advertising and media / edited by Bobby J. Calder.
    p. cm.
  Includes bibliographical references and index.
  ISBN 978-0-470-11986-0 (cloth)
  1. Advertising media planning.   2. Advertising.   I. Calder, Bobby J.
II. J.L. Kellogg Graduate School of Management.

  HF5826.5.K46 2008
  659.1'11—dc22                        2007052392

Printed in the United States of America.

10  9  8  7  6  5  4  3  2  1

# CONTENTS

# FOREWORD

PHILIP KOTLER

$\mathbf{M}$edia-based advertising has been first among equals for the traditional Ps of marketing for over a hundred years. Indeed the advertising agency model of translating a company's marketing strategy into carefully crafted *messages* that are inserted into media vehicles that *reach* the targeted consumer with appropriate *frequency* has perhaps been the most defining characteristic of modern marketing. The product/brand manager works with the agency account, creative, and media specialists to communicate to the consumer the benefits of the product. It is a world that generations of marketers have grown up in.

All this is changing. Today, the standard approach to advertising faces many challenges. The most obvious is consumer overload. The sheer amount of advertising "clutter" has grown to be a burden on consumers. Estimates vary but it is clear that consumers are exposed to thousands of messages a day. At the very least, this means that consumers process ads in an ever more cursory way. Certainly companies attempt to make their ads stand out more, but this is an increasingly uphill battle.

Even more challenging is the fact that consumers themselves are changing. Consumers engage more and more in ad avoidance. They actively seek to limit their exposure to advertising. Digital video recorders (DVRs) are only the tip of the iceberg of this phenomenon. Younger consumers engage in surfing behavior specifically intended to decrease the burden of information overload. They want to take in only information that they actively select. A new millennial generational cohort of consumers may even have trained itself to be fairly oblivious to the advertising around them. And the messages that manage to get through may be subjected to a more critical eye based on a sophisticated, not to say cynical, consciousness of potential manipulation by marketers. It is coming to be as likely for an ad to be posted on YouTube for comment, or ridicule, as it is for the ad to elicit a really strong intention to buy the product.

There is a great need to rethink the traditional approach to advertising. There is a need to think through basic issues such as how to design messages that do not necessarily depend on the consumer consciously processing the message's content. There is a need to think about information that consumers get not from ads but from media coverage of companies and products. There is a need to think about the relative effectiveness of ads carried on traditional media versus ads carried on new digital media. There is a need to think about how ads can be customized to be more relevant to individual consumers. There is a need to think about how ads can be more interactive, facilitating more two-way communication. In general, there is a need to think about how the consumers' engagement with the medium affects their response to advertising. All of these issues and more are explored in this book.

This book reflects a continuing interest at the Kellogg School in the future of marketing and advertising. And the realization that changes in media management and media technology will play a profound role in this future. Our MBA program has both a major in marketing and a major in media management. Students frequently combine the two. We have a Media Management Center for research studies that is jointly affiliated with the Kellogg School of Management and the Medill School of Journalism. We have developed relationships with experts in a variety of companies for dialogues about the future of marketing and advertising. The variety of companies represented by contributors to this book reflects this.

It is important to remember that this book is not intended to be the last word on marketing and advertising. Quite the contrary, our hope is that it is among the first words on the change that is taking place and what the future might look like. The book does not present a pat, business trade book approach, telling you how things should be done. The reader is invited to think along with us.

# INTRODUCTION
## ADVERTISING AND MEDIA

BOBBY J. CALDER

$\mathbf{N}$ot too long ago, this title would have signaled the discussion of narrow issues in the backwaters of marketing. Today, it is the new frontier. The past was cheap media and relatively easy advertising. The future? Well, the future is worth thinking about, but not predicting. That is what this book is about.

Throughout most of the twentieth century, consumers and companies had a bargain. In return for cheap, easily accessible media, consumers agreed to look at ads. It was not a bad deal for either side. It made a company's job of communicating and building brands easier and consumers got cheap information and entertainment. The highpoint was three TV networks that came over the air for free with the turn of a 1 to 13 dial. All the consumer had to do was sit back and watch the ads go by. From there, TV began to fragment into hundreds of networks and the cable bill became a major consumer expenditure. The change was not overnight, the official date will have to wait for hindsight, but the era of cheap media and relatively easy advertising was over. If you are reading this, you have probably gotten the word.

It is difficult to sort out cause from effect, but the changes are clear. Most visible is the decline in network TV viewing and ad avoidance with digital video recorders (DVRs). No longer is the *sine qua non* of marketing communications the 30-second TV spot. Marketers are increasingly turning to online and mobile advertising, alternative media, product placement, branded entertainment (integration), and other "marketing services" such as customer relationship management (CRM) and direct marketing. Advertising agencies now generate more revenue from these than from traditional media—more than 50 percent at Omnicom, Interpublic, and WPP. But traditional media are taking on new life as well. ESPN is a TV network but it is also a magazine, online site, radio network, mobile network, and more. It is a *media brand*. And like *National Geographic* and many others, it offers myriad ways of communicating with consumers. Technology is the wild card in the deck. A hypermedia environment is likely to compound any corporate missteps.

Most marketers have a sense of being in uncharted territory. This book is an effort to explore the new landscape and to help point out some promising directions. The overarching theme is the search for "engagement." Most marketers today face strong competition from products that are well positioned and at parity in quality. The job of marketing communications is increasingly to find ways of not just delivering a brand benefit message but also of engaging the consumer, of getting the consumer to feel the brand is relevant to their lives. What the new landscape offers, the good news, is an abundance of promising directions for achieving this.

In the first chapter, Ed Malthouse and I examine in some detail the *concept of engagement* and its connection to media. We argue that engagement is not another marketing buzzword. There are those who would like to see it as a buzzword, probably so they can move on to the next one, but it is not. Whether you call it engagement or something else, the challenge marketing faces is to promote not only a liking for the brand but a sense of engagement with it. It is not a new challenge, but it is one that today has more urgency for more brands. We present an approach to measuring engagement and show the relationship of media engagement to advertising effectiveness.

Mike Schreiber of NBC Universal, and a Kellogg graduate, then looks at how TV is moving from a lean-back medium to be more of a lean-forward medium. The development of *interactive TV* offers considerable promise in this regard. Marketers in the future may be able to engage consumers with their brands as much with the old medium of TV as with online and other new media.

Scott Berg of Hewlett Packard makes the case for moving on to the *new media*. He provides insight into the opportunities and the potential pitfalls. Engagement will come from burning your boats and learning to use online and other new media.

Claudio Marcus of Visible World, and another Kellogg graduate, adds a different dimension. He and his company are pioneers in customizing video for TV and online. Commercials no longer need to be static. *Tailored ads* can be dynamically designed to fit specific consumers. A path to greater engagement lies in moving away from treating consumers as a mass audience.

Jim Webster, against this backdrop, reviews the evolving field of *audience measurement*. Accountability is the watchword among marketers today. It is essential for measurement to keep pace with changes in the advertising and media landscape.

Angela Lee revisits the core advertising discipline of *message design*. She points out that in the past advertisers assumed that consumers were processing and absorbing brand messages. Increasingly, we must face the possibility that consumers do not dwell on brand messages. It may be better to design messages intended for less conscious processing by consumers.

The next three chapters look at the company's larger environment. Michelle Roehm and Alice Tybout turn to marketing communications in a world of hypermedia. They provide specific advice as to what a company should do when confronted with a *crisis situation*. Then Daniel Diermeier considers how a company should manage its *corporate reputation* on an ongoing basis by monitoring all of the media communications surrounding it. Clarke Caywood calls for an expanded role for *public relations* in recognizing that marketing communications should be targeted at a wide variety of stakeholders in a highly interdependent world.

Jim Newcomb of Boeing, and a Kellogg graduate, shows that the use of sophisticated media can bring increased engagement with *B-to-B products* as well. He points out that marketing typically does not extend very deeply into the personal selling process that is at the core of B-to-B. Marketing can play a greater role, however, by using intensive and immersive media.

Charles Spinosa and David Le Brocquy of Vision Consulting join me in contending that the search for engagement will require more than an advertising strategy. Companies need a parallel commitment strategy that uses contacts between employees and customers, and even employees with each other, to turn the brand promise into something that is enacted by employees. This requires more than CRM or internal communications. It requires *commitment conversations with the customer*. The organization itself becomes an interactive medium of marketing communication.

Julie Roehm, who has led change efforts at companies like Ford and Wal-Mart, gives advice on how to get organizations to face change. Perhaps the biggest obstacle to taking advantage of the new advertising and media landscape is to get the company to embrace *marketing change*.

Finally, Richard Kolsky and I take up the relationship between advertisers and media companies. Very often there has been a wall limiting the interaction of advertisers and content providers. Yet, this flies in the face of the current trend toward *advertising and media content integration,* as in product placements. We try to provide an approach to dealing with both the practical and the ethical issues that arise from closer relationships between journalistic and artistic content providers and advertisers.

This book is thus intended to provide a road map to the emerging new world of advertising and media. It is not a list of prescriptions or predictions. It is a map of potential paths to greater consumer engagement.

# CHAPTER 1

# MEDIA ENGAGEMENT AND ADVERTISING EFFECTIVENESS

BOBBY J. CALDER and EDWARD C. MALTHOUSE

In an era of extreme advertising clutter and consumer avoidance, perhaps no other recent concept has captured more interest from marketers than *engagement*. This interest is symptomatic of changes in the field. Traditionally, marketers have thought about advertising as a process of translating a brand, expressed as a benefit, a promise to the consumer, a value proposition, or a positioning in the consumer's mind into a message that is delivered to the consumer through some medium. This advertising will be effective to the extent that the consumer values the brand idea and the message does a good job creatively of communicating the idea. Two things are critical, the quality of the brand and the quality of the message. The media used is more of a tactical matter of achieving the desired reach and frequency against the consumer target group. The present interest in engagement brings something new to this picture.

You can think about engagement in two ways. One way, and the focus here, is on *engagement with the advertising medium*. If the journalistic or entertainment content of a medium engages consumers, this engagement may affect reactions to the ad. In the past, the medium was thought of as being only a vehicle for the ad, a matter of buying time or space to place the ad to expose the audience to it—a matter of buying eyeballs. But this ignores the fact that the medium provides a context for the ad. If the media content engages

The authors wish to thank the Magazine Publishers of America, the Newspaper Association of America, the Online Publishers Association, the Knight Ridder Foundation, the Meredith Corporation, Starcom United States, and the Media Management Center at Northwestern University for supporting our research. We wish to thank Suzanne B. Calder for comments on the manuscript.

consumers, this in turn can make the ad more effective. Another way of thinking about engagement is in terms of *engagement with the advertised brand itself.* We return to this at the end of the chapter; the focus here is on how engagement with the medium affects advertising effectiveness.

The Advertising Research Foundation (ARF) defines engagement as follows: "Engagement is turning on a prospect to a brand idea enhanced by the surrounding media context" (ARF 2006). This definition highlights the synergy between the brand idea and media context as the key issue for marketers. What is not clear from the definition is what engagement *is,* as opposed to what it might do.

## WHAT IS ENGAGEMENT?

We all know what engagement feels like. It embodies a sense of involvement. If a person is engaged with a TV program, he or she is connected with it and relates to it. But the concept is hard to pin down beyond this. Ultimately, we need not only to pin it down but also to measure it.

Let's start with what engagement *is not.* Our conceptualization of engagement is different from others who often characterize it in ways that we regard as the *consequences* of engagement. Marc (1966), for example, defines engagement as "how disappointed someone would be if a magazine were no longer published." Syndicated market research often asks whether a publication is "one of your favorites," whether a respondent would "recommend it to a friend" or is "attentive." Many equate engagement with behavioral usage. That is, they define engaged viewers or readers as those who spend substantial time viewing or who read frequently.

While all of these outcomes are important, we argue that they are consequences of engagement rather than engagement itself. It is engagement with a TV program that causes someone to want to watch it, to be attentive to it, to recommend it to a friend, or to be disappointed if it were no longer on the air. Likewise, it is the absence of engagement that will likely cause these outcomes not to occur. But, while these outcomes may reflect engagement, many other things can produce the same outcomes as well. A person may watch a TV program for many reasons. Your spouse may watch it with you to be companionable. Someone in the household gets a magazine so you look at it in spare moments because it is on the coffee table. You like the local newspaper and even recommend it to people moving into the area, but you do not have time to read it yourself. All of these outcomes or consequences are due to something else besides engagement. They should not be confused with engagement. Moreover, to the extent that an outcome is due to engagement, the outcome still does not tell us what engagement actually *is.*

To think about what engagement really means, come back to engagement as a sense of involvement, of being connected with something. This intuition is essentially correct. It needs elaboration to be useful, but it is correct in that it captures a fundamental insight—engagement comes from *experiencing* something like a magazine or TV program in a certain way. To understand engagement, we need to be able to understand the experiences consumers have with media content.

The notion of focusing on consumer experiences has itself become a hot topic in marketing, and the question that follows is: What is an experience? A simple answer is that an experience is something that the consumer is conscious of happening in his or her life. The philosopher John Dewey (1934/1980) captured the nuances of experience best:

> . . . we have *an* experience when the material experienced runs its course to fulfillment. Then and then only is it integrated within and demarcated in the general stream of experience from other experiences . . . is so rounded out that its close is a consummation and not a cessation. Such an experience is a whole and carries with it its own individualizing quality and self-sufficiency. It is *an* experience. (p. 35)

There is always experience, but Dewey points out that much of it is "so slack and discursive that it is not *an* experience" (p. 40). Much of what we do has, in Dewey's words, an "anesthetic" quality of merely drifting along. An experience is the sense of doing something in life that leads somewhere. Experiences can be profound but typically they just stand out from the ordinary in the stream of experience.

Experiences are inherently qualitative. That is, they are composed of the stuff of consciousness. They can be described in terms of the thoughts and feelings consumers have about what is happening when they are doing something. As such they are primarily accessible through qualitative research that attempts to "experience the experience" of the consumer (for more on this view of qualitative research, see Calder 1977, 1994, 2000). Thus, we can seek to capture the qualitative experience of, for instance, reading a magazine. This experience will have a holistic or unitary quality but can be broken down into constitutive experiences that have their own holistic quality. As we will see, one such experience for magazines has to do with consumers building social relationships by talking about and sharing what they read with others, the *Talking About and Sharing* experience. You have undoubtedly had the experience of reading something then using it in conversation with others. To the extent that this experience stands out in the ordinary stream of experience, it constitutes a form of engagement with the magazine.

To further clarify what is unique about the engagement concept, it is useful to distinguish experiences that are closely related to engagement from other experiences. For this, we turn to some ideas from psychology.

### Engagement and Experiences

Although much of our work is anchored in qualitative research on experiences, a theoretical model proposed by Columbia University psychologist Tory Higgins (2005, 2006) provides a useful framework for thinking about the relationship of engagement and experience. We follow Higgins and a long tradition in psychology of conceptualizing experience as either *approach* toward something or *avoidance* of something. Experiencing something positively means feeling attracted toward it; experiencing something negatively means feeling repulsion away from it. This holistic experience of approach or avoidance is what we want to understand.

Figure 1.1 presents a model of the approach–avoidance experience. One factor affecting the experience is the hedonic value associated with the object of the experience—what is desirable or undesirable about it, the pleasure/displeasure taken in it. This factor, call it *liking,* primarily affects the direction of the experience toward approach or toward avoidance. The second factor affecting the experience is engagement. Engagement is thus one of two components of experience, and it is different from the liking component of

**Figure 1.1**
**Engagement as Motivational Experience**

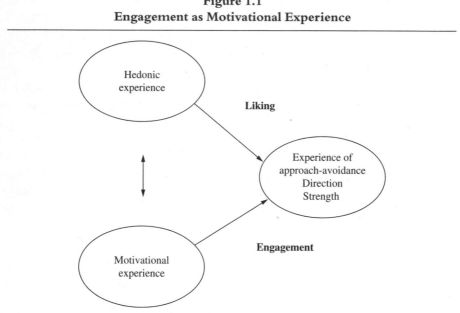

Adapted from Higgins (2006).

experience. I may like the local newspaper, but not be particularly engaged with it. Or, I may be engaged with it, but not particularly like it.

Engagement stems from the underlying motivational component of the experience. According to Higgins (2006), it is a second source of experience that:

> does not involve the hedonic experience of pleasure or pain per se but rather involves the experience of a motivational force to make something happen (experienced as a force of attraction) or make something not happen (experienced as a force of repulsion). Although the hedonic experience and the motivational force experience often are experienced holistically, conceptually they are distinct from one another. (p. 441)

It is thus useful to separate the hedonic side of the experience from the motivational side and to view engagement as the motivational side of the experience.

Media engagement is to be distinguished from liking, that is, the experience of the desirable or undesirable features of a particular magazine, program, or site. In contrast, engagement is about how the magazine or other media product is experienced motivationally in terms of making something happen (or not happen) in the consumer's life. Note that the magazine experience we described earlier, consumers building social relationships by talking about and sharing what they read with others, is just this sort of experience. It is more about what the content does for the consumer than what the consumer likes about it per se.

These considerations lead us to view engagement as the sum of the motivational experiences consumers have with the media product. The individual experiences contribute more or less to an overall level of engagement. We therefore analyze engagement in the way shown in Figure 1.2. Separate motivational experiences underlie an overall level of engagement. One of these might be the *Talking About and Sharing* experience. It is this overall level of media engagement and its constitutive experiences that could affect responses to an ad in the medium. Engagement and experiences may also affect things like usage of the media product, but this should be viewed as a consequence or side effect.

Besides providing some conceptual clarity for thinking about engagement, this discussion also points up the reason why media engagement may be important to marketing. All things being equal, it is probably a good idea to place ads in media vehicles that consumers like (have a positive hedonic experience with). However, there is much more at stake with engagement. If consumers are engaged with a media vehicle, and are having at least some strong

**Figure 1.2**
**Analysis of Engagement and Experiences**

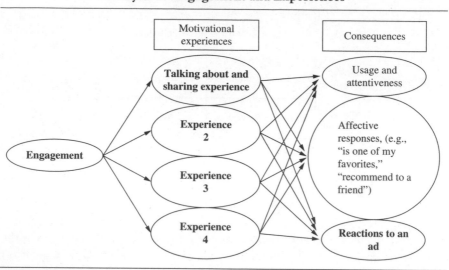

motivational experiences, an ad potentially becomes part of something the consumer is trying to make happen in his or her life.

## Identifying Experiences

Engagement is comprised of motivational experiences. To understand and measure engagement, we need to identify relevant experiences. It is useful to think about these experiences in the following way. As already indicated, some experiences may be positive, about *Approach,* whereas others may be negative, about *Avoidance.* Another useful distinction is that some experiences may reflect *Intrinsic Motivation* and others *Extrinsic Motivation* (see Deci and Ryan 1985). In the former case, the consumer's goal is the activity—it is an end in itself. In the latter case, the activity is the means to an end—the goal is extrinsic to the activity itself. The difference between these two cases is the person who relaxes with the Sunday newspaper over brunch versus the person who busily scans the newspaper looking for something to do later in the evening or for travel tips for a vacation. Figure 1.3 identifies the four types of experiences relevant to engagement.

We refer to Approach experiences, where the activity itself is the goal, as *Transportation.* Here the consumer's goal is either to be transported into a different state, from bored to happy for example, or to be transported into taking

**Figure 1.3**
**The Four Types of Engagement Experiences**

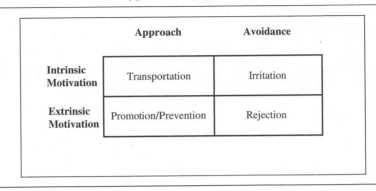

| | Approach | Avoidance |
|---|---|---|
| **Intrinsic Motivation** | Transportation | Irritation |
| **Extrinsic Motivation** | Promotion/Prevention | Rejection |

part in an activity. The latter is especially significant in the case of media. It is the experience of being absorbed into a story or program and shutting out the real world. Researchers (Green and Brock 2000; Green, Strange, and Brock 2002) have defined this form of transportation as "a convergent process, where all mental systems and capacities become focused on events occurring in the narrative (2000, p. 701)." Csikszentmihalyi (1990, 1997) describes the more general variant of the experience as the individual being caught up in the "flow" of an activity and absorbed into it.

Approach experiences where the goal is extrinsic to the activity are of two kinds. Higgins (1997) distinguished between Promotion experiences and Prevention experiences. The Promotion experience involves the pursuit of hopes and aspirations; the goal is to gain or attain something. The Prevention experience involves duties or obligations, what one ought to do; the goal is to avoid losses.

In our work on media experiences, we have focused on Promotion experiences. Prevention experiences are to some extent just a different way some individuals approach a goal. The *Talking About and Sharing* experience noted previously may be experienced more as a Prevention experience by some consumers (as in using the media content to be sure that one does not get left out of a conversation or appear ignorant). This distinction deserves more attention in future work. Wang and Lee (2006) demonstrate that exposure to an ad in the context of either a Promotion or a Prevention experience can differentially affect a given ad.

Avoidance experiences are of two types. When the goal is extrinsic to the activity, we have the simple case of Rejection. The person wants to have something not happen as a consequence of the activity. When the person wants to avoid the activity itself, we refer to this as Irritation. The person feels forced to perform the activity and is annoyed by this and adverse to it. Irritation experiences are mitigated, but not irrelevant, in the case of media use because consumers generally exercise choice in this area. In both of these cases, the experience contributes negatively to engagement, that is to say, to disengagement. To see the difference between Rejection and Irritation think about local TV news. A person who sees watching the news as a waste of time because the things it covers are trivial is experiencing Rejection. Probably this person rarely watches the news or views it incidentally. A person who watches the news but feels disheartened by the frequency of negative stories is experiencing Irritation.

This classification of experiences provides a framework for identifying the breadth of experiences that may underlie media engagement. Another dimension to this, however, is depth (Figure 1.4).

Every individual's experience is idiosyncratic to herself and the specific object of that experience. An example of an idiosyncratic experience is, for example, you reading a certain magazine. For marketing purposes, we cannot hope to deal with experiences at this level. It is more feasible to try to identify common or shared experiences that cut across people and apply to a wide variety of media products. We can seek to deal with readers of the top 100

**Figure 1.4**
**Levels of Experience Description**

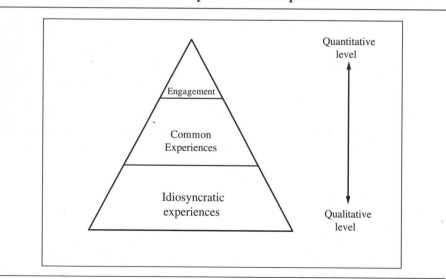

**Table 1.1**
**Dutch Media Monitor Experiences**

| Experience | Description |
| --- | --- |
| Information | Offered something new, gave useful information, taught me about what is going on |
| Stimulation | Excited me, made me curious, made me enthusiastic |
| Negative emotions | Irritated me, was unclear, disturbed me, made me sad |
| Transformation | Gave me enjoyment, made me cheerful, made me forget everything for a moment, was relaxing |
| Pastime | Filled an empty moment |
| Identification | Recognized myself in it, felt involved, empathized with it |
| Social | Subject of conversation |
| Practical use | Useful tips/advice, motivated to do something |

magazines, for instance. For these readers, we can try to identify experiences that are common in the sense of being similar, though certainly not exactly the same, across readers and magazines. We seek to identify experiences that large numbers of consumers have, to varying extents, with different media products. At a higher level still, these experiences reduce to an overall level of engagement, and this is highly comparable across people.

There is one last point about identifying experiences. It is possible to take a top-down approach or a bottom-up approach. For instance, Fred Bronner and Peter Neijens (2006) at the University of Amsterdam have taken more of a top-down approach with their Dutch Media Monitor Experience study. Based on a review of the literature, they identified eight experiences as important for media and developed metrics (scales) to measure them (see Table 1.1) Our approach is more bottom-up. We try to identify common experiences from qualitative research on idiosyncratic experiences—the bottom level in Figure 1.4. This tends to lead to a longer list of somewhat narrower experiences. Aside from this, however, the two approaches seem to yield comparable results.

We now describe our approach in more detail. Following this we describe specific media engagement experiences and consider the evidence that media engagement impacts advertising effectiveness.

# IDENTIFYING MEDIA EXPERIENCES

Media experiences, as noted, can be described at different levels. At the most basic level, there is the concrete experience of the particular content of a given media product. While this level of description may well be of interest, it is too saturated with specific details and unique characteristics of the particular content to be useful for comparison purposes. If our goal is to compare across different media products, we need a more abstract or generalized description of experiences, albeit one that tries to preserve something of the underlying idiosyncratic quality of experience.

We approach this in the following way. As a first step, we conduct qualitative research in the form of individual in-depth interviews with users. Each interview focuses on a specific media product, such as a specific magazine. But we seek to describe the experiences talked about in the interviews at a level that is common across the media category, for example, across magazines. We essentially seek to paraphrase the specific things that people report experiencing with individual media products in a way that preserves the common essence, or gist, across products but does not include details peculiar to individual products in the category. For example, exactly what people say about *Better Homes and Gardens* magazine is different from exactly what others say about *Parents* magazine, but at a higher-level people may be describing the same experience. They may be describing the extent to which they would say, paraphrasing across users, that "I get ideas from this magazine." We refer to this description as an *experience item*. The "ideas" in the item could be about designing a flowerbed or keeping a toddler occupied on a long trip—in either case, the reader is having a *Utilitarian* experience.

The logic of our approach is as follows. From qualitative interviews we induce a large number of experience items. Then we employ quantitative methods to explore the relationships among the items. If some experience items are highly interrelated, this indicates that they are alternative measures of the same experience. No single item is a perfect measure because no one item captures a single experience in total. We refer to these sets of items as experience metrics or scales and use them to measure experiences.

We have applied this approach to magazines, newspapers, TV, and online sites. The following examples are from our research of some media experiences. Although our research has focused on identifying experiences for different categories of media, for present purposes we describe experiences that occur similarly with several kinds of media. For each experience, we include some of the statements made by consumers that characterize the experience.

### Talking About and Sharing Experience

- Reading/looking at this magazine/newspaper/TV programming/site gives me something to talk about.

- I bring up things I have read/looked at in this magazine/newspaper/TV programming/site in conversations with many other people.
- I use things I have read/looked at in this magazine/newspaper/TV programming/site in discussions or arguments with people I know.
- A big reason I read it is to make myself more interesting to other people.
- I show things in the magazine/newspaper/site/program to people in my family.

This is a Promotion experience (though as noted earlier it could well have Prevention overtones for some consumers). The goal is to become more interesting to other people. Media enables people to be more interesting because they can talk to others, and even to themselves, about what they read or view. In some cases, topics could be about strange or silly things: "Did you see where some guy tried to dry his dog by sticking it in the microwave oven?" "Can you believe that some couple in New Zealand wants to call their son '4real?' Imagine when the poor kid goes to school." Some people like to argue about or debate current events. "Why on earth would the governor do this when all the facts show that it is the worst possible decision?" "How could the quarterback have been so stupid?" "Why is the team trading that player?" The media content engages the consumer in the experience of being more interesting conversationally.

### Utilitarian Experience

- I learn about things to do or places to go in this magazine/newspaper/TV programming/site.
- This magazine/newspaper/TV programming/site gives good tips and advice.
- It shows me how to do things the right way.
- I get good ideas from this magazine/newspaper/TV programming/site.
- You learn how to improve yourself from this magazine/newspaper/TV programming/site.
- It helps me make up my mind and make decisions.
- This magazine/newspaper/TV programming/site provides a lot of "how-to" information.

This is another Promotion experience. A good example of content that is engaging in this way occurs with the experience of cooking TV programs, cooking magazines, newspaper "food" sections, and the like. Consumers use the advice or tips to do something in their own lives—new techniques, ingredients, recipes, and so on. Likewise, a gardening magazine could help a person decide what flowers to plant in a shady location. An online astronomy site could tell someone how to find a certain star. A TV program could provide the viewer with diets and exercises to try out.

### Makes Me Smarter Experience

- It addresses issues or topics of special concern to me.
- It updates me on things I try to keep up with.
- It's important I remember later what I have read/looked at.
- Even if I disagree with information in this magazine/newspaper/TV programming/site, I feel I have learned something valuable.
- I look at it as educational. I am gaining knowledge.

The Makes Me Smarter experience is similar to the Utilitarian experience, but is focused more on keeping up with certain topics than on how to do something specific. Keeping up with international affairs by using certain publications or programs is a Makes Me Smarter experience, as is keeping up with celebrities, next year's automobiles, fashion, technologies, and so on. An article in a computer magazine describing the next generation of storage devices is providing a Makes Me Smarter experience, while an article describing how to install a program is perhaps more of a Utilitarian experience. A given media product may well produce both kinds of experience.

### Credible and Safe Experience

- They do a good job of covering things. They don't miss anything.
- I trust it to tell the truth.
- It does not sensationalize things.
- You don't have to worry about accuracy with this magazine/newspaper/ TV programming/site.
- It is unbiased in its reporting.
- I would trust this site with any information I give it. (more for online sites)
- I feel safe in using this site. (more for online sites)

This is more of a Prevention experience. The goal is about not being misled. This is distinct from the Makes Me Smarter experience, which is more about having confidence that topics and stories the consumer thinks are important are covered.

### Timeout Experience

- I lose myself in the pleasure of reading/looking at this magazine/newspaper/TV programming/site.
- It is a quiet time.
- I like to kick back and wind down with it.
- It's an escape.
- The magazine/newspaper/TV programming/site takes my mind off other things that are going on.
- I like to go to this magazine/newspaper/TV programming/site when I am eating or taking a break.
- I feel less stress after reading it.
- It is my reward for doing other things.
- This magazine/newspaper/TV programming/site improves my mood, makes me feel happier.

This is a Transportation experience. The experience is one of having a break and forgetting about everything else, of being transported into a better mood or state of mind. With some kinds of media, it is also possible to separate out the experience of being transported into the narrative world of the content.

### Visual Imagery Experience

- I look at the pictures in it and think "Wow."
- Most often I look at the pictures/videos before anything else. I like to look at the pictures/video even if I don't read the story.
- I sometimes show a picture in it to someone else.
- I like to look at the pictures for a while.
- I love the photography on this show.
- The photography is one of the main reasons why I watch this show.

This is another Transportation experience. The experience is one of being absorbed visually into the content. Travel magazines may feature photography that makes readers feel as if they are there. Other magazines often feature pictures of beautiful homes and food that give a similar vicarious experience. Even newspaper photographs can convey this sense of being there. Television can obviously be visually intensive as well.

### Regular Part of My Day Experience

- It's part of my routine.
- I use it as a big part of getting my news for the day.

- I usually read/look at it at the same time of the day.
- This is one of the sites I always go to anytime I am online.
- I follow a routine pattern each time I read it, reading the same sections in the same order.
- It helps me get my day started in the morning.

For some, breakfast is not complete without watching a morning news program. Watching is part of a ritual: turn on the program, make coffee and breakfast, and watch or perhaps listen. For others, the morning newspaper is the habitual breakfast companion. Some people have a news site (e.g., cnn.com or nytimes .com) or aggregators such as Yahoo as their homepage. These sites become a habitual way of checking news. Some people have a ritual of watching the late-night news before going to bed. They do not feel ready for bed until they have watched it. Similar experiences occur with all sorts of other media content. This is a Transportation experience in the sense that the media content puts people in a comfortable, calming state of mind. For some people, as noted next, the news can result in an Irritation experience that is the opposite of this calming effect.

### Overload, Too Much Experience

- Reading/looking at this magazine/newspaper/TV programming/site makes me feel like I am drowning in the flood of information that comes out each day.
- It tries to cover too much.
- Too many of the articles are too long.
- It has too many special sections.
- I wish this newspaper had fewer pages.
- Unread copies of this newspaper pile up.

This is a Rejection experience. It is especially strong for many consumers for newspapers, as reflected in some of the preceding statements. Consumers wish to avoid the deluge of information that they feel they are being exposed to continuously. The experience is a negative one, a feeling of drowning in too much information and wanting to escape. This experience also touches on the issue of control (especially with online media). Consumers resent having information forced on them.

### Ad Interference Experience

- The number of ads makes it harder to read/look at the magazine/news-paper/TV programming/site.

- I make a special effort to skip over and avoid looking at ads.
- I am annoyed because too many of the ads on this site have too much movement.
- I don't like the number of pop-up ads on this site.
- All too often the ads are dull or boring.
- I hate the inserts they put in it.
- Sometimes the ads are overdone or even weird.
- The ads are so similar in style they blend together.

This is an Irritation experience. The consumer does not want to look at many of the ads in the media product but feels forced to. The same experience can occur with other kinds of content. For instance, with TV many consumers experience violent stories in this way. The local news leads with the automobile accident and you cannot avoid seeing it. It should be noted that advertising is not necessarily part of a negative experience. In fact, advertising can contribute to positive experiences as well.

These experiences are good examples but represent only a few of the experiences consumers can have that engage them with media content. As already noted, some of these experiences arise more with some media than others. The following is an experience characteristic of online media.

### Community Connection Experience

- A big reason I like this site is what I get from other users.
- I'm as interested in input from other users as I am in the regular content on this site.
- Overall, the visitors to this site are pretty knowledgeable about the topics it covers.
- This site does a good job of getting its visitors to contribute or provide feedback.
- I'd like to meet other people who regularly visit this site.
- I've gotten interested in causes I otherwise wouldn't have because of this site.

As indicated, this Promotion experience is most associated with online sites. The experience is one of being able to connect to others and participate in a larger social collective.

These examples illustrate the variety of motivational experiences consumers can have with media products. Keep in mind, however, that these are constitutive experiences. *An* experience with a media product will ordinarily be a combination of different constitutive experiences. While *an* experience is unitary, it does appear that its constitutive experiences affect advertising independently of each other. Wang and Calder (2006) have shown, for example, that a Transportation experience affects an ad independently of the effects of a Promotion experience with the media vehicle. Breaking down the holistic overall experience is useful for marketing purposes. We now turn to the measurement of experiences.

## METRICS FOR MEASURING MEDIA EXPERIENCES AND ENGAGEMENT

Advertising and media organizations should measure experiences and engagement for several reasons. First and foremost, experiences with media content can affect reactions to advertising. We present evidence for this in the next section. Marketers need to understand the experiences offered by various media vehicles when placing ads. We also offer some evidence that ads appearing in vehicles that are experientially congruent with the ads will be more effective. So it may be that advertisers should consider media experiences even in creating the ad itself. As for media organizations, they should monitor consumer experiences as a marketing management tool. Recall that experiences, in part, drive usage of the media product. A drop in the *Talking About and Sharing* experience could be an early warning and a diagnostic tool, alerting the media organization to take action before usage levels also decrease. At a more micro level, a media organization may wish to test new content to determine whether certain experiences can be improved. For example, an online site might develop a feature to increase the *Utilitarian* experience. It is necessary for all of these reasons to be able to measure media experiences and engagement.

An organization wishing to measure experiences has a choice between *à la carte* and *table d'hôte* options, depending on its objectives. Consider an advertiser who wants a media vehicle high on certain experiences, or a media company that wants to focus on certain experiences to attract consumers and/or advertisers. Both could measure these particular experiences in an *à la carte* fashion, measuring just the experiences that are relevant to them. For a magazine, let's say, metrics might be added to an ongoing reader survey. The magazine would only have to add a set of questions specific to the experiences they are focusing on. If one of the experiences was the *Timeout* experience described in the previous section, measurement could be accomplished by asking survey participants to rate how much they agree or disagree on a five-point scale with three to five statements such as:

- I like to kick back and wind down with [magazine name].
- I lose myself in the pleasure of reading [magazine name].

- [Magazine name] takes my mind off other things that are going on.
- I feel less stress after reading [magazine name].

The average of the ratings of these four statements measures a survey respondent's *Timeout* experience.

In our research, we have developed scale items like this one for a variety of experiences. The resulting metrics or scales have been shown to have good psychometric properties. For most experiences with a particular medium, we have been able to show that the statements "hold together" as a scale in multiple studies using different data collection methods and across many publications within the medium. For example, in the case of online web sites, we have run three separate experience studies. The first studied 39 general news, business, local news, and aggregator web sites using a marketing research panel. After identifying the experiences, we conducted two studies in which online users were intercepted at various web sites in order to confirm that the scales factored properly and had acceptable reliabilities. The experience scales are thus useful for a variety of sites and data collection methods. Likewise, we have run multiple studies for newspapers, magazines, and TV news.

An organization may wish to add or substitute statements that are more specific to their media product. Care should be taken, however, to find items that relate to the motivational experience of interest. Ideally, the reliability and validity of these items should be tested.

Experience scores can be factor analyzed to identify an overall engagement measurement. For example, Calder, Malthouse, and Schaedel (in press) measured eight experiences with news web sites (the sample of sites included About.com, Washingtonpost.com, PalmBeachPost.com, Reuters .com, DallasNews.com, etc.). The experiences were selected à la carte for relevance to the nature of the sites. We first used a confirmatory factor analysis to show that the eight experiences were distinct and reliable. Next, factoring the eight experiences yielded the structural relations shown in Figure 1.5. Notice that in this case two overall higher-level engagement factors emerged. One was personal engagement with the site reflecting a number of experiences such as the *Temporal Regular Part of My Day* experience. The factor loadings shown in Figure 1.5 indicate that this experience counts for a little less in the overall personal engagement experience than the *Stimulation and Inspiration* experience. Personal engagement is comparable to the sort of individualistic experiences found with magazines and newspapers. In the case of these news web sites, however, another type of overall engagement emerged, which we call *interactive* engagement.

**Figure 1.5**
**Online Engagement and Experiences Measurement Model Used**
**for Testing Effects on Advertising**

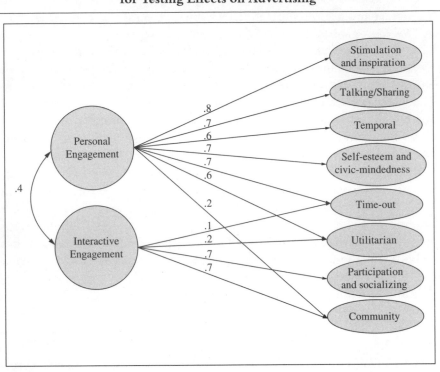

Experiences such as the *Community Connection* experience described earlier factor more heavily into this. The second-order factor scores for personal and interactive engagement can be used in subsequent analyses, as we illustrate with the study described next.

Advertisers and media companies may wish to conduct a more comprehensive assessment of experiences and engagement. Ideally, this assessment might be obtained from syndicated marketing research firms who could measure a broad cross section of experiences spanning many media vehicles. Due to the larger number of questions, this might have to be a stand-alone engagement study as opposed to adding a few questions to another survey. The Appendix at the end of this chapter makes some table d'hôte recommendations for magazines, newspapers, online sites, and TV programming based on our research. These recommendations enable an organization to measure several types of experiences that are common for a medium.

In the case of media products with a wide breadth of content and high degree of similarity with other competitive products across publications, our table d'hôte recommendations provide a good starting point. It is more difficult to make table d'hôte recommendations for specialized media products. You may wish to omit some experiences or even identify new, more relevant ones. For example, the distinction between the *Utilitarian* and another experience we call *Inspiration* may be too subtle for some purposes. Utilitarian is about feeling a media product gives actionable advice and tips while Inspiration is about making consumers feel they can do important and meaningful things in their life. If an article telling the story of a woman who lost 50 pounds is typical of a magazine's content, it is probably relevant to Inspiration. If the typical article gives specific diets and exercises, then it is probably providing a Utilitarian experience. For some publications about, for example, shelter, health, parenting, the two are distinct and very important. For others, such as news weekly or business publications, the two blend together and this should be factored into the measurement approach.

Our point is that both an advertiser and a media company should think carefully about the experiences that it wants to measure. Our table d'hôte suggestions will be helpful in this.

## ENGAGEMENT AND ADVERTISING EFFECTIVENESS

It may be useful at this point to give a brief summary of the role of media engagement in advertising. The effectiveness of advertising depends on the brand being advertised, the quality of the ad itself, and characteristics of the execution such as the size of the ad and placement in the medium (e.g., back cover, inner front cover, top of the web page). Marketers have not, however, considered one factor in an explicit way—the consumer's engagement with the surrounding media content. The emerging view is that media should not be treated as merely the passive vehicle through which consumers are exposed to ads simply because they are viewing or reading media content. The actual *contact* with the consumer is formed by both the ad and the surrounding media context. The journalistic or entertainment content of the media product itself provides experiences for the viewer or reader that may affect the advertising.

What is the evidence that media engagement and its constitutive experiences can actually impact advertising effectiveness? There have been many demonstrations that the context in which an ad appears can affect consumer reactions.[1] Here, we shall focus more specifically on what is known about how context characterized by media experiences affects reactions. First, we summarize several studies that demonstrate the basic effect. Having established that engagement and experiences affect ads, we examine how often this occurs generally and how important such context effects are relative to other factors such as the size and placement of the ad. Finally, we examine the hypothesis that advertising can be more effective when ads are *experientially congruent* with the media vehicle.

Many different studies have shown that experiences with media content can affect reactions to ads. For example, Malthouse, Calder, and Tamhane (2007) have shown that the extent to which readers experience the content of a magazine as Utilitarian or as Makes Me Smarter is related to standard copy-testing measures for a test ad (Figure 1.6) for a fictitious bottled water product (controlling for any spurious effects due to interest in bottled water and sensitivity to ads in general). As can be seen, both the product and the ad are very straightforward. Yet, these and other experiences with the media context affect consumer reactions to it. A control group was used in this research to strengthen the case for a causal connection.

Likewise, Calder, Malthouse, and Schaedel (2007) have shown that web site users who are engaged with web sites are more positive toward an online travel agency (Orbitz) ad and are more likely to click on the ad. Interestingly, both the types of overall engagement described previously, personal engagement and interactive engagement, as well as many of the constitutive experiences, affected reactions to the Orbitz ad. This research also showed that interactive engagement, which is more uniquely characteristic of online media, affected the ad independently of personal engagement. In other words, both types of engagement contributed to ad effectiveness. A control group was again used in this research to make a stronger case for causality.

The evidence for the impact of media engagement and experiences on advertising is persuasive. But how important is the effect? Existing research is limited to ad testing effects, though the online research mentioned previously did show behavioral effects on click-through behavior. Another way of getting at impact, however, is to compare the effects of media experiences with the effects of other advertising variables that are usually considered important for effectiveness and that enter into the cost of advertising. In another study of over 3,000 actual magazine advertisements, we show that the effects of experiences on ad recall and measures of the actions taken because of seeing the ad are very general, holding across this large sample of ads (Malthouse and Calder 2007). We also show that the experience effects are roughly comparable in strength to execution factors including the size (half-page, full page, etc.), placement (run-of-book, back cover, inner back cover, etc.) and the number of colors in the ad.

**Figure 1.6**
**Media Experiences Increase the Effectiveness of a Generic Test Ad**

The implications of these findings for marketers is potentially profound in that the media selection and price of most advertising is currently determined by audience size and execution factors such as position and ad size, without consideration of engagement in any formal way. Take an example where two magazines have the same rate base and charge the same amount for an ad, but one magazine is more engaging: its readers find the content more Utilitarian. The research suggests that an ad appearing in the more engaging magazine will be more effective than the same ad appearing in the other magazine.

## Congruence between Advertising and the Media Vehicle

Perhaps an even bigger payoff from paying attention to media engagement lies in adjusting the ad itself to the experience of the media vehicle. It seems entirely reasonable to us that an ad that matches the experience of the medium may benefit even more from that experience. We call this the congruency hypothesis. It needs more research, but studies suggest that it is a real possibility. The study described below is particularly intriguing in this regard.

To examine whether some ads benefit from engagement and experiences more than others, we turn to the idea of congruence between an ad and content. Dahlén (2005) reviewed the literature on media context effects and identified possible rationales for why context should affect reactions to ads. One is the congruity principle: "the medium and the advertised brand converge and become more similar in consumers' minds" (p. 90).

Defining congruity is difficult because there are many different, and potentially conflicting, ways that an ad can be congruent with a vehicle. An ad could be congruent in one respect and dissimilar in another. For example, a vehicle and an ad could both have a consistently emotional tone, but the vehicle could have more of a traditional look while the ad has a more modern look. Congruency could even be viewed simply in terms of "endemicness," whether the ad is for a product that fits the literal subject matter of the magazine, for example, table saws in woodworking magazines.

Consistent with our focus on media experiences, however, we studied one form of congruence—the congruence between the experiences with a magazine and the experiences with the ad itself. We applied the logic of measuring experiences to the experience of ads and asked whether congruence between the two experiences impacts advertising effectiveness.

We studied four magazines (*Better Homes and Gardens (BHG), Country Home, Fitness,* and *Parents)* and four actual ads (Ware, Bahary, Calder, and Malthouse 2007). All four magazines are read primarily by women, but come from different magazine categories. The four ads are shown Figure 1.7 and could plausibly appear in any of the four magazines.

After selecting the magazines and ads, we recruited readers of each of the magazines to come to an online research site. On the site, they viewed a copy of the cover of one of the four magazines and read typical content from it. As shown in Figure 1.8, they could actually page through the magazine. One of the pages contained one of the four ads. The readers were asked about their

## Figure 1.7
## Ads Used to Test the Ad Experience–Media Experience Congruence Hypothesis

**Figure 1.8**
**Online Magazine Testing Procedure**

Visual Imagery and Timeout experiences (and four other à la carte experiences) with the magazine and about their reactions to the ad. The magazine experiences were related to ad effectiveness as in other studies. But in this study, we also had another group of readers who were shown the ads without any surrounding editorial content. Each reader was shown one of the ads and asked to rate their Transportation (both Visual Imagery and Timeout) experience with the ad.

We evaluated congruence in the following way. The difference between the average Visual Imagery experience with a magazine and the average Visual Imagery experience with an ad gave a measure of the experiential similarity between the ad and the magazine, as shown in Table 1.2. The distance between *Better Homes and Gardens* and the Behr paint ad is small (0.14) indicating that this ad is experientially similar to, or congruent with, this magazine. In contrast, the distance between *Better Homes and Gardens* and the Neutrogena ad is larger (1.28) indicating incongruence.

The congruity hypothesis predicts that the smaller the distance between the ad and magazine, the more effective the ad. We tested this empirically by relating the average ad effectiveness scores to these congruity measures. The graph in Figure 1.9 shows that there is a strong relationship. The more the Visual Imagery congruence between the magazine and the ad, the more effective the ad.[2]

We thus have evidence that experiential congruence is related to advertising effectiveness. This finding has important implications for both advertisers and media companies. Since the experiential congruence of an ad with the

**Table 1.2**
**Experiential Similarity: Four Magazines and Four Ads**

| Magazine | Behr | Neutrogena | Woolrich | Neosporin |
|---|---|---|---|---|
| *Better Homes and Gardens* | 0.14 | 1.28 | 0.32 | 0.09 |
| *Country Home* | 0.27 | 1.41 | 0.19 | 0.22 |
| *Fitness* | 0.50 | 0.64 | 0.96 | 0.55 |
| *Parents* | 0.54 | 0.60 | 1.00 | 0.59 |

media vehicle affects reactions to the ad, it may be that advertisers should sometimes attempt to maximize congruence. This can be done either by developing creative executions with consideration of the experiences in the intended vehicles or through the selection of vehicles. The thought that understanding the experiences offered by a vehicle should guide the creation of an ad is certainly nontraditional thinking. It is something that deserves more consideration.

**Figure 1.9**
**The Relationship between Visual Imagery Congruence and Advertising Effectiveness**

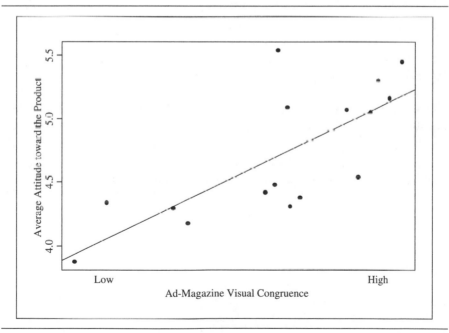

At a minimum, measures of experiential congruency could be incorporated into the media selection process. The experiences associated with particular ads could be ascertained through copy testing. These ad experience metrics and media experience metrics could be used to identify the media products that are maximally congruent with a particular ad or ad campaign. The distance approach used in this research provides a formula for calculating a *Magazine Fit Index* that could be used in this way.

Engagement is not just something that distinguishes one media vehicle from another. It is not just that one magazine offers more engaged readers than another. This research indicates that consumers have experiences with ads in the same way that they have experiences with editorial content. Advertisers need to think about ads, as well as media vehicles, in terms of engagement. And in a section below we will expand this point to the brand itself. Both media companies and advertisers need to give more thought to the congruence of ads with vehicles by considering the fit of ad experiences to media experiences.

## POTENTIAL NEGATIVE EFFECTS OF ENGAGEMENT

We have painted a rosy picture of media engagement and experiences. Unfortunately, things may be a little more complicated. Imagine that you are highly engaged in watching a TV program. A pod of ads appears. You may or may not pay attention to any of the ads. If you do attend to an ad, will your high level of engagement always lead to a more positive impression? Could the effect sometimes even be negative?

The critical issue of course is *intrusion*. It is possible that an ad may intrude on a media experience. Intrusion may produce a negative response from consumers because the advertising harms the experience of the media content. This in turn could lead to a negative reaction to the advertising, compromising its effectiveness. The consumer may feel that the ad has intruded on the experience with the content and accordingly may have a less positive reaction to the ad.

Research has demonstrated that such negative effects can occur. A recent study (Parker and Furnham 2007) looked at an ad embedded in the TV program *Sex and the City,* an episode entitled "Was It Good for You?" They compared reactions to the ad with reactions to the same ad in a nonsexually themed program (*Malcolm in the Middle*). The results of the study indicated that the sexually themed context decreased recall of the ad. It seems safe to assume that the sexually themed programming was engaging to the viewers (especially since they were students). This and similar studies thus suggest that engagement may not always enhance advertising.

Engagement can result in positive effects but sometime it can cause negative effects. Wang and Calder (2006, 2007) are doing ongoing research aimed at understanding this better. The research focuses on Transportation experiences, in particular, the experience of being deeply caught up in the world of the story. In the case of print media and ads, they show that transportation enhances ad effectiveness when an ad is at the end of a story but decreases effectiveness if the ad appears in the middle of the story. As shown in Figure 1.10, an ad at the end of the story benefits from the positive transportation experience but an ad in the middle interrupts the transportation experience and is evaluated more negatively because of this. But it is not the placement of the ad per se that matters. It is the degree of intrusion. Suppose an ad is for a product that is particularly relevant to the consumer. The consumer should pay more attention to this ad, which is good, but this also makes the ad potentially more intrusive. Wang and Calder show that even when an ad is at the end of a story, if the product is goal-relevant for the consumer, a high transportation experience with the story decreases the ad's effectiveness compared to the same ad with a low transportation media experience.

**Figure 1.10**
**Positive and Negative Effects of the Transportation Experience Depending on Ad Placement**

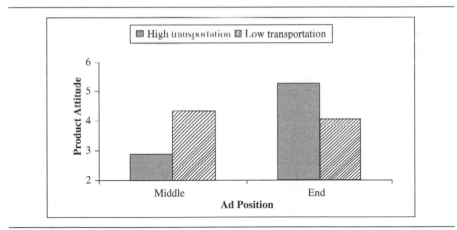

It seems that many things can make ads more intrusive on media experiences. Wang and Calder (2007) look at an ad in a pod of ads appearing at a climatic point in a TV program, an episode of *ER*. In this case, the ad was *less* effective for people who experienced high transportation with the program. The same ad was also tested in a pod of ads appearing at a nonclimatic point in the program. The pod was at a point just after a key story line climaxed and just before another story line picked up. In this case, the ad was *more* effective for people who experienced high transportation with the program.

Congruence also appears to play a role here. In both the *Sex in the City* and the *ER* TV studies, media–ad congruence in terms of whether the ad was sex or health themed mattered. The effect of the media experience on the ad was only obtained if the ad was congruent. This may simply reflect the fact that attention to TV ads is low and that without congruence an ad was simply ignored. Or it may be that congruence accentuates intrusion.

Clearly, further research along these lines is needed. It does seem clear at this point, however, that the intrusion factor should be of real concern to marketers. And, not surprisingly, this concern should perhaps be greater for TV than for other media. One interesting finding in this regard comes from the work of Bronner and Neijens (2006). They had people report both media experiences and their experiences with advertising for different media. The correlation between TV media experiences and the TV advertising experience was lower than for print. This could be due to the more intrusive nature of TV advertising.

Media engagement and experiences can make ads more effective. But if the ad intrudes on the media experience in any way, the ad may perform better in a less engaging media context. To date, research has been designed to show that this is a possibility, but not how likely it is. What is needed is a better understanding of how the experience of the media product and the experience of the ad fit together and how intrusion can interfere with this process. With more research, we would be in a better position to judge how likely negative effects are and when they might occur.

## ENGAGEMENT WITH THE BRAND

We have focused on engagement with the medium. This is important to marketers because media engagement affects advertising and offers a new avenue to making advertising more effective. But engagement is also important in terms of engagement with the brand. Much of what we have said here applies equally to brands. After all, media products are brands just like any other product. Popular as the notion of brand experience has been over the past few years, we believe that a more careful analysis of how the concept of experience applies, what it means, and how it can be measured, along the lines proposed here, could be useful in marketing a great many products. For brands, experiences need to be identified at a deeper level (lower in the hierarchy in Figure 1.4), but the same principles apply.

The marketing of a great many products, not just media products, can be based on identifying, measuring, and improving overall engagement with the product and its constitutive experiences. In fact, we have previously suggested how the marketing enterprise can be organized in this way (see Calder and Malthouse 2003, 2005b; Malthouse and Calder 2005). Figure 1.11 illustrates the process, which we refer to as integrated marketing for reasons that will become apparent.

In an integrated marketing process centered on identifying, measuring, and improving consumer experiences, the brand becomes the concept that defines and describes *an* experience that the marketer intends the consumer to have. It is developed out of an understanding of what the consumer's experience currently is and how the product could be more relevant to that or other

**Figure 1.11**
**Integrated Marketing as the Identification, Measurement, and Improvement of Experiences**

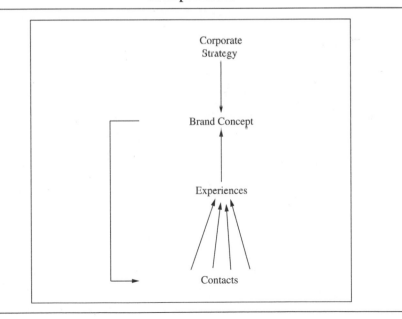

experiences. The focus is on the experience of the consumer, on the product in the context of the consumer's life experiences, and not on the product per se. Again, the brand is the concept that the marketer wants the consumer to have, the concept of how she or he should experience the product. Notice the loop in Figure 1.11, from experience to brand and back from brand to experience. The brand concept is based on experience and then is used to produce the experience and if necessary to improve it.

In this view, *contacts* are anything that creates experiences. A contact could be an aspect of the product that leads to an experience. Or it could be anything else that affects a relevant experience. An ad can be a contact if it affects experience. *If a media vehicle helps engage consumer experiences, the ad is a better contact.* Advertising, or any particular kind of advertising, like TV advertising, is not privileged. Any way of touching the consumer is equally a contact. If new media and new technologies can be used to engage consumers more, advertising should move in this direction. If old media can be managed to build better brands, in just the way suggested here, media engagement will help the old media to remain important in the future as well.

Marketing in our view should, above all, become an exercise in specifying the best set of contacts for matching consumer experiences to the experiences called for by the brand. The identification and measurement of experiences is crucial. The process shown in Figure 1.11 can thus be seen as a continuous feedback loop with experience identification, measurement, and improvement at its core.

## FUTURE OF BRANDS

Marketers love buzzwords and there are already those who say that *engagement* and *experiences* are yesterday's buzzwords. Those looking for the next silver bullet may soon move on. One final thought, however.

We all know that marketing increasingly operates in a world of parity products. The danger of winding up with a commodity product is a clear and present danger to most companies. Faced with this, is there really any choice but to look at the experience of the consumer and to focus on what would make a consumer have *an* experience with the product? Can marketing not be centered on finding and creating experiences for consumers? The future of brands depends on finding and creating experiences, and not just experiences based on liking, but experiences reflecting engagement with what consumers are trying to make happen in their lives.

# APPENDIX

This appendix first gives some additional experiences. See Malthouse et al. (2007) for a complete listing for magazines, Calder and Malthouse (2004) for newspapers, Calder and Malthouse (2005a) for web sites, and Peer, Malthouse, Nesbitt, and Calder (2007) for TV news. We then make our table d'hôte suggestions for advertisers or media organizations wishing to do experience studies.

## Inspirational Experience

- It makes me feel like I can do important things in my life.
- Reading it makes me want to match what others have done.
- It inspires me in my own life.
- Reading this magazine makes me feel good about myself.

The *Inspirational* experience is about believing that one can do something. A good example of the *Inspirational* experience is in the "I Did It!" column of the *Better Homes and Gardens* magazine, featuring normal people who completed impressive projects on their homes. The emphasis is not on how they did it, but rather on the fact that *they* did it.

## Civic Looks Out for My Interests Experience

- Reading this newspaper/watching the news makes me feel like a better citizen.
- I count on this newspaper/station to investigate wrongdoing.
- Reading/watching makes me more a part of my community.
- Our society would be much weaker without newspapers/TV news.
- I think people who do not read this newspaper or one like it are really at a disadvantage in life.

People believe that news organizations are vital to the well-being of a community because they connect them with others in the community. They believe news organizations can serve as a balance against the powerful; in particular, investigative reporting that exposes government corruption or illegal business practices gives the reader this experience.

## Positive Emotional Experience

- The magazine/show definitely affects me emotionally.
- Some articles/stories/episodes touch me deep down.

- It helps me to see that there are good people in the world.
- It features people who make you proud.

Some people feel touched emotionally by stories or programs they read or watch. For example, seeing a children's choir during the holidays or the neighbor who helped someone in need can create this experience.

### Entertainment Experience

- It always has something that surprises me.
- It often makes me laugh.
- It is definitely entertaining.
- Once you start surfing around this site, it's hard to leave.
- I like stories about the weird things that can happen.
- I really do have a lot of fun visiting this site.

This Transportation type experience is about feeling entertained and absorbed in a site, magazine, newspaper, or TV programming. Many TV networks and programs focus on this experience. Certain newspaper content such as the Metropolitan Diary column in the *New York Times* or newspaper stories about unusual topics deliver this experience.

### Ad Attention, Turned On by Ads Experience

- I like the ads as much as articles.
- I look at most of the ads.
- I like how colorful the ads are.
- I click on the ads from this site more often than most other sites I visit.
- This site has ads about things I actually care about.
- I use the ads in this newspaper to understand what is on sale.
- I value the coupons in the newspaper.

With some publications or programs, the advertising can be an important part of the content and can be an important reason for buying the publication, visiting the site, or viewing the program. Looking at the ads is a core part of the experience of reading a fashion magazine. Likewise, the ads in hobby magazines and programs could be relevant to readers/viewers in this way.

*Participation and Socialization Experience*

- I contribute to the conversation on this site.
- I do quite a bit of socializing on this site.
- I often feel guilty about the amount of time I spend on this site socializing.
- I should probably cut back on the amount of time I spend on this site socializing.

This experience applies mostly to online sites and taps into the feeling that the site is replacing real-world activities. "Second Life" is a good example. Other media create a community around a topic (e.g., *American Idol*) that is so involving to its members, they feel they almost spend too much time with it.

Our table d'hôte suggestions for measuring experiences for different media are given in the table that follows. A magazine, for example, might well want to ask about the 10 experiences for which the cells in the table contain the numbers of specific experience items recommended for magazines. The numbers refer to the experience items noted previously or in the text. The experience items would be presented as agree-disagree questions.

Thus, for magazines the *Talking About and Sharing* experience lists "1" as the first recommended item. This refers to "Reading this magazine gives me something to talk about" which is the first item (number 1) in the text where this experience is discussed. Likewise, for Other TV the *Entertainment* experience lists "1, 2, 3, 5" where "1" is "It always has something that surprises me" from the experiences listed previously.

To be comparable with other studies, we recommend using the questions listed next. If comparability is not a goal (i.e., the study is for internal tracking purposes), add or drop experiences and/or exchange items to meet the needs of the study.

Cells that have the notation "LA" indicate that the experience is less applicable in a particular medium. For example, the *Overload, Too Much* experience is less applicable to magazines because usage is more voluntary. "SA" indicates selectively applicable. The experience is highly relevant for some publications within a medium, but not for most. The *Civic Looks Out for My Interests* could be highly relevant for certain news magazines, but will not be central for most hobby, shelter, health, parenting, or women's magazines. *Inspirational* will be relevant for certain cooking and fitness shows, but not for much TV programming. Similarly, *Positive Emotional* will be highly relevant to the Hallmark network, but less so for a sports TV network. Empty cells indicate we do not have recommendations at this time.

| Experiences | Magazines | Media Web | News-papers | TV News | Other TV |
|---|---|---|---|---|---|
| Talking about and sharing | 1, 2, 3 | 1, 2, 3 | 1, 2, 3 | 1, 2, 3 | 1, 2, 3 |
| Utilitarian | 1, 2, 3 | 1, 2, 3 | 1, 2, 3 | 1, 2, 3 | 1, 2, 3 |
| Makes me smarter | 1, 2, 3, 4 | 1, 2, 3, 4 | 1, 2, 3, 4 | 1, 2, 3, 4 | 1, 2, 3, 4 |
| Credible and safe | 1, 2, 3 | 1, 2, 3, 6, 7 | 1, 2, 3 | 1, 2, 3 | |
| Time-out | 1, 2, 3, 4 | 1, 2, 3, 4 | 1, 2, 3, 4 | 1, 2, 3, 4 | 1, 2, 3, 4 |
| Visual imagery | 1, 2, 3 | 1, 2, 3 | 1, 2, 3 | 1, 6, 7 | 1, 6, 7 |
| Regular part of my day | | 1, 2, 3, 4 | 1, 2, 3 | 1, 2, 3 | |
| Overload, too much | LA | LA | 1, 2, 3 | LA | |
| Ad interference | 1, 3, 5, 7 | 1, 2, 3, 4 | 1, 2, 6 | 1, 2, 5 | 1, 2, 5 |
| Community connection | LA | 1, 2, 3, 4 | LA | | |
| Inspirational | 1, 2, 3 | 1, 2, 3 | LA | | SA 1, 2, 3 |
| Civic looks out for my interests | SA | 1, 2, 3, 4 | 1, 2, 3, 4 | 1, 2, 3 | SA |
| Positive emotional | SA 1, 2, 3 | SA | LA | 1, 2, 3 | SA 1, 2, 3 |
| Entertainment | SA | 1, 2, 4, 6 | 1, 2, 3, 5 | | 1, 2, 3, 5 |
| Ad attention, turned on by ads | 1, 2, 3 | 1, 2, 4, 5 | 2, 6, 7 | | |
| Participation and socialization | | 1, 2, 3, 4 | | | |

## NOTES

1. See Malthouse et al. (2007), Calder et al. (2007), and Ware et al. (2007) for empirical tests of this claim and for extensive references to other studies. For magazines, see Malthouse et al. (2007). For newspapers see Calder and Malthouse (2004). For online sites, see Calder et al. (2007). Also see Bronner and Neijens (2006).

2. See Ware et al. (2007) for a more thorough analysis controlling for other factors such as the quality of the ad, interest in the product category, and reader engagement with the magazine.

## REFERENCES

Bronner, Fred, and Peter Neijens. 2006. Audience experiences of media context and embedded advertising: A comparison of eight media. *International Journal of Market Research* 48: 81–100.

Calder, Bobby J. 1977. Focus groups and the nature of qualitative marketing research. *Journal of Marketing Research* 14: 353–364.

Calder, Bobby J. 1994. Qualitative marketing research. In *Principles of marketing research*, ed. R. Bagozzi, 40–72. Cambridge: Blackwell.

Calder, Bobby J. 2000. Understanding consumers. In *Kellogg on marketing*, ed. D. Iacobucci, 151–164. New York: Wiley.

Calder, Bobby J., and Edward C. Malthouse. 2003. What is integrated marketing? In *Kellogg on integrated marketing*, ed. D. Iacobucci and B. Calder, 6–15. Hoboken, NJ: Wiley.

Calder, Bobby J., and Edward C. Malthouse. 2004. Qualitative media measures: Newspaper experiences. *International Journal of Media Management* 6: 124–131.

Calder, Bobby J., and Edward C. Malthouse. 2005a. Experiential engagement with online content web sites and the impact of cross-media usage. Proceedings of 12th Worldwide Readership Research Symposium, October, Prague, Czech Republic.

Calder, Bobby J., and Edward C. Malthouse. 2005b. Managing media and advertising change with integrated marketing. *Journal of Advertising Research* 43: 356–361.

Calder, Bobby J., Edward C. Malthouse, and Ute Schaedel. In press. Engagement with online media and advertising effectiveness. *Journal of Interactive Marketing*.

Csikszentmihalyi, Mihaly. 1990. *Flow: The psychology of optimal experience*. New York: Harper & Row.

Csikszentmihalyi, Mihaly. 1997. *Finding flow: The psychology of engagement with everyday life*. New York: Basic Books.

Dahlén, M. 2005. The medium as a contextual cue: Effects of creative media choice. *Journal of Advertising* 34: 89.

Deci, Edward L., and Richard M. Ryan. 1985. *Intrinsic motivation and self-determination in human behavior*. New York: Plenum.

Dewey, John. 1980. *Art as experience*. New York: Perigee. (Original work published 1934).

Green, Melanie C., and Timothy C. Brock. 2000. The role of transportation in the persuasiveness of public narratives. *Journal of Personality and Social Psychology* 79: 701–721.

Green, Melanie C., Jeffrey J. Strange, and Timothy C. Brock. 2002. *Narrative impact: Social and cognitive foundations*. Mahwah, NJ: Erlbaum.

Higgins, E. Tory. 1997. Beyond pleasure and pain. *American Psychologist* 52: 1280–1300.

Higgins, E. Tory. 2005. Value from regulatory fit. *Current Directions in Psychological Science* 14: 209–213.

Higgins, E. Tory. 2006. Value from hedonic experience and engagement. *Psychological Review* 113: 439–460.

Malthouse, Edward C., and Bobby J. Calder. 2005. Relationship branding and CRM. In *Kellogg on branding*, eds. A. Tybout and T. Calkins, 150–168. Hoboken, NJ: Wiley.

Malthouse, Edward C., and Bobby J. Calder. 2007. The robustness and importance of media context experiences on advertising. Working Paper, Northwestern University, Evanston, IL.

Malthouse, Edward C., Bobby J. Calder, and Ajit Tamhane. 2007. The effects of media context experiences on advertising effectiveness. *Journal of Advertising* 36: 7–18.

Marc, Marcel. 1966. Using reading quality in magazine selection. *Journal of Advertising Research* 6: 9–13.

Parker, Ellie, and Adrian Furnham. 2007. Does sex sell? The effects of sexual programme content on the recall of sexual and non-sexual advertisements. *Applied Cognitive Psychology* 21 (9): 1217–1228.

Peer, Limor, Edward C. Malthouse, Mary Nesbitt, and Bobby J. Calder. 2007. *The local TV news experience: How to win viewers by focusing on engagement*. Technical Report, Northwestern University Media Management Center, Evanston, IL, www.mediamanagementcenter.org/localTV/localTV.pdf.

Wang, Jing, and Bobby J. Calder. 2006. Media transportation and advertising. *Journal of Consumer Research* 33: 151–162.

Wang, Jing, and Bobby J. Calder. 2007. Understanding how media context affects advertising. Manuscript submitted for publication.

Wang, Jing, and Angela Y. Lee. 2006. The role of regulatory focus in preference construction. *Journal of Marketing Research* 43: 28–38.

Ware, Britta, Judy Bahary, Bobby J. Calder, and Edward C. Malthouse. 2007. The magazine maximizer: A model for leveraging magazine engagement dynamics. Proceedings of the 13th Worldwide Readership Research Symposia, October 21–24, Vienna, Austria.

## CHAPTER 2

# MAKING TV A TWO-WAY STREET: CHANGING VIEWER ENGAGEMENT THROUGH INTERACTION

### MICHAEL SCHREIBER

Television is undisputedly the most effective mass-market marketing vehicle and will maintain that title for many years to come, if not forever. However, marketing itself has changed with the advancement of technology and development of new advertising mediums. Whether you are talking about promoting a primetime show or advertising a bar of soap, marketing has become a true dialogue between the advertiser and the consumer. Marketing has become a search for a conversation, thus resulting in a heightened level of consumer engagement. For over 50 years, marketers and programmers have been using mass-market vehicles such as TV to broadcast messages and content to the masses. Even the term *broadcast* itself seems antiquated and outdated. Even though TV and its associated viewer engagement have evolved over time, it is still a generic search for eyeballs and impressions through repetition. However, change is underway. Over the past 10 years, there has been a shift with the help of the fastest growing medium, the Internet. Consumers have begun to interact with brands through web sites and online ads and have trained themselves to use the Internet for transactions. The Internet has dramatically closed the gap between the point of sale and marketing. This type of engagement is directly linked to the interaction with brands and product, the holy grail of advertising. The subsequent challenge has been to use those lessons from the Internet and aim to increase viewer engagement in the most powerful medium, broadcast TV. Can the same interaction model really engage a TV viewer in the same way? Does TV interactivity result in viewer engagement? This chapter explores those questions and uncovers the latest efforts around interactivity through the TV industry.

## HISTORY OF TV AND VIEWER ENGAGEMENT

Analyzing the future of TV must start with an examination of the medium's history. Television has always been a one-way street—a true "broad"-cast. It was born in the 1950s, broadcasting to only those families in households that could afford large monster TV sets that were more like furniture than a consumer electronic device. It was true appointment viewing with neighbors from all around gathering week after week to bear witness to these amazing moving pictures. As the technology continued to develop and eventually reduced the cost of TV sets, it quickly became the prominent mass-market vehicle for content owners and marketers. Audiences were engaged and hungry for this new medium. They grew up in radio, listening to descriptive stories and relying on their imaginations. This new medium brought three major TV networks, born out of their radio heritage. With only three major channels to choose from across the country, TV shows became national events and viewer engagement was quite high. For example, shows such as the *Tonight Show* with Johnny Carson would pull in as many as 60 percent of all TV viewers (60 percent TV household share) which is a number even the Super Bowl today cannot compete with. The nature of TV viewership was a true broadcast, meaning that everyone got the same broad experience without customization or interaction.

Moving forward 30 years, the evolution of the TV medium in the late 1970s brought the innovation of wiring homes for a new offering called cable TV. Once a home was wired with co-axel cables as an alternative method for receiving TV signals and didn't rely on broadcast spectrum, capacity for channels expanded greatly. With this added capacity, programmers were given a blank canvas and created a slew of targeted TV networks focused on specific demographics and interests. Thus networks such as MTV, Discovery, CNBC, SciFi, Nickelodeon, Lifetime, CNN, and so on were born. Some of the channels focused on specific populations such as teenagers or women while others focused on interest areas such as science fiction or world news, but all provided a separate 24/7 broadcast experience. Not wanting to be left behind, many of the major broadcasters (i.e., NBC, CBS, and ABC) also began to build new niche networks, for example, MSNBC. This shift brought about the development of over 20 new channels. As the capacity and delivery efficiencies developed, aided by the advent of satellite operators, the number of networks leapt to 300 to 500 channels.

Cable TV took the formerly holy grail of media, broadcast TV, and broke it down into a fragmented universe of broadcast alternatives. Such fragmentation was great for the viewer, but led to immeasurable audience levels that challenged networks' presentation of their value to advertisers. Typically, networks have to relay specific attributes of the content and demographics of the perceived audience to sell ads and the niche nature of cable TV allows for more targeted content leading to a more engaged audience. For example, the business and financial news network, CNBC, does not get substantially large ratings (in comparison to broadcast TV or even some of the major cable news networks), but its audience consists of CEOs and senior business and financial professions who claim that they need to watch CNBC to stay current for their job. This perceived connection to a network is a dream for advertisers, not only because of the affluent engaged audience, but because this audience of decision makers influence and shape the decisions of others. That is just one of many interesting effects of cable TV.

Another interesting point to note in the evolution of cable TV, is the notion of the "wired home." With over 70 percent penetration of cable TV in the United States most homes are wired to the cable or satellite system through a set-top box in the home. With that model in place, the cable company has control over which content, services, ads, and so on are served to each household and potentially each individual. This power, among other things, creates the ability to hyper-customize and further target the content and advertising offerings. For example, cable operators sell local ads within their service area down to the zip code and pending privacy law, down to the household. This ability became a major driving force in the efforts to develop functional extensions for programmers and advertisers, which we will explore in more depth later in this chapter. Since cable TV has grown, broadcast TV has been working to increase its engagement and customization to match cable's success without alienating its base audience. Despite the growth and advancement of cable TV over time, broadcast TV is and will remain the most efficient way to reach mass audiences of viewers. It will take a long time, if ever, until traditional broadcast TV loses its crown as the most powerful mass marketing vehicle.

Moving forward another 30 years to the present day, we explore the growing availability and accessibility of Internet video. As we know from the past decade, the Internet provides a seemingly unlimited number of choices and niches for a consumer of information. As the Internet grew in the 1990s, it was engaging but focused on the delivery of information and e-commerce services and was not heavily pulling TV audiences away from cable and broadcast viewership. However, as technology advanced and bandwidth increased, the U.S. penetration of broadband users has reached close to 70 percent. Broadband and online video has become a driving force in media. In particular, online video has been gaining an audience among the highly valuable

younger demographics who are turning to the Internet for professionally produced or user-generated short-form on-demand content. The engagement in
both video sites and community sites, such as MySpace, has led to an unprecedented level of engagement with the younger generation who often spend
hours a day on their personal web pages or interacting with friends online.
The lack of quality of online video has not deterred audiences and is just a
temporary hurdle given the constant evolution of technology. The benefits
are obvious: not only does the Internet provide virtually unlimited choice,
but it also provides a heightened level of interactivity ranging from the ability
to select your video entertainment on-demand to the ability to influence the
outcome of your entertainment or the creation and distribution of your own
video products. This nirvana of viewer engagement has visibly started to crack
away at both the broadcast and cable TV audiences as well as their advertisers'
budgets. Engagement with content and the ads embedded within are always
more valuable to an advertiser than ads in a passive viewing experience. This
high consumer engagement has shifted significant portions of ad budgets away
from traditional TV and reallocated them to online video. As consumers and
new electronic devices start facilitating the convergence of the computer content to their TV screens, broadcast and cable TV see an even greater threat.
The challenge at hand for the broadcasters and advertisers is not only to move
into those fragmented online businesses by acquisition and organic growth,
but to increase the level of engagement with traditional broadcasts and commercials. Herein lies the major challenge for broadcasters, the simultaneous
increase in engagement in their broadcast and their advertisers' content.

Marketers have always claimed that interaction with and testing of their
products leads to a more engaged consumer who is more likely to purchase
their product. Can broadcasters and TV advertisers learn from this to solve this
challenge? They certainly are trying to make TV an interactive experience, a
two-way street, in an effort to build engagement.

## MAKING TV A TWO-WAY STREET

Some basic definitions prove useful here. *Interaction* refers to any immediate
action a viewer takes after being directed by something in a TV broadcast.
Some industry leaders do not consider true TV interactivity unless the viewer
responds to your action. In some ways, consumer-buying behavior is the TV
interactivity because viewers get directed to buy a certain product and then
they go out and buy it. This is a bit of a stretch and traditionally disregarded
because it is not often an immediate action, but does lead us to the philosophy
behind the first real interactive TV (iTV) efforts, direct-response advertising.

Direct-response advertising started in the late 1960s with the advent of toll-free phone numbers. A viewer would see a 30-second commercial advertisement or a telethon with a toll-free number and take immediate action by calling and ordering a product or service directly over the phone. This was really the first true iTV as it represented pure interactivity. Before people were ever dreaming about calling in to vote for their favorite American Idol, they were calling in to pledge a donation to the call center advertised on their TV.

A discussion around the birth of interactive TV would not be complete without the examination of the rise and fall of WebTV, Microsoft's killer iTV software application from the 1990s. When Microsoft bought the fledgling WebTV Networks Inc. in 1997, they thought they were tapping into a goldmine, with the combination of interactivity and broadcast TV, however, even a decade later this code still has not been fully cracked. When Microsoft got behind the product, a number of consumer electronics manufacturers (OEMs) including Sony and Philips, starting building set-top boxes for WebTV. Two main products were introduced, called WebTV Classic and WebTV Plus, which were both versions of a proprietary browser that formatted web sites and text for view on the TV set. The idea was that people could use their TV to browse the Internet and watch TV at the same time. Sounded like a great idea, so why didn't it work? The TV industry is full of powerful players such as broadcast networks and cable operators who wield tremendous power and who are quite protective of their turf. Working with these stakeholders is key for the interactive TV model to flourish. No one can be a maverick, not even Microsoft. At launch, the WebTV set-top box immediately undermined the control that the cable operators had worked so hard to achieve and upset the programmers/broadcasters because it facilitated the extraction of audiences from their linear networks to the Internet. Thus, Microsoft learned, although a little too late, that coordination and sharing were key to building a ubiquitous interactive TV model.

Another example of iTV, Tivo, played a slightly different role, changing the TV landscape forever, but faltering on some similar issues. One big difference between WebTV and Tivo is that Tivo did build the killer application for TV. When Tivo launched their first mass-market set-top box in 1999, it was seen as a niche product for only tech-savvy users. However, as the product began to grow and gain mass-market notoriety, cable operators and broadcasters took notice. Recording TV shows on a hard drive quickly became a norm and later considered a consumer right. Cable operators again felt threatened and broadcasters and their advertisers became upset with the ability to fast-forward and bypass commercials. They are still a viable company and product, but nowhere near as dominant as they could have been. Instead of focusing full board on disseminating their still superior software to the main stakeholders in the value chain, Tivo focused on selling hardware at retail, which is a tough business to scale and inevitably competed directly with the cable set-top box. Their popularity and innovative software helped them build an installed base of a couple million users, but they began to plateau when the other major stakeholders began to compete. Cable operators licensed independent software providers to build competitive offerings for their boxes and thus the generic digital video recording (DVR) was born. DVRs are now reaching about one-fifth of all households. Even though WebTV and Tivo did not turn into the blockbuster businesses they were originally considered, they did prove a significant hypothesis in the market, namely that consumers become more engaged with the medium when presented with interactive features and when they have more control over their viewing content. Broadcasters and advertisers had always had this hypothesis, but had not had an opportunity to test and prove it in the mass market.

Under the premise, which has developed throughout the history of media, that viewer engagement is paramount, coupled with the knowledge that interactivity creates engagement, many programmers/broadcasters and advertisers have started to embrace new technologies and outlets for interactivity. These efforts typically fall into five models based on a communication method: One-Screen (TV), Two-Screen (Computer), Three-Screen (Wireless), Multi-Screen, and Blended-Screen. Each model evokes a slightly different degree of participation and engagement.

## One-Screen Interactivity

One-screen interactivity is considered the ultimate in iTV in terms of engagement. It refers to direct interactions through your TV without accessing a phone, personal computer, or mobile phone. It is as simple as voting for a contestant or purchasing a product just by pressing a button on your remote. When interactivity and thus engagement are that easy, viewers have been proven to follow. But it is also one of the hardest methods to organize based on all the powerful stakeholders involved. One-screen interactions are facilitated directly through a viewer's TV or set-top box by using the remote control. The set-top box or TV itself has software embedded in it that can produce overlays and prompts over the programming and ads. Responses can be used to make a local change on the set-top box, such as the recording of a program, or can be used to return information which is then aggregated and sent back to the cable operator through the cable lines for voting or inquiry information. For example, a TV prompt could appear in the corner of the screen and ask you, "If you are interested in learning more about the product in this commercial, please press A." A message then gets sent back to your TV's set-top box from your remote and your decision is recorded. At that point, another prompt appears with the information requested and perhaps details on the retail store in your neighborhood where you can go to buy the product.

When interactivity comes directly from the TV's set-top box, audience's engagement tends to reach its highest levels based on the participation rates. The most recent and advanced installation of this technology is being built and evolved in cooperation with a number of stakeholders, including software providers, advertisers, cable operators, and programmers. These latest offerings add live one-screen voting and polling interactivity to the programs or requests for more information prompts to advertisements. As you can tell from the number of stakeholders involved in orchestrating a one-screen interactive application with a show and/or advertisement, these are challenging to organize. The required level of cooperation from multiple partners is sometimes prohibitive, but the result is extremely high participation rates. In the spring of 2006, the Bravo cable network launched the first mass-market one-screen iTV application for their new show, *Top Chef*. Launched in conjunction with Time Warner Cable, the application was built and delivered through the viewer's set-top box and gave Bravo the ability to ask the viewers trivia questions in which the viewers would choose their answer by pressing a button on their remote. The answers were then returned to the cable operator, aggregated, and displayed on screen in conjunction with the correct answer. It was reported that this application reached participation rates close to 30 percent. This means that almost a third of all the applicable viewers used their remote to interact with the broadcast. This was unprecedented in terms of response rates, and started to solidify the hypothesis that one-screen interactivity leads to high engagement.

## Two-Screen Interactivity

Two-screen interactivity is when interactions with a TV broadcast are facilitated through a personal computer that is connected to the Internet. Viewers are beginning to multitask more and more at home. One of the effects of such multitasking is the use of a personal computer and the Internet while watching TV. This has led to a number of programmers and advertisers integrating web-based interactivity into their creative content. This does not refer to the simple promotion of a web site, even though that could loosely be considered interactivity. Rather, two-screen interactions are set up for real-time interactivity during the broadcast, such as prompts that direct viewers to go online and play along with an online quiz or voting system that is tied and timed to the broadcast. Sometimes the winners or results are read live on air before the show ends. For example, NBC developed an online quiz game for the Golden Globes in which consumers could play along and answer questions about the celebrities appearing on stage. The users that received the best scores were then awarded a prize at the end of the broadcast.

Although, two-screen applications do create a significant level of engagement with those who choose to play along online, participation rates overall are not traditionally high due to the level of effort for each consumer to engage. Users need to not only have a computer that is connected and available, but they must remember the web site address and type it in themselves. These tasks seem simple, but when most people are relaxing on their couch, these little tasks become the reason for disengagement.

### Three-Screen Interactivity

Three-screen interactivity uses a phone, primarily a mobile phone, as the communication device. Three-screen interactivity is probably the fastest growing form of iTV, second to one-screen interactivity. The hit TV show, *American Idol*, is the best and most widely known example of three-screen interactivity. Fox, in conjunction with Cingular, pioneered the mass use of three-screen interactivity in the United States when they first premiered in 2002. After each broadcast, you can call in or send a short-code text message through your mobile phone to the numbers presented on the broadcast to vote for your favorite singer. The singer with the lowest votes through the phone and text messages is then eliminated during the next broadcast. Combine the top-rated show in the United States with three-screen interactivity and you have a major force and growth engine. Mitch Feinman, of Fox Mobile Entertainment, recently discussed *American Idol* voting through test messaging. He said, "In Season 1, we had 12,000 text messages, compared to 65 million in the most recent season. I think that gives you a sense of the trajectory of this medium." ("Latch on to interactivity," Carly Mayberry, *The Hollywood Reporter*, 12/1/06). The producers claim the finale gets more votes than the U.S. presidential election. The combination of a hit show and an effective engagement tool has proven to be successful, especially within the younger demographics. *American Idol's* success is based on a number of elements, but there's no question that interactivity helped drive its dominance.

### Multiscreen Model

Multiscreen interactivity is based on the combination of two or more of the previous models. For example, the show *Deal or No Deal* on NBC uses a multiscreen model by offering viewers the ability to participate in their "Lucky Case" sweepstakes game each show either by text message from their mobile phone or online submission through their computer. The combination of multiple models does help increase participation over all, however, this model still does not reach participation rates of one-screen.

## Blended Screen Model

Blended-screen refers to new applications that have just begun to be tested, where one communication device assists in controlling another device. The best example of blended-screen interactivity is using your mobile phone to control your set-top box from anywhere as if it is the remote. This blends both one-screen and three-screen. A prompt can come up on any screen broadcasting a certain program and ask you similar questions as one-screen application, but you do not have to be on your couch or even in your house to respond. Your mobile phone will communicate with your set-top box from anywhere and you can participate.

# iTV: THE ENGAGEMENT BUILDER

The connection between interactivity and engagement can be measured by overall participation rates, but simple numerical participation rates do not help explain the causal factors that lead to such engagement. The next section lays out these traits and benefits and their associated growth possibilities, especially for the programmers and advertisers. First, the programmer's perspective is discussed. Programmers benefit from one thing—higher ratings. Higher ratings translate into better advertising rates and high licensing fees, the two main pillars of revenue for broadcasters. Taking it one step further, the more the viewers are engaged in the programming, traditionally, the better the ratings. That's where the engagement traits of iTV come in.

## Benefits to Programmers

*Richer Experience*    iTV provides viewers with a richer and more relevant TV experience. When viewers can interact with the broadcast through their remote, phone, or computer, they feel more connected to the program and not only watch longer but also come back for the next episode. Programmers have started using the highest concentration of iTV in reality TV scenarios to create an enhanced experience for the viewers. This enriched viewing experience not only engages the viewer, but creates a level of stickiness that can lead to high ratings.

**Differentiation**    Another benefit for the programmer and program's producer is differentiation. A program with interactivity options is always going to be more attractive to programmers and viewers, than one without, assuming all else is equal. The producer's willingness to work with the broadcaster to incorporate interactivity is always a good sign in the effort to differentiate the program from its competition.

**Relevance**    Relevance is another benefit of interactivity and engagement. If you believe that you can influence the outcome, the show has just become that much more relevant to your life. Fox has become a leader in relevance with *American Idol*, as discussed previously. They have also become the standard-bearer of results shows. When you give the audience a chance to participate and decide the outcome, they will come back for the results. Fox recognized how engaged their audience had become due to this interactivity and quickly built a vehicle to capture them a second and third time in the same week, thus reality TV results shows were born.

In the summer of 2006, NBC took this concept one step further and launched the first-ever one-screen iTV voting application for broadcast TV for the show *Last Comic Standing*. Essentially, with the help of Time Warner Cable, the second largest cable operator in the United States, NBC built an application to capture votes straight from the viewer's remote. These votes were then used to decide who will be voted off the show. This was the first time a one-screen iTV application was used to influence the outcome of a primetime broadcast program. Viewers did not have to pull out their phone or even memorize a phone number or web site. All they needed to do was continue to lean back on their couch and press a simple button on their remote to cast their vote, ultimately deciding who would be the *Last Comic Standing*. That type of connection and relevance with the audience, not only keeps the viewer engaged throughout the entire program, but gets them to come back for more, including the results. All in all, when a viewer feels like he or she is influencing the outcome of a show, the program becomes that much more relevant to their lives and develops into an "appointment viewing" experience, in which viewers schedule their evenings around a certain program.

**Stickiness**    One of the other big challenges for programmers is keeping the viewer engaged through the full duration of the program and having them stick around for the next show—stickiness. For example, local news programs will often promote the juiciest stories at the beginning of the show and then air them at the end of the show. This technique is an effort to retain the audience through the program. Viewer engagement through iTV can also help with stickiness. Voting and polling overlays help keep viewers around as they await the results and/or the next question, but prompts can also be used to build a connection to the next program or the scene after the commercial pod.

*Community*    Creating community is another theme that benefits the programmers. Community features are ever popular after the recent growth of social web sites such as MySpace, YouTube, and Facebook, and the effects are real and create engagement. If viewers believe that they are part of a community, they are more likely to stay engaged. iTV can provide this sense of community. Viewers can communicate with each other and foster a response to an advertiser or programmer. There are a number of community vehicles, such as online instant messaging through the set-top box. This vehicle enables viewers to interact with each other or members of the cast during the broadcast. Additionally, iTV features can facilitate the creation of fan clubs, distribution lists for e-mail and mobile alerts, and host chat rooms, all of which create a sense of community.

*Personalization and Customization*    Creating the perception of what I like to call a "narrowcast" from a broadcast vehicle has always been a struggle for broadcasters, but interactivity allows the broadcaster to get one step closer to a narrowcast experience through personalization. Whether the viewer is setting up a recording schedule for a digital video recorder, building a customized on-demand homepage, or creating alerts via the set-top box, they are effectively customizing their entertainment experience. One example that is still being perfected, but has great potential, is the personalization of an on-air ticker. For example, if you are an avid CNN viewer, then you probably do not get much benefit out of the ticker because most of the news is irrelevant to your life. With this feature, the viewer would go to the programmer and/or cable operator's web site, or directly through an interface on your set-top box, and select favorite news topics. The result would be a personalized news ticker overlaying CNN's broadcast ticker and it would only scroll stories on those topics you have selected. In effect, the viewer becomes more engaged in the ticker and potentially the ticker's sponsor. Furthermore, customization can go a number of directions, especially with the help of the cable operator and the high-level targeting abilities of each set-top box.

Another example of customization is the broadcast of the Olympic Games. As one of the largest U.S. sport properties, it can be hard to program all the activity of the Olympic Games into one broadcast, given that so many events are going on simultaneously. Programmers wrestle with questions such as, "Which events do you show, which ones do you delay, and which ones do you not show at all?" iTV customization features can help solve this problem and create additional engagement by letting the viewer decide. During the 2006 Winter Games in Turino, Italy, Time Warner and NBC teamed up with an iTV software manufacturer to build a custom application that gave the viewers the choice of which event to watch as well as an option to watch multiple events at once on the same screen.

The NFL also took a similar approach for football games starting in 2006 as part of the NFL Sunday Ticket offering. Working with DirecTV, they created an application where the viewer could pick the match-up that was of most interest or even watch multiple games at once. When the viewer can customize their experience, engagement inevitably increases because the content is that much more relevant to their interests. This sense of choice and relevance, not only excites programmers due to the added engagement, but generates interest from advertisers who feed off engagement as well as the association with freedom and choice.

*Information*    Viewers like to be informed and learn about their shows, the fictional characters within, and the real lives of the actors. Online web sites dedicated to specific shows were originally set up to serve this purpose. These sites traditionally had in-depth information about the program, the actors, behind the scenes stories, and so on. This is a type of passive interactivity that has been used since the Internet became mainstream. Taking this concept one step further is the mobile web site. Many programmers are building mobile sites for their shows to present similar information. For example, during a program, you may see a promotion directing you to visit the web site or mobile site for more information. Better yet, the cable operators can assist by building this detail into the information section on the program guide or can prompt the viewer, using overlays, during a program when there is more information about the actors and/or the scene. Sponsors are big fans of such features. For example, while watching an episode of *24* on Fox, a prompt may show up on the bottom third of the screen and tell you that the truck the Jack Bauer character is driving in the scene is a 2007 Nissan Pathfinder with a sticker price of $28,500. Later in this chapter, the advertising benefits of interactivity and their associated lift in engagement are explored. Another installation for informational prompts could be a pop-up video feature popularized by VH1 that played classic music videos with overlaid "thought clouds" that would appear with interesting facts about the production, artist, or the musical genre. These same features can be laid over programming and viewers can decide whether they would like to activate it or not.

**Commercial Opportunities** Outside of the commercial benefits for third-party advertising sponsorships that are discussed later in the chapter, there are a number of commercial opportunities for broadcasters that arise via interactivity. Programmers can offer the direct sale of merchandise from the program currently being viewed. For example, selling the Box Set DVD from the past season within the premier of the current season tends to be effective.

Home shopping broadcasts have always been based on interactions with the audience. Recently, the Home Shopping Network (HSN) partnered with Cablevision to build one-screen interactivity into their shopping broadcasts, so viewers can purchase the showcased products through their remote without even picking up the phone.

Another commercial opportunity lies in the ability to charge a fee for a vote or response. Most broadcast networks have looked to exploit this option after the success of *Deal or No Deal*'s Lucky Case Game which started producing real revenue for the network and the wireless carriers with the $0.99 per submission fee. Some cable networks are taking this to the next level and broadcasting full interactive trivia shows with instant cash prizes. These shows are set up to attract viewers to call-in or text-in responses for $1 each, which ends up being very similar to a lottery. Some other forms of iTV commercialization include dating services such as personals on-demand and video game services via the set-top box.

## Benefits to Advertisers

Another stakeholder who significantly benefits from iTV engagement is the on-air advertiser. TV commercials have always been a passive experience where advertisers promote their slogans and/or product benefits. They rely on creativity and repetition to drive engagement and ultimately recognition and purchasing habits. Thus, there has always been a premium placed on the quality of the creative content (i.e., the execution of the message). Some executions use humor, others use spokespeople, such as celebrities. There have not been many alternatives to traditional commercials for on-air advertisers that do not cheapen the brand while helping to engage the viewers.

However, the one thing that advertisers do know is that more engagement in their ads or the programming surrounding their ads leads to more effective ads. For example, traditionally, ads with higher engagement lead to significantly higher recall rates than passive ads. Equipped with this understanding, advertisers tend to be on the lookout for viewer engagement techniques. Thus, iTV has become a major initiative for advertisers even more so than for programmers. Advertisers want viewers to interact with their brands. iTV turns a passive viewing experience into a brand interaction experience. It creates a deeper connection between a brand and a viewer. Viewers typically have a negative reaction to advertising in general because it typically interrupts their viewing experience. But a better advertising experience that offers the consumer choice and information is a different playing field. iTV provides direct consumer interaction that was never possible in the past through TV advertising. If a marketer can be offered the chance to have the viewer take an immediate action based on the ad, then a direct connection and engagement is achieved. Additionally, placing an iTV ad within a program that is utilizing iTV itself creates a full interactive experience for the viewer.

In terms of the iTV models, two- and three-screen installations have existed for a while, such as 1-800-number direct-response ads and the more recent generic ads driving viewers to an e-commerce web site. However, one-screen interactivity is bringing all of that activity directly to the remote. Additionally, one-screen interactivity has proven over and over again, through response rates, the ease with which the viewer can interact. For example, it is much easier to push a button on your remote, than get out your phone, remember a number, and call in to a voicemail system to record your selection. Additionally, remembering a web site and typing it into your computer is not the most fluid experience. Response rates as high as 30 percent, from some of the early one-screen implementations, quickly heighten advertisers interest. As a comparison, direct-mail advertising, which is quite expensive, tends to have response rates in the 0.5 percent range.

However, it is hard to get national breadth with one-screen interactivity. The main reason for this is that one-screen iTV is run through the cable operator or the satellite provider, like Direct TV. These operators have a large footprint, but will never have a national footprint because they share locations with their competitors (i.e., different operators service different markets with some markets dominated by multiple operators.) True "national" iTV would require an unprecedented amount of cooperation between stiff competitors, which is quite unlikely in the near term. The other option is for broadcasters to untangle the regulations and build an over-the-air standard for iTV to be delivered through traditional broadcast signals.

One-screen advertising applications are currently more common with cable operators. Operators have negotiated, from the networks, the rights to control and sell approximately 30 percent of the advertising that is run on cable networks on their systems to local advertisers. Since the cable operators control this local advertising inventory, they have the flexibility to place their own interactivity within those local commercial pods, without the hassle or extra coordination with the programmers. This can be quite attractive to local advertisers and has led to quite a bit of innovation in local iTV advertising. The only drawback to such applications is that it does not give viewers the full interactive experience, "interactive programs with interactive ads."

Some examples of how advertisers are currently benefiting from the innovations that one-screen interactivity provides are discussed next.

***Sponsored Applications*** The easiest and most frequent use of iTV advertising is sponsoring the actual iTV feature in general. These are just association advertisements that sponsor the iTV features within programming. They are not necessarily applications built specifically for an advertising event, but still are very valuable in the world of viewer engagement and interactivity. For example, within the Olympics iTV application, mentioned earlier, in which viewers can choose the event they want to watch, advertisers could sponsor that feature with messaging such as, "Choose Your Own Event, brought to you by Visa." This type of sponsorship will grow in concert will the growth of iTV, in general.

***One-Way Overlays*** One-way overlays are the simplest version of advertiser-built iTV applications. They are simple graphical overlays that pop up in the corner or bottom third of the screen. These can be placed over programming, with the networks' permission, or over traditional national or local commercials. For example, a national appliance retailer can run its traditional commercials, but then work with the cable operator to overlay a message on the bottom third of the screen denoting this week's special refrigerator sale. If the viewer is interested in the sale, they can press "A" on their remote and another overlay arrives with details on the sale and maybe even the closest store locations. These can become powerful tools to engage viewers as advertisers dream up new uses and applications.

***Requests for Information*** Requests for information (RFIs) are probably one of the most utilized one-screen iTV applications. RFIs combine new advertising technology with one of the oldest advertising methods, direct mail. Typically, the way it works is that an overlay pops up over a commercial that asks if the viewer is interested in receiving more information about the product advertised. If the viewer presses "Yes," the software in the set-top box triggers a message back to the cable operator to send out a brochure to the viewer's home address, which the cable operator has in its system as the billing address. Then another overlay pops up to inform the viewer that information has been sent and should arrive via mail in the next few days. RFIs have seemingly endless possibilities from sending a brochure for a new real estate development to sending samples of shampoo.

*Video on Demand Showcases*    Cable operators have the ability to program their video-on-demand (VOD) menus to offer what they please. They have begun to reserve areas within these destinations for advertisers to place longer advertisements, product showcases, or "infotainment" segments. Car manufacturers have taken hold of this opportunity and built it out. They are producing two- to five-minute extended commercials to give interested viewers more information about their cars within these VOD showcases. Some of the major advertisers actually pay the cable operators to build entire sections for their different brands. For example, General Motors has built out a showcase on Comcast systems. It lets viewers who are in the market for a new vehicle browse the different long-form advertisements about their cars. Jeep has taken a slightly different approach by actually producing live action productions complete with story lines—all running within VOD menus as well. Showcases can even be used for classified ads, recruitment ads, and perhaps personal ads in the future.

*Telescoping*    Telescoping is when an overlay appears at the end of a commercial and asks the viewer if he or she would like to see more information about that product or view a long-form product showcase. Telescoping provides a heightened level of engagement in the advertisement, which the advertisers love, but at the same time it pulls people from the broadcast, which the programmers are against for obvious reasons. If an interaction is going to pull a viewer from the broadcast, then it is inevitably decreasing the programmer's ratings. However, cable operators can use their local ads as they please. This innovation has potential as a powerful iTV application, but it has become a heated debate between programmers and distributors.

*Bookmarking*    Bookmarking is another application that can take a viewer to an advertiser's VOD showcase or directly to a long-form advertisement. It is really a compromise that is more tolerated by programmers, but still not a perfect application. The application basically prompts the viewer if he or she is interested in learning more, but then bookmarks the request for later, instead of taking the viewer out of the broadcast immediately. There are three main options for the viewer to then use the bookmarks once created:

1. Once the show is over, a prompt reappears with the option to go to the product showcase that was bookmarked.
2. As soon as the viewer changes the channel, a prompt asks if he or she wants to view the latest bookmarks.
3. Bookmarks are added to a list of favorites for view at a later date (programmers prefer this version, of course).

Both telescoping and bookmarking need to be closely managed, due to a number of potentially predatory uses. For example, national programmers could run promos in local slots on their competitor networks with telescope applications that bring a viewer back over to their networks and away from their competitors'. For example, if you ran a local ad with a telescope iTV feature inside of a CSI program and promoted the option to switch over to TNT because the latest episode of *Law and Order* is just about to start, this would lead down a potentially slippery slope among competitors.

***Customized Ad Selection***   What if the viewer could choose which ad he or she was interested in watching? For example, either in a linear broadcast, or more likely in a VOD presentation, a viewer can be prompted and asked whether he or she would be more interested in a car commercial, a financial services ad, or a wireless carrier ad. What would you choose? This prompt is a great way to let consumers decide how they are advertised to. All the talk about hypertargeted advertising technologies and dynamic insertion of ads based on demographics becomes obsolete when the viewer actually chooses the ad. The downside is that customized ad selection is not the best experience for the viewer. Viewers have already accepted the fact that ads appear within favorite shows, but they probably don't want the idea presented to them at the beginning of the program. It may create some negative sentiment, but it hasn't really been tested enough to fully understand. Some viewers would be interested in the customization of ads, but some would be frustrated with the extra step.

***Direct Purchase***   As discussed in the programming section, iTV can be utilized to actually purchase the products directly from the broadcast. Advertisers could work with the cable operators and develop the option to buy the product directly through the broadcast. For example, a prompt can come up over a vacuum cleaner commercial that asks the viewer if he or she would like to buy the product. If the viewer selects "Yes," the cable operator can add the charge to the subscriber's bill and send the customer's shipping address to the advertiser for shipment, all at the click of a button. This is not unlike the e-commerce bubble from the Internet's early days. The Internet, in effect, brought marketing directly to the point of sale and made both accessible from your home. Direct purchase through the cable box does the same thing without the hassle of a computer or even a credit card.

### Summary

In conclusion, the added viewer engagement that interactivity provides is just as much a benefit for the advertisers as it is for the programmer. Arguably it may be even more powerful for advertisers because it provides them a platform for the dialogue that they are so desperately seeking. With the use of a number of these tools, TV advertising can become an inviting interaction versus an unwanted interruption. Advertisers were realistically the pioneers of iTV with direct-response ads touting 1-800-numbers, but now that technology has caught up with them, they have a number of new models and outlets to explore and perfect.

## TV INTERACTIVITY = VIEWER ENGAGEMENT

The Internet has changed marketing forever. It has facilitated the interaction between marketers and their respective consumers. More importantly, the Internet has taught us some powerful lessons about interactivity. The main lesson in interactivity is that direct interaction with the consumer leads to heightened engagement, the holy grail of advertising. As we uncovered throughout this chapter, the translation of this lesson into traditional mediums, such as TV, can be quite powerful. Turning static viewers into interactive participants at the click of the remote has energized programmers, operators, and advertisers. TV interactivity is truly driving viewer engagement, but as discussed, the benefits vary based on the model enlisted. The two- and three-screen interactivity models have been the most widely used, mainly because of their relative ease of execution, while one-screen interactivity is proving to be the most effective, yet the hardest to organize.

This leads to a final question: If TV interactivity generates such heightened viewer engagement, why isn't iTV ubiquitous? iTV and the resulting viewer engagement seem to benefit the entire value chain from producers whose show performs better to the advertisers who sell more products. The issue seems to be that iTV requires a heightened level of cooperation between a number of powerful players in the TV industry who are typically not comfort-able working together. Two- and three-screen models are leading the way be-cause they do not require as much cooperation and are easier to implement. But one-screen gets quite tricky because it requires cooperation between the cable operator and the broadcasters, two entities that traditionally have been in a power struggle, despite knowing they depend on one another.

What is the future of iTV? A good majority of the real-life examples de-tailed throughout this chapter, especially the one-screen examples, were merely pilots or exploratory rollouts with the intention of understanding the effectiveness of the platform. It quickly became evident that we are now just at the tip of the iceberg. Technology will continue to develop and standardize, meeting the needs of programmers and advertisers. Viewers will become more familiar with the prompts and steps required to participate, thus training them-selves for the future. And the industry powerhouses will learn to cooperate and share. The challenges will rapidly work themselves out over the next dec-ade as iTV evolves and strives to reach its full potential.

# CHAPTER 3

# ADVERTISING IN THE WORLD OF NEW MEDIA

SCOTT BERG

**H**ernando Cortez the great Spanish explorer came to what is now the state of California in 1519. His goal was to conquer the New World even though he and his crew were greatly outnumbered by the Indians in the region. In order to motivate his crew to fight and not surrender, Cortez set all of his boats on fire—thus, eliminating any means of retreat.

In many ways, this story of Cortez displays the changing world of media and how it is affecting consumers and companies. On one hand, you have traditional media types such as TV, radio, newspaper, magazines, and outdoor, which have been the main communication channels for the past 50 years. These communication vehicles were controlled by media companies and the messaging by the advertiser. Fast-forward to today, and you have the virtual explosion of digital technology and content that has led to more channels of communication, the consumer increasingly in control of content, channels, and messaging. Advertisers and media companies in a sense must "burn the boats" from traditional methods of advertising and begin to embrace new media types, business models, distribution channels, and content delivery. We must not forget the fundamentals of the past, but understand that as more and more content becomes digital versus analog, the opportunities for communication completely change. If advertisers and media companies fail to migrate to the new media world, the boats will still burn—the only difference is they will be on the boats.

So what and who is driving this unprecedented change? A number of factors are contributing to the cyclone of change, but this change started many, many years ago, before anyone had ever thought of the Internet, mobile phones, blogs, and so on. In 1948, John and Margaret Walson strung a cable from a TV antenna to their store and other local residents in order to provide TV reception to himself and others in rural Pennsylvania.[1] This simple invention, designed to provide TV reception to a few households, set the stage for significant future change in the media industry that would impact millions of people across the world. This technology provided the initial foundation for the future development of niche content cable TV stations and programs including news, sports, movies, international, cultural events, and music to name a few. So instead of being forced to watch network-only TV programming from ABC, CBS, and NBC, consumers were now able to watch different content based on their individual tastes, needs, and requirements. Rather than being forced to watch TV news at 6:00 and 10:00 PM every night, they could now turn on CNN at any time and get a complete news update.

If you were to "bucket" the categories that have occurred related to the changes and growth in the media industry, they can be summed up into a few major categories.

## TECHNOLOGICAL ADVANCEMENT

Different technological developments including increased computing power, expansion of microchip technology, software development, and the creation of the Internet have all had and will have a monumental impact on the current and future changes in media. These advancements have led to smaller and more sophisticated technology components at much cheaper prices, thus allowing consumers to economically purchase a host of media and communication devices for entertainment and business.

### Computer Technology

The personal and business computer have revolutionized the consumer and business world. From being able to create documents, spreadsheets, databases, web sites, or e-mail; access the Internet; communicate via chat, video, or speech; and the list goes on and on . . . the computer turned the business and personal world upside down. How we all managed without computers seems incredible given its widespread use and proliferation.

### Music and Video Players

Music and video players such as Apple's iPod or Microsoft's Zune allow customers to carry thousands of songs, photos, information, and video content in the palm of their hands. Gaming devices such as the Sony PSP device allow consumers to play real-life sophisticated games with graphics that are as good as most TVs. These devices also allow Internet access, communication channels, and the like. Many devices are marketed with a single purpose (e.g., playing games, video, or music), but have the ability to do much more given low-cost component pricing.

### Mobile Devices

There are devices that can take pictures, record video, play music and video content, access the Internet, download content, and make phone calls to anyone in the world. And all that computing and chip technology fits in a device that is a bit larger than a credit card. You now have the ability to have all of your e-mail sent to you anywhere in the world via a handheld device. Or in Japan, the widespread use of cellular technology allows customers to view live and prerecorded TV content while they are traveling on the subway to and from work. For better or worse, this technology has allowed businesses and individuals to be available anytime and anywhere.

### Internet

Of course you can't talk about technology without mentioning the Internet. In many ways the Internet, which gives us the ability to distribute and download content for individuals and businesses and to communicate with others, provides access to purchase goods and services, and so on, has revolutionized the world. It is safe to say that the Internet has provided the biggest jolt of change to the traditional media model.

## MIGRATION TO DIGITAL CONTENT

Just as technology has changed the way we interact and consume content, having content shift from an analog platform to a digital platform allows us to manipulate and consume content through a variety of mechanisms. Digital content essentially allows for things to be stored in a format that can be read by computers, music players, and other devices. Music and movies that are on DVD or Apple iTunes format are examples of how content is stored in a digital format. Having access to your financial records online, being able to purchase items on the Internet, play a video game, communicating via e-mail, blogs, chat, or even using Voice Over Internet Protocol (VOIP) technology has its basis in digital format. Because most things are stored or based in a digital format, the devices discussed earlier can access information that is relevant to individuals and businesses, making commerce, communication, and entertainment a rich and valuable experience.

### User Control and Participation

Having devices and digital content that can be accessed by users ultimately leads to consumer and business demand. And the consumer has spoken by demonstrating strong use and participation. For instance:

- Over 12 billion text messages are sent yearly worldwide.[2]
- Over 2 billion people (or one-third of the worldwide population) have mobile phones. And the second billion was added in the past year.[3]
- There are 188.1 million Internet users in the United States.[4]
- There are 139.4 million broadband users in the United States.[5]
- More than 2.69 trillion e-mail messages are sent every year.[6]
- In 2006, 808,000 units of the game World of Warcraft were sold in the United States.[7]
- Presently, 57 million people read blogs and 12 million people actually keep a blog in the United States.[8]
- In 2006, 34.2 percent of U.S. Internet users made an online purchase.[9]

There is little question that consumers have embraced the world of information and entertainment. People now have a channel to express their opinions, share information, connect with others who share the same passions, and learn about and interact with content they have never been able to before. No longer do they need to have music served to them the way a music company or radio station believes it should be heard. They can become their own disk jockey by programming their iPod to the music they want to listen to, in the order they want to listen to it, and so on. They can skip commercials by using a Tivo device, program the device to record the content they desire, and watch the content when it's convenient. The consumer can play a video game with anyone in the world, look at the news in another country, or view a video that someone uploads to YouTube. Consumers are now firmly in control, and they are driving this evolution by voting with their pocketbooks (or should I say Pay Pal account?).

## VIEW OF THE PAST

It wasn't that long ago that media planning was actually considered to be a necessary evil in most agencies and an afterthought by most clients. It was the last step in the process after the marketing strategy, creative development, pro-duction, and so on were completed. In fact, over the past decade, many media departments were "spun out" of the creative agency to become freestanding entities within the company. This reorganization in the business model al-lowed advertisers more choice in determining the appropriate media agency to service the account versus just having the creative agency manage the media.

The other glaring thing about media in the past was the lack of media types and choices available. However, although media was very elementary in those days, the seeds of change were being planted.

## TV

Network TV stations (ABC, CBS, NBC, and FOX) continued to garner the lion's share of individuals watching TV. The old TV guard continued to pro-vide programming including such themes as NBC's *Must See TV* on Thursday nights. And although the networks still maintained significant audience num-bers, their audience numbers were beginning to shift as more consumers chose cable TV programming. Not only were the old guard of cable channels such as United States Network, CNN, and MTV gaining audience numbers, many new niche cable TV channels were being created as well, thus giving more choice to consumers. These channels gained audience numbers by offering theme-based content. For instance, the Sci-Fi channel runs programming that appeals to science fiction fans and TV Land reruns sitcoms and other content from years past. These, and many other niche programming channels, have continued to eat away at the audience numbers the networks dominated for so many years.

## Radio

The growth of the radio marketplace got a shot in the arm when FM radio became more mainstream. The playback experience was superior to the AM frequency that had dominated the medium previously. As with the advent of cable TV, new radio station formats became prevalent during the past 20 to 30 years, with the talk radio and Latino music formats adding more diversity and choice for listeners. And although many new formats have been added, there has been a slow but steady decline in overall radio listeners during the past decade. The advantages of radio advertising are that it can be targeted to a regional listening area or a specific demographic audience and it is relatively inexpensive per exposure.

## Magazines

In 2006, 262 new magazines made there way into the U.S. marketplace, an increase of 2 percent over 2005.[10] Thousands of magazines are published in the United States each year. The categories of publication can be wide in nature or extremely finite. And although magazines have seen a decline in advertising revenue, daily newspapers have been hit even harder.

## Newspapers

Of all media types, newspapers have probably taken the largest hit as more and more consumers go online to get their news (Figure 3.1). The time that consumers spend reading newspapers has been sliding in recent years. Newspapers have attempted to counteract this decline in readership by beefing up their web sites through video streaming and up-to-the-minute news content publishing.

## Outdoor or Out-of-Home

Out-of-home (OOH) continues to evolve and has been expanding to include a variety of additional and new sites. Traditionally, OOH was the standard

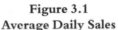

**Figure 3.1**
**Average Daily Sales**

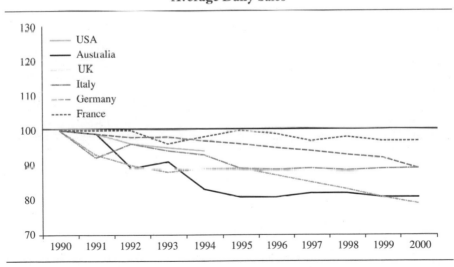

*Source*: ZenithOptimedia.

billboards on highways, posterboards on residential streets, or the famous OOH signs that light up the Broadway sky in New York City. Signage at sports complexes, music venues, benches, on cabs and buses, and so on have also continued to increase as companies try to utilize any and all space available to them to generate revenue and product brand awareness.

## Internet

The Internet has become the most overall disruptive media channel in recent years. The decrease in use of many media types by consumers can be directly tied back to the increase in use of the Internet. It might sound funny to put the Internet in a "view of the past," but we are now fully in the second decade of Internet use by companies to market products and services so it belongs in this category. The technology behind the Internet has had significant impact in the use and time spent on the Internet. When the Internet was first introduced, dial-up service was the normal gateway to the Internet for many consumers. This technology and lack of bandwidth proved challenging for most activities including e-mail, surfing, photo and video viewing, downloading, and the like. However, the introduction and roll out of broadband service by cable providers, Internet services, and telecom companies has increased bandwidth allowing customers immediate access to the Internet, faster downloads, viewing, and interaction with content.

Broadband penetration is estimated to be 48.3 percent (or 139.4 million people) in the United States (Figure 3.2).[11] Most consumers are spending more time on the Internet as they discover the vast content and information that it holds.

When Internet advertising first began to take form, the most traditional types of advertisements were relatively simple sponsorships or banner advertising. Both of these provided the ability to link back to the respective advertiser's web page or promotion page where more information could be conveyed to the consumer. Banners and sponsorships are still very prominent in most interactive campaigns. But with new technology and broadband access, the advertisements and campaigns are much more complex with video and flashtype creative features being used versus the static banners and logos from the past.

The area of most significant growth in the past few years has been *search marketing*. Most advertisers and agencies now understand the power of utilizing key words to drive consumers to their web site for more information.

If done properly, a search program can drive an extraordinary volume of clicks to a web site as well as significant sales volume. One of the key variables

**Figure 3.2**
**Total Online Population (in Millions)**

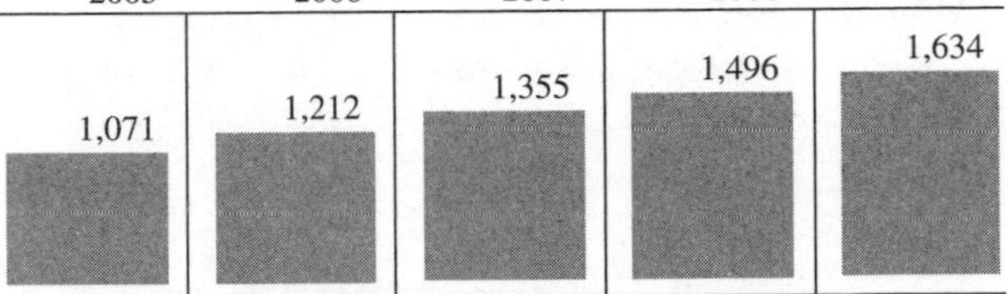

| | 2005 | 2006 | 2007 | 2008 | 2009 |
|---|---|---|---|---|---|
| | 1,071 | 1,212 | 1,355 | 1,496 | 1,634 |
| North America | 220 | 233 | 247 | 261 | 275 |
| Western Europe | 218 | 239 | 261 | 282 | 303 |
| Eastern Europe | 73 | 86 | 99 | 112 | 125 |
| Asia Pacific | 427 | 494 | 562 | 627 | 690 |
| Central/South America | 77 | 90 | 104 | 117 | 132 |
| Middle/East Africa | 55 | 69 | 83 | 96 | 110 |

*Source*: Computer Industry Almanac.

in getting a powerful search program is to ensure the listing is relevant and comes up at the top of the page when someone searches for the term. The farther up the page, the greater click-through activity will occur because the first slot is the most clicked-through area on the page.

Because search terms are purchased through a bid/buy auction system, it is critical for advertisers to understand the key terms that consumers will search on in order to maximize their return on investment.

All of the previously mentioned major media types are important avenues to reach the consumer with a marketing message. The big question every advertiser and agency faces prior to determining "where" to communicate is "who" they are communicating to. Without a thorough and complete understanding of the target audience, the entire media investment could be wasted. Some of the key targeting elements that currently go into determining the basis of a well-defined media strategy include:

- *Demographic data*—Age, ethnicity, sex, geographic location information, home ownership, type of vehicle, number of household members, employment status, and type of employment
- *Psychographic data*—Including values, the way individuals view things, their interests and beliefs
- *Financial data*—Household income, home value, net worth, financial scores, debt repayment history, and so on

- *Purchase behavior*—Type of credit card used, average purchase size, types of brands purchased, frequency of purchases, direct versus indirect purchase behavior, brand loyalty, and the like
- *Media consumption habits*—How does the target audience receive information on the product awareness, consideration, preference, and ultimate purchase? What media types are used to convey this information, what does the consumer value?

This and much more specific data available on the customer (demographics) go into creating a media strategy and plan that will maximize the results of the financial and human capital commitment made to the campaign. Usually the differences in a target audience are easy to discern when you compare media plans side-by-side. Differences such as the type of media used, the weight placed on specific media, the length of time a media property is used, and the type of program or initiative executed in the media are all critical differentiators between target audiences.

Changes in both media companies and media agencies have followed the changes that have occurred in the industry as a whole. For instance, media and the work done by media-specific agencies used to be the last consideration when a campaign or initiative was being planned. Creative agencies tended to be the lead in all initiatives. But as media channels have changed, grown, and become more complex, media agencies are now sitting at the marketing table, if not sitting at the head of the table leading the overall campaign strategy with the creative agency. And over time, the media department that used to be located within the creative agency, is now more than likely a separate entity. It is not unusual for the creative account to go to one agency and the media to a totally separate specific-media agency. This separation of duties clearly shows the importance of media agencies in the strategy and execution of a campaign. Media is now a specialty just as creative has been in the past at traditional agencies. In addition, the celebration of excellence in media through media-specific industry award shows also proves media is at the forefront of marketing strategy. The Cannes Advertising Festival, Addy Awards, *Media-Week*, and *Advertising Age* all now promote excellence in media through awards or special reports.

Media companies or conglomerates have also undergone dramatic changes. The past three to five years have seen upheavals in the portfolios of many media companies. Time Warner, for instance, sold off 18 magazine publications from its stable of properties and has shifted the savings into expanding interactive properties. Employment layoffs are common among print-heavy companies because the growth in print sales has slowed or is in decline. Television properties are trying to take advantage of content by streaming it on the Internet. Interactive and search-only properties are trying to staff up based on increased consumer and advertiser demand. What the final scenario looks like is anybody's guess, but needless to say, the media industry is probably just at the beginning of this change cycle.

## VIEW OF THE FUTURE

Now that we've seen a glimpse of the past, what does the future look like? One popular media and marketing executive, Rishad Tobaccowala, CEO of the Denuo Group and chief innovation officer of Publicis, put it this way:

> Increasingly, marketing has been outsourced to the consumer or customer as they self-market. By combining word-of-mouth, research on the web, and other information, people are marketing to themselves in category after category from automobiles to computers to electronics to travel. The job of the marketer is to facilitate and become a part of this self-marketing. Increasingly, well-educated people go to doctors with web pages printed out on what is wrong with them and ask for a prescription to be written! Marketing will become facilitation.

Media and marketing funding in general will continue to grow as advertisers find more productive and unique areas to reach the consumer. The funding may shift from one media type to another and the lines between what is and is not media may become gray, but marketing drives sales . . . and sales drive profits. ZenithOptimedia, one of the leading media agencies in the world, has predicted that advertising expenditures will continue to increase over the next few years (Figure 3.3). And as advertising expenditures increase, all marketers will be looking at new ways to increase efficiency and optimization of media. Let's look at some of the projected changes.

### TV/Video

It would seem in a world where DVRs become the norm, TV consumption would decrease. But a deeper look shows that those who have a DVR installed actually watch slightly more TV content versus those who don't have a DVR (Figure 3.4). The simple reason is that the consumer has the power to determine what they want to watch, when they want to view it, while at the same time having the option to fast-forward through the commercial breaks. In a recent report, 53 percent of all DVR users skipped through the commercial breaks[12]—a staggering number for advertisers and TV networks to deal with.

**Figure 3.3**
**North America (in Millions)**

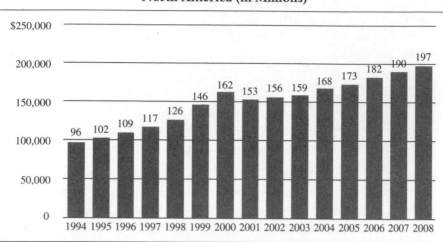

*Source*: ZenithOptimedia Advertising Expenditure Forecast, March 2006.

***Intertwined Content and Commercial Messages*** As more consumers skip commercials through the use of technology, advertisers, agencies, and TV networks will continue to be more creative about integrating content and advertising messages into the actual content. From the obvious product placement (the Coke cups on the table of the *American Idol* judges) to more sophisticated

**Figure 3.4**
**Percentage of Homes with a TV That Have a DVR**

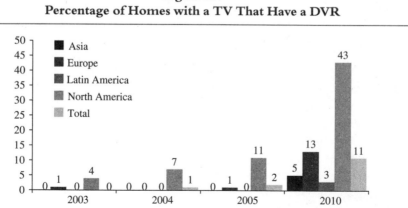

attempts where the consumer is seamlessly being shown the product's features and benefits intertwined within the storyline of the show. The latter are challenging and difficult to execute, but networks will begin to look more and more to these integration efforts to increase bottom-line revenue.

*Content Expansion*   With the Internet maturing, broadband connections expanding in not only household penetration but also bandwidth, video and TV content will be more prevalent than ever. No more will you have to set aside time to program your DVR or make an "appointment" to view a particular TV show. Some cable and satellite operators allow you to view the content when it's convenient for you. This service is being offered on a limited scale today on some cable networks and is beginning to take hold on the Internet. The big question that looms is: Will the revenue model support the growing content? For instance, will there be advertising to support the show, will the consumer be charged an additional fee to view the show, or will it be a combination of the two? In addition, we won't be held to view only U.S.-based content. The Internet provides the opportunity to have content from all over the world available to the consumer. So watching more content produced, for instance, in China will become more common in the not-so-distant future.

*Content Distribution*   As mentioned previously, the expansion of the Internet will create many more opportunities for video content (TV, video commercials, short- and long-form user generated content, etc.) to be played on the desktop, laptop, or mobile device in addition to being played on a traditional TV screen. The world is changing to a three-screen world—computer screen, TV screen, and mobile screen. Content will be available anywhere, anytime, and through any number of devices—the consumer will be in total control. And with increased distribution capabilities, the entire marketplace will have significant challenges including:

- *Content ownerships rights*—Who owns what? When and where can it be viewed?
- *Business model*—How and who makes revenue? Who gets charged for content? Will consumers pay for content or will advertisers subsidize the cost of content?
- *Infrastructure*—Which type of infrastructure will become the standard or will there be a number of standards? How might those standards integrate with one another and with devices?

***Increased Competition***   YouTube has certainly shown that anyone can produce and distribute content. Competition will continue to increase with all sorts of players getting into the marketplace including:

1. Print publications offering expanded interactive sites that distribute video content as well as articles. In addition, they will provide more current information in order to lure consumers back.
2. Television networks who will continue to expand their online video distribution through their branded web sites.
3. Internet portals, for instance, Joost (www.joost.com), Yahoo! (www.yahoo.com), and so on who will aggregate content across the Internet including video.
4. Start-up and current video distribution sites which will provide aggregation of content specific to video (including user generated content, video content, etc.).
5. Cable companies who will offer replayed content via the TV set-top box, but store the content on the cable company's servers.
6. DVR companies, computer manufacturers, and the like who offer the consumer control of the content on an in-home hard disk they can then play at their convenience.

And who knows who else will put out a shingle to broadcast TV or video.

Everyone hopes prices in media will decrease with increased competition for access to consumers. However, we could see a short-term market in which the end consumer actually has to pay more for cables services if TV networks are forced to raise fees. This would be the result of declining prices or demand in commercial advertising rates which traditionally subsidize the cost of programming.

***New Income Sources***   As increased competition lowers prices in the marketplace not only for advertisers but also for viewers, TV and video companies will need to adapt to create additional income sources. Product placement and integration are the hot button for TV studios, but you might also see brand characters or icons being integrated into a show's storyline. Interactive TV that allows the consumer to purchases items seen in the show might provide revenue to the networks. For instance, if you see a handbag that a character in a sitcom is carrying, you would be able to click it to see the price. If you want to buy it, you would hit "buy" and it will be sent to your home.

***Traditional Marketplace Shift***    The traditional once-a-year purchase of most of a company's yearly TV advertising will begin to play less of a role in the future. Given the significant shifts into other forms of media, more precise measurement of other media types, and the challenges of understanding long-term media needs, more TV advertising will probably be purchased in the short- and long-term scatter markets over the next 10 years.

## Radio

In the past, radio was always a great way to reach a target audience based on fairly segmented broadcast content. The inexpensive nature of a 30-second spot has allowed advertisers to reach a target audience in a cost-effective manner. However, demographics, usage trends, and technology have had an impact on the radio marketplace. The future trend continues to show that overall radio consumption will decrease in the future.

As the use of terrestrial radio continues to decrease and satellite music devices and the Internet become more integrated into automobiles, consumers will turn to these devices for more content and programming options relative to their needs.

However, alternative niche formats will continue to expand. For example, as the Hispanic market increasingly expands and becomes concentrated in new markets, Spanish language formats will become more prominent.

***Satellite Radio***    Satellite radio will probably begin to rely more heavily on advertising and product integration revenue to subsidize the current fee-based subscription revenue. Hiring more expensive on-air personalities will increase expenses and these will need to be offset with additional revenue. The easiest way to increase revenue will be to offer minimal advertising inventory to advertisers.

***Audio Content Distribution***    Just as TV is pushing the boundaries of distribution, so will radio. Simultaneous broadcast of radio on the Internet is already in practice today. The lines between the two will continue to blur. Are people listening to the radio on the Internet counted as "interactive users" or are they counted as "radio listeners?" And what if someone is listening to the radio station via the Internet from another country or region? How do advertisers match the proper message to this consumer? Much work and consistency in definitions, process, and technology will need to take place.

## Print

Since the late 1990s, the time spent by consumers with print publications has steadily been decreasing. And print readership usage will continue to decrease as more people get information from alternative sources such as the Internet. This significant shift in consumption habits will continue to have a profound effect on the print industry. For instance:

- The number of new print publications created each year will decrease as investors worry about whether new (and current) publications can create a sustaining advertising revenue model.
- In order to reduce expenses, print publications will look for unique ways to reduce production expenses including: reducing the physical size of publications—both in number of pages and the dimension of the publication, reducing quality of paper and ink, and so on.
- End users will probably see a steady increase in subscription and renewal costs of print publications. And special subscription price offers might not be as "enticing" as they once were.
- Major media conglomerates will continue to shed print publications that are not meeting revenue and profit targets. These publications will either be sold off or shut down entirely.

The future is still bright for print publications that survive. Those consumers who continue to read print publications will be extremely brand loyal. They will find the publication a source of information, entertainment, or knowledge that they can't live without. Advertisers will know the subscribers are more than likely to pay attention to their advertising message given this loyalty.

The bonanza for print media properties will be the continuation and expansion of syndicated content to other media vehicles such as mobile and interactive properties. Content on a print publication's web site will become increasingly real-time, very dynamic, and will integrate video. Advertisers will integrate messaging and content from the print advertising to the publication's web site. Advertising revenue will shift where the web site generates an equal or greater amount of revenue than the print publication.

## Digital

Entire books are devoted to discussing the future of the digital media landscape. The digital media frontier is literally being written and rewritten every day—with new technologies, opportunities, and the like. Here we briefly cover the most talked about and potentially explosive growth areas.

***Search Marketing***    The expansion of search advertising has been an incredible phenomenon. More than 6.9 billion searches were conducted from August 2005 thru August 2006. Of that, Google and Yahoo! led the pack of search engines at 47.5 percent and 28.1 percent, respectively.[13] Search spending (including paid inclusion, contextual, paid search, and fees) was $7.067 billion in 2006 and is anticipated to climb to $11.571 billion by 2010.[14] Advertisers and media agencies have just begun to realize the significance that both paid search and organic search have in the success of branding and demand generation. So what's the future of search? Quite simple—expansion! As more and more mid-size and small companies and international companies get on the search bandwagon, more advertising dollars will shift to the medium. And the science of search will expand as well. As opposed to searching for something as you do today, search will morph into discovery. So not only will you find specifically what you were searching for, but search companies will also provide you items you might like to discover as well. Search will also begin to expand in that you will not just receive the text link in your search results but relevant photographs, video, or audio as well. Search will expand into other media types—most notably mobile phone technology. It will become much easier and faster to search using your mobile device—especially when you're searching for directions, an address, or phone number. Look for more targeted search engines to pop up in the near future. As opposed to searching a mass search engine like Google for music, you might find a specific music search engine that does a better job of compiling the results you want. The upcoming challenge in search is the severe lack of skilled professionals and agencies who understand the search process, mechanisms, and tool sets.

***Mobile***    There are an estimated 2 billion mobile users globally.[15] Handset shipments of mobile phones across the world has been expanding and will continue to expand (Figure 3.5).

However, mobile companies are in the infancy stages of developing a compelling advertising revenue model that provides value to the advertiser while not upsetting the mobile end customer. And while the amount of cell phone advertising globally is relatively large at $2.496 billion, the U.S. advertising is only at $904 million.[16] The opportunity for search and the integration of marketing messaging into those queries looks promising. But note, an advertiser who "crosses the line" between what the end customer believes is acceptable and unacceptable interruptions and messages will be harshly criticized by the

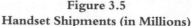

**Figure 3.5**
**Handset Shipments (in Millions)**

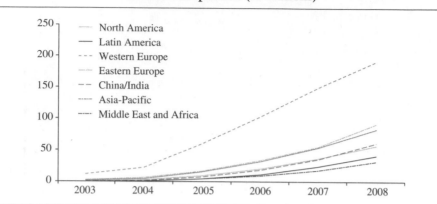

*Source*: Ovum 2004.

public. The area that perhaps holds the most promise related to mobile marketing is how advertisers can actually provide value to the consumer . . . by offering them information, insight, assistance, and other services in exchange for a message. Areas that are beginning to get traction include the use of mobile phones to conduct banking, utilization of mobile as a "debit" card attached to a checking account, and viewing specific mobile-only video content.

***Gaming***    In 2007, the estimated advertising revenue from the gaming industry is expected to be $502 million, expanding to $969 million by 2011 (Figure 3.6).[17] It might not seem like a lot, but this media type is in its infancy and is very compelling in audience/user base size. From individual game sales to massive multiplayer online games, the opportunity for integrated media in gaming is significant. Burger King's successful and applauded "King Games" that were sold at retail with a meal purchase have been a big hit. And the gaming technology itself is expanding rapidly.

Sony, Microsoft, and Nintendo product launches are big news with gamers of all ages. It is interesting to note that 44 percent of all gamers are in the 18 to 49 age group and 25 percent are above the age of 50 (Figure 3.7).

Watch as advertisers attempt to seamlessly integrate their brands and products into gaming platforms. As yet, the time frames associated with game production are long, and many advertisers are leery of committing marketing dollars and messaging this far in advance. The real opportunity in the future is

**Figure 3.6**
**Estimates of Active Gamers in the United States in 2005 (in Millions)**

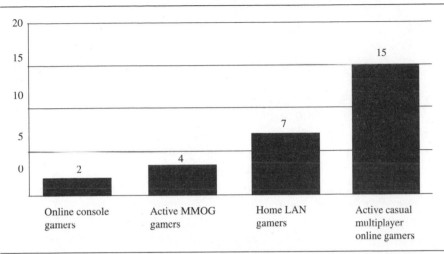

*Source*: Yuanzhe (Michael) Cai and Peter Shackelford, 2005.

online game play, where advertising messages can be woven throughout the gaming experience in a near real-time execution.

***Virtual Worlds***    SecondLife (www.secondlife.com) in the United States and CyWorld (www.us.cyworld.com) in Korea are two examples of the newest craze in gaming—virtual worlds. The premise behind these sites is a bit of

**Figure 3.7**
**U.S. Computer and/or Video Game Players by Age and Gender, 2006 (% of Respondents)**

| Age | % |
| --- | --- |
| <18 | 31 |
| 18–49 | 44 |
| 50+ | 25 |

| Gender | % |
| --- | --- |
| Male | 62 |
| Female | 38 |

*Source*: Ipsos Insight commissioned by Entertainment Software Association (ESA), May 2006.

fantasy mixed in with social marketing. The individual creates an online persona avatar and walks around a virtual world, mingling with others in the game. These sites have received a lot of PR attention lately, however, the big challenge with these sites include:

- *Costs*—It's expensive to create and maintain a business site in a virtual world.
- *Brand experience*—How do you convey the proper brand experience within this virtual environment?
- *Return*—It's difficult for most marketers to sell product in the virtual world, thus, it's difficult to get a positive return on the marketing investment.
- *Content*—The most popular content on these sites tends to be challenging (e.g., many sexual oriented and gambling areas).

Advertisers are dipping their toes into the water with virtual worlds. Look for these sites to either improve the commercial aspects and benefits to advertisers or to be sparsely used by advertisers as a mechanism of communication.

***User Generated Content***   All the advertising in the world can't compete with a recommendation from someone you respect and trust. And that concept is behind the flurry of activity around blogging and word-of-mouth media. Blogging has been growing exponentially with an estimated 12,000 new blogs being created daily (Figure 3.8).[18] Everyone wants to be heard, they want to see their name, and talk about what interests them. On the other hand, people like to read what others have said on topics that interest them; they want to hear other's opinions and thoughts. This is the power of blogging. Many corporations now have blogs on their web sites to encourage interaction between customers and employees. A blog gives the company a platform to talk about upcoming products, discuss and address issues and concerns, and get opinions from customers while forging a stronger bond with the customer. Public relations and media are intertwined with blogs. And companies will continue to exploit them to further connect with the customer. Company-oriented blogs will increase in number and corporations will try to further enhance their marketing strategies with more resources focused in this specific area.

YouTube, Flickr, MySpace, Wikipedia (and user-generated blogs) have all taken the world by storm. What do they have in common? The content is generated and created by end users. If you don't believe user generated content (UGC) is a powerful force in terms of marketing, consider this. Of the top 15

**Figure 3.8**
**Weblogs Tracked March 2003–October 2004 (in Millions)**

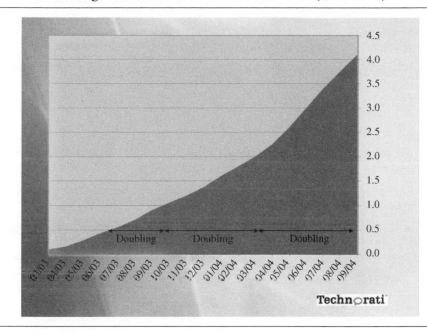

*Source*: www.sifry.com/alerts/archives/000245.html.

web sites (as measured by unique visitors), three of them are UGC sites—Fox (My Space), Wikipedia, and YouTube (Figure 3.9)

Will this growth continue? Absolutely! And it will grow at an accelerated rate. Why? Growth is due to the types of behaviors people are exhibiting:

- *Social networking:* People want to connect with others. A great example of this is FaceBook (www.facebook.com) that started out as a site where college freshman could get to know members of their class before arriving at school. And today, it's still used for this purpose, but now others are allowed to post to FaceBook in order to connect as well. MySpace (www.myspace.com) is another example where people can connect to others with similar interests.
- *Publishing:* As mentioned earlier, blogs have exploded. Look for more content including a dramatic expansion of e-books, e-magazines, and the like as more people realize they can become "published" simply by posting to the Internet.

**Figure 3.9**
**User-Generated Content—Wikipedia, MySpace, and YouTube Have Moved to Top of Internet User Pack**

| Rank | Property | Total Global Unique Visitors (MM) 10/06 | Y/Y Growth |
|---|---|---|---|
| 1 | Microsoft | 503 | 4% |
| 2 | Yahoo! | 475 | 5 |
| 3 | Google | 470 | 9 |
| 4 | eBay | 239 | (4) |
| 5 | Time Warner | 220 | (1) |
| 6 | Wikipedia | 164 | 99 |
| 7 | Amazon | 138 | 8 |
| 8 | Fox | 124 | 347 |
| 9 | Ask | 113 | (2) |
| 10 | YouTube | 95 | 2,542 |
| 11 | Apple | 94 | 34 |
| 12 | CNET | 93 | 1 |
| 13 | Adobe | 92 | (3) |
| 14 | Lycos | 91 | (5) |
| 15 | New York Times | 70 | 16 |

*Source*: comScore Media Metrix Global data.

- *Sharing:* The idea of being able to post photos of your children, your latest party or event on sites like Snapfish, Flickr, or Yahoo Photos allows people to share and connect moments in time almost instantaneously. For instance, posting a picture or showing the video of a child's first steps so the grandparents can experience the same emotional connection to the moment is powerful expression. And as broadband connections and the use of video conferencing becomes more prevalent, look for more individual consumers to carry on live video-to-video "phone calls" to share and connect in a more personal manner.

- *Creative expression:* Mashups, cell phone video, and individual videos created by small video cameras, and widgets are empowering expressions of individual creativity. Comedian Judson Laipply's video "The Evolution of Dance" http://youtube.com/watch?v=dMH0bHeiRNg is an example of how people can literally create an online phenomenon of creative expression. As of May 2007, the video had received well over 47 million views. Or how about the Diet Coke/Mentos experiment videos http://youtube.com/watch?v=hKoB0MHVBvM or the Honda video http://youtube.com/watch?v=g2VCfOC69jc. Both of these are examples of how a brand was inserted into a video in a unique manner. Coke and Mentos were associated by a couple of guys who decided to do a cool video. Honda specifically designed the video themselves. But what a sensation these commercial videos have caused. The popularity of video will continue in both terms of quantity produced as well as quality. The growth in video inventory on web sites and the opportunity to place videos on sites will also drive increased use of videos by marketers and media agencies.

**Banner Advertising**   It's strange to think of traditional banner advertising as "old" in the digital age, but in reality it is a matured vehicle in many ways. That being said, many companies are just now starting to increase budgets in the digital space, so banner advertising will continue to grow and expand in the future. Banners are evolving with more interactive and creative messaging and in general a better user experience. The transfer of images and messages that wreaked havoc with web advertising in the past has subsided as broadband has become more popular. But banner advertising is not without its challenges. Pop-up blocking software, Internet scams, and privacy issues are all areas that could hurt the effectiveness of banner advertising in the future.

## Out of Home

Out of home (OOH) is a broader term used to recognize this category's growth over the past 10 years. Traditional billboard advertising has come of age and expanded to include: mall or store advertising, "wild" postings (posters and such that are usually seen at ground level in major metro areas), mobile signage, airport billboards and posters. OOH spending is estimated to stay somewhat flat in the future.

But the technology of OOH should expand with traditional flat, static billboards being replaced with new digital outdoor signs that play video and use intensive graphics. These new digital signs have tremendous advantages because they can be programmed with multiple messages appearing throughout the day based on traffic patterns, demographics, and other factors. Therefore, multiple advertisers and multiple messages can be utilized to communicate messages. These boards are becoming more sophisticated and user interaction will probably become the norm at some point. For instance, being able to "listen" to the board by tuning your radio into a specific frequency, or have consumers engage with the board by uploading content to the board, are all things that can be done today on a limited basis, but look for this technology to increase in the future.

Advertisers will still continue to use OOH for branding efforts, but many are trying the medium for more direct sales and demand generation activities. The issue that has and will continue to be a challenge is accurately measuring the results—how much OOH contributes to brand awareness, consideration, and ultimately product purchase.

### Product Placement

The challenge with product placement has always been making it look organic within a particular media type, for example, TV. This is much easier said than done in a media world that moves quickly. But when done correctly, product placement can provide strong advocates for a company's brand and products. But product placement is and will continue to evolve as advertisers and media agencies demand results. Most large brands do not have an issue with brand or logo awareness. What advertisers usually want product placement to achieve is to show the product being used in a fulfilling and positive manner. This can be achieved if written directly into a script or if the product is demonstrated. Demonstration type shows include *Martha*, *Oprah*, *Hometime*, and others. These shows typically describe the challenge, what the product does to help solve the issue, and then actually demonstrate the use of the product. And usually these demonstrations have the added benefit that the host is someone who the consumer trusts and believes. The host in essence is recommending a product. And the most important influence in many decisions is a recommendation from family, friend, or trusted advisor.

## MEDIA MIX CHANGES

So with all this change in the individual media pieces, what is happening to the overall media mix? It's dramatically changing and will continue to change in the future.

Figure 3.10 demonstrates the typical media mix that most advertisers adhered to in the past. The future media mix is much more sophisticated, taking into consideration various types of viable media platforms for advertisers to target. Traditional media types such as TV and print will and are ending up with a smaller share of the media dollar, while digital (specifically interactive and search) will see gains in the not-so-distant future.

Here are a few of the changes that are occurring:

- *Digital*—More dollars will move to digital as consumers continue to look online for information, content, and purchasing.

Figure 3.10
Media Mix Changes

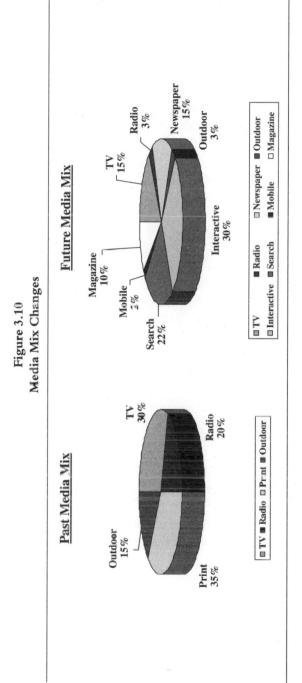

Past Media Mix

TV 30%
Radio 20%
Print 35%
Outdoor 15%

☐ TV ■ Radio ☐ Print ■ Outdoor

Future Media Mix

Radio 3%
Newspaper 15%
Outdoor 3%
TV 15%
Interactive 30%
Search 22%
Mobile 2%
Magazine 10%

☐ TV  ■ Radio  ☐ Newspaper  ■ Outdoor
☐ Interactive  ■ Search  ■ Mobile  ☐ Magazine

- *Search*—More dollars will move to search as smaller and mid-size companies learn the extreme financial value of search and search technology (e.g., mobile search, expansion of search technology).
- *Print*—Dollars will shift out of print, the historical mainstay of the media mix. Magazine advertising (especially monthly issues) will decline but newspaper advertising will probably stabilize as advertisers use newspapers to drive specific demand through price point messaging.
- *TV*—Advertising on TV is probably the toughest area to predict. Network advertising has continued to increase in price as overall viewership has declined. Advertisers are finding it difficult to justify the cost as they shift more dollars to digital platforms. However, if TV continues to evolve and utilizes the Internet and changes the business model, video advertising could begin an upward trend.
- *Out of home*—OOH will increase slightly as more venues and unique sites are added to engage consumers. Overall, demand for any particular media type will ultimately depend on the effectiveness of the media type based on the goals of the individual advertiser. If a particular media type does not perform, look for quick changes and shifts in the media mix to those areas that do work. In addition, as new technologies and other media types develop, additional shifts in the mix will continue.

Other changes that appear likely include:

- *Skill sets*—Perhaps the greatest challenge in the future for advertisers, media companies, and agencies will be acquiring diverse skills—mathematical, statistical, creative, problem solving, technology, CRM, database, computer programming, strategy and planning, marketing, project management, global business, and procurement. In a sense, media staff and management will be required to be multifaceted experts with the ability to work across, influence, and educate the entire organization. They will drive more of the marketing strategy and help management determine the proper implementation and investment of media and marketing dollars.
- *Media agencies*—Staying relevant is the most important challenge for media agencies in the future. Changing skill sets, pressure on margins, advertisers demanding better pricing for media, international footprints, and the ability to measure all aspects of the media mix are some of the major areas media agencies will need to focus on. Acting as the intermediary between advertisers and media companies may be threatened if media companies begin offering advertising for sale through auction models.

These types of auction models are being tested by Google, eBay, and others. If successful, media agencies will need to prove their value to clients in order to stay in the game.

- *Creative agencies*—The hurdles that face creative directors and agencies certainly are similar to media agencies—skill sets, understanding the changing media landscape/opportunities/technology. But perhaps the challenge that underlies all of this is the ability to continue to connect creatively to the consumer as media types become more varied and diverse. This is no small task. Creative directors must also become adept at knowing how to communicate through the different vehicles.

## Media Industry Changes

The changes in the media industry have had significant impact on media companies. Print companies are selling titles, decreasing publication sizes, and trying to expand into new media types. Horizontal and vertical consolidation will be a consistent theme in the current and near future. It's already happening:

- Google's impending purchase of DoubleClick—a leader in ad serving to online sites.
- Microsoft's impending purchase of aQuantive—a digital marketing company.
- Time Warner's divestiture of 18 small and less profitable magazine titles from its current print portfolio.
- Tribune (the owner of newspapers such as the *Los Angeles Times* and the *Chicago Tribune*) company's purchase by private investor Sam Zell.

Media companies will develop new forms of income to replace shrinking gross revenue from declining sales of some products. At the same time, they will continue to take extreme measures to reduce expenses by producing content that can be utilized in multiple revenue streams, reducing programming production costs and updating processes that can increase productivity. Media companies will begin to "cooperate" more with one another in order to provide unique opportunities to advertisers. For instance, TV companies will increasingly partner with online providers to resell content to consumers, thereby providing new advertising opportunities.

## Advertisers

So what's an advertiser to do? Stop advertising? No, quite the contrary. The advertiser must now think more like a mutual fund manager. Just as mutual funds buy and sell different stocks based on current and future performance, advertisers will need to apply this same type of management when it comes to building a media portfolio. As a mutual fund manager looks at asset classes, so too must an advertiser. The advertiser needs to build a portfolio of media products that meets the needs of the particular business problem or sales issue trying to be solved. Other areas advertisers will be increasingly concerned with in the not-too-distant future include:

- *Emerging markets*—For international advertisers, the ability to tap into faster growing marketplaces will be critical to drive a company's future growth.
- *Long tail marketing*—Marketers such as Amazon.com have made the long tail profitable, providing that not-so-often-considered item to very few consumers and doing it over and over and over again.
- *Media integration (or demand management) into supply chain management*— Many companies have spent large sums of money developing sophisticated customer databases that create just-in-time supply chain management. Dell is the most quoted example of this successful theory in which the components to make a computer arrive just after the product has been ordered. This effectively reduces carrying costs, allows the company to get the most up-to-date price for the product, and so on. Demand management will tie the media results directly into the supply chain. Thus, if supply is high for a particular product, automatically a media/marketing message and placement will take place and be executed into the market. This integration will allow for product to more seamlessly flow through the company, and allow for pricing to be gradually dropped (thus maximizing profit margins).
- *Eyes on the future*—Keeping a very close eye on new technologies, shifts in consumer media consumption and maximization of every media dollar spent will keep advertisers on their toes for the future. Media is and will continue to morph. It will be up to advertisers to understand, decipher, and apply this knowledge to maximize shareholder value.

Media agencies, media companies, and advertisers are at the apex of a new media wave. The road will be long, hard, rocky, and fraught with many challenges and failures. But just as Cortez chose to burn his boats in order to motivate his crew to survive in the early 1500s, so too must we "burn the boats" in order to succeed in the future of media.

## NOTES

1. http://inventors.about.com/library/inventors/blcabletelevision.htm.

2. *2015 Global Media Trends*, video (New York: ZenithOptimedia).

3. *Horizons Newsletter* 1, no. 2 (2007), p. 1.

4. *Advertising Age Digital Marketing & Media Fact Pack*, April 23, 2007, p. 30.

5. Ibid., p. 28.

6. See note 4, p. 44.

7. See note 4, p. 45.

8. See note 4, p. 21.

9. See note 4, p. 32.

10. www.magazine.org/Press_Room/MPA_Press_Releases/21559.cfm.

11. See note 4, p. 28.

12. www.marketingvox.com/archives/2006/05/04/jupiter_dvr_ad_skipping_threatens_8b_ in_advertising/.

13. See note 4, p. 39.

14. See note 4, p. 42.

15. See note 4, p. 46.

16. See note 2.

17. See note 4, p. 42.

18. www.sifry.com/alerts/archives/000245.html.

## REFERENCE

Cai, Yuanzhe (Michael) and Peter Shackelford. 2005. *Networked gaming, driving the future.* Dallas, TX: Parks Associates, www.parksassociates.com/research/ reports/tocs/2005/networked_gaming.htm.

# CHAPTER 4

# REINVENTION OF TV ADVERTISING

CLAUDIO MARCUS

**O**ver the past couple decades, the Web has become an incredibly engaging communications medium in large part because of the ability to readily tailor content relative to viewer, community, and timely information. Now imagine what TV would be like if it was able to adapt its content based on who is watching what, where, and when. Advancements in broadcasting technology are making such a scenario increasingly possible. Although it may take many years for TV programming to become as nimble as a dynamic web page, TV advertising will lead the way. It is already possible to develop and deliver TV ads that adapt in real time based on their intended audience, or timely conditions such as local weather, product affinity, or consumer response. Over the next decade, TV advertising will undergo a major technology-enabled revolution. Some marketers and agencies will learn to thrive in this new environment, others will simply fail to adapt.

*Webster's Dictionary* defines *television* as the electronic transmission of video images. Over the past five decades, TV has increased in both abundance and popularity. Consumers are now faced with more video programming options and viewing platforms than ever before. Despite the increasingly complex media world that consumers now navigate, we live in a TV-centric world. Traditional TV viewing levels remain at an all-time high with the average American adult viewing more than four hours per day. More time is spent with traditional TV than with all other media combined. Despite rapid growth in Internet use, U.S. adults still spend less than 25 percent as much time on the Internet as they do watching TV.[1]

Nevertheless, evidence of impending change is mounting. A McKinsey & Company study found that U.S. teens spend less than half as much time watching TV and spend 600 percent more time online than the typical U.S. adult. And, according to a recent Forrester Research report, people ages 18 to 26 already spend more time online than watching TV.[2] The advent and growth of online video will mean that consumers will have even greater choice and more control over what, how, and when they watch. Various technologies have begun to reshape how TV is delivered and consumed. At this point, it seems clear that while the common definition of TV will need to evolve to include new modes of electronic transmission of video images, TV, both in its traditional and new platforms, will likely remain a popular element in consumers' lives.

## EVOLVING TV LANDSCAPE

Since its inception some six decades ago, TV has quickly grown to have an enormous impact on modern society. To better understand what lies ahead for TV advertising, it is useful to understand how technology has shaped TV as we know it. These insights can then guide our understanding of how current and near-term advances in technology will likely affect the future of TV.

The first five decades of TV technology adoption (see Figure 4.1), saw the rapid initial adoption of TV, transition to color TV, and some applications that began to provide some degree of viewer empowerment. Even in the early context of relatively few available TV networks, the number of available TV programs quickly extended viewer choice. Soon thereafter, the emergence of cable TV made content more abundant and more varied while the TV remote control made it easier for viewers to quickly search for programs. Subscription-based cable and satellite networks initiated pay-per-view programming, becoming early examples of TV program offerings available on demand of consumers. Some 20 years before the turn of the century, the video cassette recorder (VCR), first enabled consumers to view prerecorded and consumer-recorded, time-shifted TV content.

An important distinction needs to be made between adoption and widespread use of new technologies. In the case of TV, overall use has become pervasive. However, even though subscription-based cable and satellite TV services are available to practically all U.S. households, not all households choose to pay for them. The magnitude of use and impact on advertising of the TV remote control or VCR has largely been unclear. It proved difficult to estimate just how many individuals regularly used a VCR, or how often, and what it may have amounted to relative to their total viewing time. It is likely to have been a small percentage of their total TV viewing experience. Still, as

**Figure 4.1**
**U.S. Media Consumption, 2002–2006 (Billions of Person Hours per Year)**

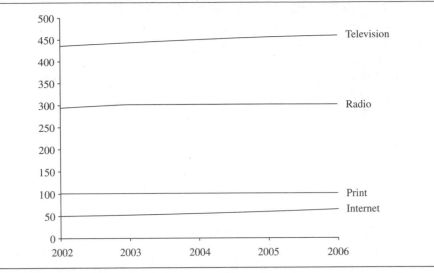

*Source*: *MEDIA*, August 2007; Magna Global estimates.

a development that introduced new consumer behavior, the use of VCRs is noteworthy and prescient of times to come.

The first two decades of this millennium will involve rapid change in how TV is delivered, driven by the increasing integration of three dynamic industries: TV, computers, and telecommunications. This competitive environment will redefine TV in new ways that are full of promise and uncertainty as to potential outcomes. The adoption of key new TV technologies (see Figures 4.2 and 4.3) will drive consumer choice to new horizons, further empower viewers to manage their personal TV experience, and potentially have even more profound societal implications.

Started with satellite and cable, digital TV delivery will soon be ubiquitous. The U.S. Federal Communications Commission (FCC) has mandated that all broadcast TV signals be converted from analog to digital by early 2009. Digital TV requires households to have a digital TV tuner or set-top box but enables a better viewing experience due to less signal degradation. Consumers will also benefit from the operator's use of the digital bandwidth to deliver more programming channels and video-on-demand content. To put it in perspective, even when delivering a high-definition channel, operators will have

**Figure 4.2**
**TV Technology Adoption (1950–2000)**

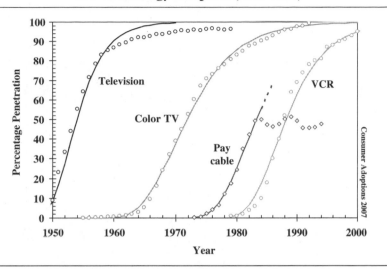

*Data Sources*: *U.S. Statistical Abstract*, Kagan, CEA; Technology Futures, Inc.

remaining bandwidth to provide at least two additional standard definition channels.[3] In short, consumer choice expands.

In conjunction with the growing deployment of digital set-top boxes, the adoption of digital video recorders (DVR) and availability of video-on-demand (VOD) have grown quickly and are projected to respectively reach 35 percent and 54 percent of U.S. households by 2011.[4] Both enable consumers to view content on their terms, namely whenever they want to watch, and make it easy to fast forward through content. Research into early adopters suggests that DVRs transform how consumers view TV, with various reports that estimate DVR users spend 40 percent to 60 percent of their total TV time watching time-shifted content and fast forward through 66 percent to 92 percent of the commercials when watching prerecorded content.[5]

Such data is seen as foreboding a gloomy scenario for TV advertising. However, a couple of important points need to be considered relative to early experiences with DVR usage. It is not yet clear whether late majority DVR adopters will behave similarly. One study conducted by a major cable operator who provided DVRs to 157 typical late adopter households reported that 57 percent of the test households returned the DVRs because "they did not want them."[6] Regardless of the potentially biased nature of the study, it raises the possibility that DVR use may be lower than currently expected. It is also

**Figure 4.3**
**TV Technology Adoption (1995–2020)**

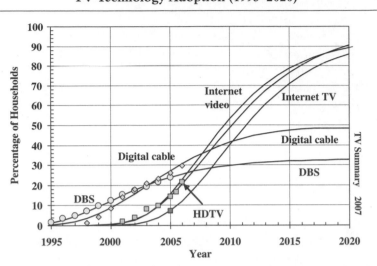

*Data Sources*: Kagan; Technology Futures, Inc.

important to take into account that the major cable system operators can control whether and how easily consumers are able to fast forward through commercials on VOD and DVRs supplied by the operators. To expand VOD programming content cable operators must secure VOD distribution agreements with the content providers. Content providers are generally interested in VOD distribution because it increases viewer convenience to access their programs. However, content providers may insist that the cable operators disable fast forwarding through advertising in VOD and perhaps even in operator-supplied DVRs. It is also worth noting that the underlying digital platform required to enable DVR and VOD capabilities also enables household-addressable TV advertising. Consequently, while DVRs and VOD present a major challenge for advertisers because technological advances deliver greater viewer control, they also present opportunities to fine tune the targeting and customization of TV ads.

Perhaps the most notable rapid adoption of TV-related technology today is that of Internet or online video. The rise of Internet video is being fueled by the rapid growth of high-speed Internet delivery, which has already surpassed more than 50 percent of all U.S. households. Use of online video is being driven by the growing availability of both traditional TV programming as well as a variety of additional video content including consumer generated videos posted on popular sites such as YouTube. As of late 2006, Forrester Research reported that more than one-third of adults age 18 and older say they view online video at least monthly and that 53 percent have viewed online video at least once. With broadband Internet access expected to reach more than 81 million U.S. households,[7] online video will soon be a fairly mainstream type of "TV." From the consumer perspective, Internet video overwhelmingly expands viewer choice and variety, delivers great control over when the content is viewed, and enables new forms of interactive and personalized video communications.

Sometimes thought of as synonymous to Internet video is Internet protocol television (IPTV). Unlike online video that literally relies on the public Internet for delivery, IPTV does not. IPTV uses Internet technology for delivery but represents an alternative method of distribution which is typically deployed over private operator networks. Major telecommunications companies have begun to deploy IPTV systems to achieve greater delivery efficiencies and free up bandwidth to provide TV-like services including a broad array of standard and high-definition TV channels and a plethora of on-demand video. However, to effectively roll-out IPTV in large scale, telecommunications companies will have to significantly upgrade their delivery networks, distribute or acquire desirable content, and effectively market in a very competitive environment.

Video delivered via phone handsets or other portable video devices enables consumers to watch video content wherever they want, even on the go. The growing battle between phone companies and major cable operators has made wireless phone services a key consumer deliverable, with feature functionality of handsets becoming a common lure to attract subscribers. Consequently, mobile phone makers and operators are eager to tap the potentially lucrative market for mobile TV. Despite the consumer and business benefits, the growth of portable video devices will be restricted by the need for bandwidth expansion and a shortage of airwaves that will likely lead to rising costs for handset vendors, telecom operators and possibly consumers.[8]

Most of the major new TV technology advances provide consumers with greater content choice and the opportunity to take greater control over what, when and how they watch TV. However, as outlined in the book *The Paradox of Choice: Why More Is Less*, too much choice may actually inhibit consumers' desire to take action. Interactive television (ITV) serves as a notable example. Available in Europe and the United States for more than a decade, ITV involves the combination of TV with interactive content, blending the traditional TV viewing experience with the interactivity of a personal computer. Despite industry hype, consumer uptake for interactive TV has been slow, with only some 10 percent of European households regularly using interactive TV services. The main reason cited for slow adoption is that ITV requires user involvement which runs contrary to the typical "lean-back" experience of TV.[9] Recent U.S. research also suggests that ITV will not attract mainstream audiences. Asked how they want to interact or interface with various technologies while watching TV programs, 73 percent of research participants said they just want to watch.[10]

The adoption of new TV technologies is redefining how consumers perceive and use TV. Consumers have much greater choice, and availability of video content will continue to expand at a rapid pace. Consumers also have increasing control as to when, where, and how they watch TV. Such emerging and growing consumer capabilities are beginning to reshape the nature of TV. The bottom line is that TV is evolving:

- *From*: Mass distribution of selected video content sent to a TV set via linear programming delivery.
- *To*: Mass, targeted and user-generated video content consumed on real-time or on-demand via a variety of video-enabled delivery channels and devices.

Time will tell to what degree consumer behavior embraces these new technologies and related capabilities, but it is clear that even the early impact is already posing significant challenges for TV advertising.

## TV Advertising Challenges

The impact of greater and broader viewer choice on TV program rating points has been nothing short of dramatic. The average number of TV channels available in U.S. households increased from six in 1960 to more than 100 in 2005. Back in 1954, nearly three-quarters of U.S. TV households watched *I Love Lucy* on Sunday night.[11] Over the past 30 years, the growing abundance of cable and satellite network programming has resulted in a decline of almost 50 percent in broadcast network TV viewers.[12] At present, the average rating for the top 100 rated U.S. TV programs is less than 3.5 percent of households viewing TV.[13] *American Idol*, one of the most regularly watched TV shows in the United States is typically viewed by less than 15 percent of TV households.

Lower program ratings have certainly not translated to lower TV media costs. From 1995 to 2005, the average cost-per-thousand (CPM) viewers watching primetime TV increased 144 percent for national network and 92 percent for local broadcast TV ads,[14] generously outpacing the 28 percent increase in Consumer Price Index (CPI) during the period.[15] The sharp decline in program rating points has meant that more TV ad insertions are needed to achieve any given level of audience reach and frequency of exposure. In such an environment, even careful media planning often leads to core target audiences being grossly overexposed to the same TV ads. TV advertising wear-out is compounded by advertisers' traditional reliance on one or few video ads, which also makes it very difficult to be relevant to increasingly fragmented and diverse audiences. Audience fragmentation is not the only challenge to effective TV advertising. The rise in adoption of DVRs and growing availability of VOD enables consumers to view programming on their terms, and this option often involves skipping through TV ads. Based on such behavior, it may appear that consumers dislike TV advertising. Another option is that consumers find most ads irrelevant and intruding on their desired content programming.

Marketers who pursue a traditional mass-market advertising approach will continue to struggle to achieve relevance among an ever-more fragmented audience. Going forward, a key advertiser challenge is how to efficiently communicate with increasingly fragmented consumer audiences but to do so in a manner that is relevant and fresh. Some major advertisers including Ford, General Motors, Johnson & Johnson, Procter & Gamble, and Unilever have begun to reconsider how much they invest in TV advertising while also increasing their investments in Internet advertising. While adjusting the media mix is likely to provide some answers, many advertisers will also have to figure out how to best use TV to market more effectively.

The simple fact is that TV plays an integral part in most consumers' lives and as such it serves as an efficient platform to reach them. Some of the same digital TV technologies that have brought on greater content choice and control for consumers will serve to bring on a new generation of TV advertising innovation that will enable the creation of ads that are more relevant to consumers and more effective for advertisers. Over the next decade, these emerging enhanced TV advertising capabilities will make it possible to harness the creative, persuasive power of video advertising with the target ability of direct mail and the responsiveness of online marketing efforts.

## Emergence of Enhanced TV Advertising Capabilities

To profit from an increasingly fragmented media environment, marketers must learn to make effective use of four key enhanced TV advertising capabilities:

1. Addressability
2. Interactivity

**3.** Customization

**4.** Dynamicism

Each of these capabilities can be effectively used by itself but they can also be leveraged together to enhance viewer relevance and advertising effectiveness.

*Addressability*    The deployment of digital TV, DVRs, and VOD, as well as online video and IPTV, enables forms of increasingly targeted video advertising. Using local cable TV, nearly 50 percent of U.S. TV households can already be targeted with cable zone level TV ads. While the number of cable TV households in each cable zone can vary greatly, ranging from a few hundred to a few hundred thousand households, each cable zone can be thought of in population size as roughly comparable to large neighborhoods, suburbs or small towns. In other words, cable zone addressability is not as specific as individual zip codes but certainly much more targeted than TV ads have historically been. As of the end of 2006, more than 150 major advertisers had conducted local TV ad campaigns that made use of cable zone addressable capabilities available from major local cable system operators.

Although most of the underlying technologies that enable addressable TV ad campaigns have been around since the early part of this decade, they have only recently gathered more implementation momentum. Major cable system operators have stepped up efforts to deploy digital set-top boxes to expand use of VOD and cable telephone among their customers. eMarketer estimated that by 2007 digital set-top box penetration of U.S. households reached more than 60 percent.[16] Cable operators are beginning to recognize that household-addressable TV advertising as a powerful weapon to enhance their cross-selling and customer retention efforts, and potentially critical in the face of growing competition from phone companies.

A relatively recent development, online video, enables addressability based on site or visitor attributes which include the use of the viewer's browser identification that can be matched with a geographic database to ascertain the zip code of the viewer. What's more, leveraging the use of a computer cookie with a unique identifier that can be matched and used to store and retrieve a variety of information, online video can be targeted to the level of an individual. IPTV will also offer such an individual level of video addressability.

Ultimately many advertisers will want and be able to deliver video ads that specifically target households or individuals. Addressability will prove especially useful for advertisers who have direct consumer relationships as it will enable them to differentiate their messaging between customers and prospects. Addressability will also enable advertisers to create highly targeted video advertising campaigns that focus on specific cross-selling, up-selling, and customer retention efforts. Advertisers in general will also be able to benefit from more refined customer acquisition campaigns that make use of third-party demographic and behavioral data to effectively target their TV ads.

The bottom line is that advertisers can already use early forms of addressable video advertising and that in a few years increasingly addressable forms of video advertising will become a relatively common tool for sophisticated marketers (Figure 4.4). To provide some perspective as to the likely availability of large scale household addressable TV advertising capabilities, Steven Burke, Comcast's COO, has stated that he expects the necessary infrastructure for full-scale household-level addressability to be in place by 2008.[17]

***Interactivity***   It is important to note that addressable video advertising is fundamentally different from interactive video advertising. The former refers to the ability to target ads to a specific audience whereas the latter implies the use of an interactive response mechanism that allows the viewer to provide or solicit additional information. Interactive video ads may entice viewers to further engage through direct involvement or access to extended content. Interactive video ads can also be designed to gauge consumer response to a particular message or offer and through proper tracking can be used to better understand the potential impact of the related video advertising efforts.

Interactive TV ads have been available for a number of years and continue to grow in deployment by cable system operators. Advanced functionality of interactive TV advertising allows the cable operators and their advertisers to target groups of customers using interactive enhancements using both standard and long-form advertising. Some key capabilities include polling which entices viewers to respond to questions or opinion polls and targeted display of tailored promotions and "call-to-action" prompts. It is also possible to "telescope" through interactive links to analog or digital channels that feature long-form ads, informational content or other interactive applications.

While interactive TV ads offer advertisers some interesting capabilities, evidence to date suggests that consumers have yet to broadly embrace them. As previously discussed, even when broadly available, viewer interactivity with programming has been relatively low with less than 10 percent of households reporting one or more monthly interaction with interactive content. Nevertheless, interactive TV ads may prove valuable for advertisers who can benefit from the opportunity to facilitate further engagement or direct response from viewers most likely to be interested in their products and services.

At this point, it is difficult to foretell how the experience of interactivity with the Web will influence TV viewing behavior, or whether online video

# Figure 4.4
## U.S. TV and Internet Addressable Video Metrics (in Millions)

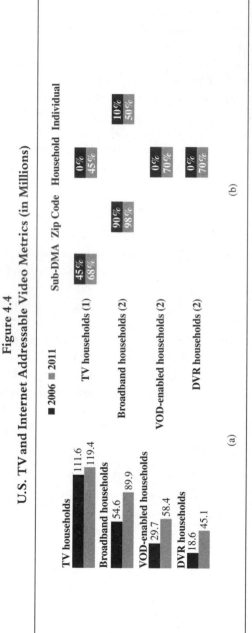

(a)

|  | Sub-DMA | Zip Code | Household | Individual |
|---|---|---|---|---|
| TV households (1) | 45% / 68% | | 0% / 45% | |
| Broadband households (2) | | 90% / 98% | | 10% / 50% |
| VOD-enabled households (2) | | | 0% / 70% | |
| DVR households (2) | | | 0% / 70% | |

(b)

*Sources:* (a) eMarketer, 2007; based on (1) Kagan Research, December 2006 as cited by the National Cable & Telecommunications Association (NCTA), 2007; (2) Nielsen Media Research as cited in press release, August 23, 2006; (b) Visible World analysis and estimates based on various industry forecasts, 2007.

will become more like passive traditional TV. Time will tell, and there may well be generational factors at play. It may be that as the generation of viewers who grew up interacting with personal computers is further exposed to a greater variety of interactive TV applications their use of interactive TV ads may become more common. Alternatively, it may be that viewers on the Web are simply better suited for interactivity, not only with content but also with advertising. Early experiences validate that individuals are much more likely to interact with online video ads. What is particularly interesting is that interaction with online video ads has been found to be greater than that for other forms of online display advertising. Research conducted by DoubleClick revealed that consumers are roughly twice as likely to play an online video ad as they are to click through on a standard online graphical ad. At least for the foreseeable future, interactive video ads will likely achieve higher response rates online than interactive ads on TV, simply because viewers online are more inclined to be engaged. On the other hand, as the online viewing experience evolves to support greater use of video, the convergence of information and entertainment or infotainment may result in an overall more passive online viewer behavior.

***Customization*** History suggests that the emergence of more efficient technology enables the creation and delivery of more customized and relevant communications in general. It was digital printing technology that brought down the costs of producing more tailored printed messages. On the Internet, more relevant communications were made possible by the development of software tools that enabled the efficient design, development, and maintenance of data and business–rule driven, dynamic content. Such technology advances enabled agencies to efficiently create and manage messages and experiences that better align communications with the intended audience, and in doing so, produce more value for the marketer.

Video is now undergoing a similar evolution. Technology-driven efficiencies in video production and editing now make it possible to create customized video messages at a fraction of the cost and time required using traditional methods. The history of film offers another important lesson. The use of digital production and editing tools in film lowered costs relative to more manual approaches, but these relative savings were quickly poured back into more sophisticated efforts, driven by increasingly complex storylines, editing, and special effects. Together, these historical lessons imply an emerging vision of video advertising that combines the storytelling power of video with the kind of targeted customization more typically associated with direct and online marketing.

*Dynamicism*   Historically, TV advertising has been so unresponsive to quick changes in messaging that most promotional advertising efforts have relied on more facile media. To put it bluntly, even newspapers, essentially wood pulp delivered by trucks, has been more responsive in enabling quicker change or updating of ads than the electronic TV medium. TV is at the cusp of becoming a far more dynamic medium, more in line with the Internet and more nimble than print media. Whether in the context of addressable, interactive or customized video ads, dynamicism refers to the ability to rapidly adapt, select and target a message based on data- or advertiser-driven input. Simple examples include automated date-driven event countdowns, dynamic updates of offer-related information and data-driven targeting of TV ad versions based on sales or inventory data. More sophisticated uses of dynamicism involve the ability to do real time customization and targeting of all or a portion of a video message based on current business, market or program-driven conditions.

# LEVERAGING ENHANCED TV ADVERTISING

When exposed to the concepts of enhanced TV advertising, the gut reaction of most advertisers and agencies is that such capabilities should enhance viewer relevance and advertising effectiveness. After all, addressability and customization have played central roles in driving higher value for direct mail campaigns, while interactivity and dynamicism have proven valuable in online marketing efforts. Yet, up to now efforts to use enhanced TV advertising have been largely experimental, mainly driven by curious individuals within advertisers or their agencies. Guided by basic common sense, this initial exploration of applications has mostly relied on trial and error. Efforts have typically focused on small tactical applications associated with specific media delivery vehicles. While these can provide useful learning experiences to familiarize advertisers and their agencies with enhanced TV advertising capabilities, such trials are not a substitute for proper examination of the core capabilities and their potential role and impact on marketing efforts.

## Value Framework

Given the magnitude of the opportunities and challenges involved, advertisers and agencies must seek a solid understanding of the underlying value drivers for enhanced TV advertising. The goal should be to establish a framework to determine how enhanced TV advertising capabilities relate to the business as well as ascertain the potential short- and long-term value. Proper assessment should include analysis of the core sources of value associated with enhanced

TV advertising capabilities as well as potential value inhibitors such as internal and external challenges that affect the likelihood for use and success.

***Addressability***    Greater media addressability enables advertisers to target their messages to a more narrowly defined audience. The primary value of address-able TV advertising is greater media efficiency since it reduces the amount of potential audience waste. A simple geographic example is that of an advertiser whose sales volume is largely concentrated in a few given markets who can selectively target TV ads to those markets rather than having to air commercials nationwide. Likewise a manufacturer of golf clubs can effectively target its audience using the Golf network or other golf-related programming.

The potential media efficiencies for addressability have to be balanced with the associated cost premium. Scale economies for advertising on national broadcast TV in the United States are such that it is typically more economical to buy a TV ad on a national broadcast network than it is to target 20 to 30 large metro areas. When it comes to cable TV, the differences are even more dramatic, as an ad on a national cable network costs roughly the same as a comparable ad in 10 to 15 large markets. As such, advertisers must consider whether the value of local market addressability outweighs the national advertising scale efficiencies.

Emerging addressable TV advertising capabilities enable use of neighborhood, zip code, household, and even individual-level targeting that means that in theory advertisers could target very narrowly defined geographic audiences. However, in practice media operators still require advertisers to buy TV ads at market-wide or DMA level that restricts the value of addressability since for any given advertiser a substantial audience waste remains likely. If and when media operators make it possible for advertisers to be able to exclusively target specific households, it will likely command a hefty premium. After all, direct mail already costs upwards of $500 on a cost per-thousand (CPM) basis or roughly 20 times the cost to buy a TV ad at market level.

Local addressability is more likely to be justified by advertisers who already use local TV. Opportunities for greater addressability will also have to be weighed relative to the role for such communications in the context of the overall media mix. Marketers will likely continue to rely on a fairly broad audience reach to establish and maintain brand awareness. Household addressable TV advertising will likely prove most valuable in campaigns whose objectives are to retain, cross-sell or up-sell existing customers, or target more narrowly defined prospect segments.

Some broad scale addressable TV advertising opportunities are already available through the use of local cable and online video advertising. Over the next few years, household- and individual-level addressability will become more widely available. While experimentation with various degrees of addressability may not provide an immediate return on investment, advertisers who best understand and prepare to leverage addressable TV will be better positioned to capitalize as broader and greater degrees of addressability become available.

*Interactivity*     The primary value of interactive video ads lies in enabling viewers to respond to the advertiser's communication. Because viewers most likely to act on an advertiser's messages are apt to be interested in the company's products and services or related promotional offers, interactive video ads offer the potential for timely engagement of suitable prospects. The growth in search advertising clearly indicates that there is value in reaching self-qualified prospects.

Beyond the potential short-term business value of enabling timely response from targeted prospects, interactive video ads also offer advertisers the opportunity to test, measure, and gain insight as to how their TV ad campaigns are performing. Because enterprises are demanding greater accountability from their advertising efforts, interactive TV advertising can serve as a platform to better assess advertising effectiveness. While brand-oriented interactive TV ad campaigns will not likely demonstrate immediate cause and effect like search or other direct-response methods, they can provide opportunities for furthering consumer engagement through telescoping to branded infotainment content, targeted long-form video advertising, or other interactive applications.

Because by definition interactive TV advertising requires the direct involvement of the viewer, its potential value requires a sufficient level of response. This makes it even more important for advertisers to establish reasonable objectives for interactive TV ad campaigns, recognizing that in many cases they may not provide an immediate return on investment. Looking ahead, the value of interactive TV advertising will likely be as much in enabling insights as to what engages diverse types of consumers, as in the scale of the actual results the interactive ads produce.

*Customization*     Consumer, product, and media fragmentation make it increasingly challenging for advertisers to rely on just a few video ads. Multiple research studies confirm that even popular commercials which initially entertain viewers or effectively cut through ad clutter suffer from wear-out.[18] Efficient TV ad customization makes it possible to create video ads that are able to adapt to diverse target audiences and viewing context.

Enabling efficient customization requires a mindset shift to an increasingly modular form of video advertising, not unlike what has transcended in direct and online marketing. For starters, the storyline of the message must lend itself to customization, which may be possible in various forms and degrees. Many, if not most, of today's brand-oriented TV ads are not particularly well suited, in large part because they were not initially conceived with message customization in mind. Going forward, advertisers must recognize that the production efficiencies associated with the development of more adaptive video ads can be substantial. With a suitable storyline, along with proper planning and preparation, dozens, hundreds, and even thousands of technology-enabled customized TV ad versions can be produced for roughly the same cost of producing just a few commercials using traditional production methods. While video customization involves a more modular approach to advertising that may be perceived as a constraint on creative storytelling, it can actually have a positive effect on the creative output. As a creative guru observed, video customization is akin to "a TV ad that is 30 seconds wide but a mile deep."

The single biggest challenge to unlocking the potential value associated with efficient video customization is the need for advertisers and agencies to shift their video advertising paradigm from a cost-per-thousand (CPM) viewers reached to a value-per-message (VPM) mentality. Media agencies carry out so-called "optimization" based on specifications associated with a target consumer profile and the relative costs for reaching the intended audience. Yet, such analysis often disregards the actual content of the message and how different audiences may perceive it. Creative agencies are charged with developing engaging messages that convey key benefits but are often constrained to producing one or few TV ad executions. The problem with doing so is that it limits the potential value of adapting the message to appeal to diverse consumer segments. In essence, advertisers who continue to rely on one or a few ads per campaign are by default discounting the potential value of properly addressing fragmented viewer audiences.

Advertisers need to recognize that driving greater returns for their media dollars will likely require incremental investments in creative development and production. Agencies will have to deal with the challenges of how to transform their standard practices to enable more efficient video customization. Likely challenges will include changes as to how video ads are created and produced. Although experimentation with various types and degrees of video ad customization may not provide an immediate return on investment, advertisers who best understand and prepare to leverage greater customization will be better positioned to maximize returns on their related media investments. It is also notable that addressable and interactive video advertising can benefit from efficient video customization, the fundamental value being the potential to further enhance message relevance for the viewer.

Another challenge to effective use of video customization is the need for greater integration between creative development and media planning since the context of the media may provide fertile ground to enhance viewer attention. Advertisers and agencies will also need to become more adept at translating consumer and media insights into creative development briefs to emphasize potential high value applications. And as the sophistication of customized video advertising campaigns increases over time, ongoing enhancements will require a greater role for analytic and modeling capabilities to help identify the most salient customization opportunities and iteratively maximize the potential value of each message.

*Dynamicism*    As the saying goes, time is money. So what is the value of being able to quickly change or adapt a TV ad? In general, response time to business or market conditions is becoming increasingly precious for all marketers. Some marketers with perishable inventory are already making inroads in using dynamic and data-driven capabilities on the Internet to help maximize the value of their available inventory. Such marketers along with others who dedicate substantial resources to consumer sales and promotion-oriented advertising campaigns are most likely to benefit from more dynamic video update capabilities. The value of dynamicism will evolve from the relatively simple opportunities to update TV ads more quickly, more often, and with less hassle than through the conventional, largely manual approach. More creative applications for dynamic video content update may also enable more engaging advertisements, less prone to wear-out and ad-skipping.

Over time, the value of dynamicism will be tied to the ability to integrate data-driven, dynamic update capabilities with addressability, interactivity, and customization. Such integration will enable targeted customized TV ad versions that adapt as needed, based on viewer, market, or business conditions. Moreover, dynamicism will usher in a new area of integrated marketing capabilities as video advertising becomes increasingly orchestrated with direct, online, and customer relationship management efforts. For example, results from targeted customized online video ads could drive customization and targeting of related TV ad campaigns.

To capitalize on the opportunities related to dynamicism, advertisers and agencies will need to become more proficient in data-driven marketing applications. While some marketing organizations have begun to develop such competencies for their direct marketing, interactive marketing, and CRM activities, rarely have such dynamic data-driven efforts involved TV ads. Effective use of dynamicism will also require strong analytic competencies. Over the long run, predictive modeling integrated tightly with dynamic response capabilities will likely become a key success factor in driving higher returns for marketing investments.

## Complementary and Comparative Value

By now, it should be obvious that while addressability, interactivity, customization, and dynamicism each offer worthwhile advertising applications, there is even greater value potential in effectively integrating the use of these largely complementary capabilities. This is one of the reasons it is important to consider the broader implications of relying too heavily on early results of tactical trial applications that may not sufficiently test any of the capabilities and poorly represent the potential value of more integrated uses. In economics, a complementary good is defined as a good that should be consumed with another good. In the context of enhanced TV advertising capabilities, it is worth noting how addressability, interactivity, customization, and dynamicism relate to and impact each other. To illustrate, consider the value of addressability when used in conjunction with other enhanced TV advertising capabilities. Adding interactivity allows an advertiser to gain insight as to who is responding and what messages they are responding to. Efficient video customization lowers the cost of creating more versions and in doing so enables enhanced use of addressability with more refined message targeting. And use of dynamicism makes it possible to have message targeting and customization that adapts to current conditions or to feedback gained from interactive response to any given advertisement. However, just because these enhanced TV advertising capabilities are complementary does not mean that they contribute equal value.

The economic theory of comparative advantage outlines the importance of taking into account opportunity costs in making resource allocation decisions. Comparative value plays a very important role in the context of enhanced TV advertising capabilities. Addressability enables the targeting of video ads to specific audiences, but the value of addressability is limited by the number of ads used. In other words, when targeting varied consumer segments in diverse program conditions, using a handful of video ad executions is likely to be suboptimal. Interactivity offers potential for viewer engagement and facilitates response to drive insights as to who is responding to the targeted efforts, but its value is also limited by the richness of the targeted messaging. Hence, addressability and customization both enhance the value of interactivity. Dynamicism can enhance the value of addressability and interactivity by enabling more immediate input and response to campaign performance, but dynamic update also benefits from efficient video customization as the latter lowers the cost of exposing viewers to the right message at the right time. The bottom line is that efficient video customization enables advertisers to better align their video ad messaging with targeted audiences, regardless of how narrowly defined an audience is or whether a viewer is able to interact with the targeted ad. While effective use of video customization poses significant implementation challenges for advertisers and agencies, its comparative value makes it an absolutely critical capability. Moreover, because achieving excellence in efficient video customization will prove to be a tough obstacle for many, advertisers and agencies who overcome such challenges will be well positioned to benefit from enhanced TV advertising.

### Gap between Mass and Customized Targeted Advertising

Often a challenge in getting started, advertisers and agencies must first find the time and money to conduct a trial of enhanced TV advertising efforts despite their all too hectic day-to-day operations and often stretched marketing resources. A *McKinsey Quarterly* article titled "Boosting Returns on Marketing Investment" suggests allocating 20 percent of overall marketing budgets to well-structured experiments with clear test protocols.[19] Enhanced TV advertising capabilities ought to be part of such test efforts. Beyond time and budget, there must be recognition that experimentation with enhanced TV advertising involves risks inherent in dealing with substantial change. So how does a marketer begin to think about leveraging enhanced TV advertising capabilities? Simple tactical trials provide experience with key capabilities and are a relatively common starting point. Assessment of the broader potential impact is less common today but can provide sound perspective about what enhanced TV advertising capabilities may be worthy of experimentation and implementation resources. Beyond a basic understanding of the key capabilities and a proper assessment of their potential value, a critical step is an analysis of the gap between an advertiser and its agencies' current competencies and work flows relative to those required for effective implementation of enhanced TV advertising. Such analysis will likely reveal insights regarding issues and trade-offs that must be addressed to overcome potential implementation obstacles. Critical questions that must be addressed include: How does a targeted capability affect the value of other related capabilities? Which competencies or processes create the greatest value and represent the highest opportunity for improvement? Is the magnitude of change proportional to the potential benefit? Does the marketing organization and its agency partners have the capacity to change at the needed pace? As marketers and agencies drill-down on the key capabilities and processes involved, they will surface symptoms relative to particular deficiencies. As in the case with medical practice, it is important to address the underlying problem and not just the symptoms. A summary of the more common symptoms and related competency or process gaps associated with enhanced TV advertising includes:

- *Symptom*: Addressable TV inefficient relative to broadcast media costs.
- *Common gap*: Focus on media efficiency rather than overall effectiveness.
- *Resolution path*: Develop understanding of addressable TV applications and the potential value impact as part of the overall media mix.

- *Symptom*: Unsure how to leverage addressable TV advertising.
- *Common gap*: Lack sufficient relevant data or analytic capabilities.
- *Resolution path*: Involve internal direct mail or CRM experts, or look for qualified external database marketing services provider.

- *Symptom*: Uncertain as to value of interactive TV advertising.
- *Common gap*: Lack of experience in response-driven marketing tactics.
- *Resolution path*: Engage direct response or interactive marketing experts, either internal or through agency partner(s).

- *Symptom*: Video customization is perceived as too expensive.
- *Common gap*: Failure to understand impact on value of media investment.
- *Resolution path*: Develop a deeper understanding of total cost and potential economic benefit of customized video ads.

- *Symptom*: Video customization is seen as complex or too much work.
- *Common gap*: Difficulty or unwillingness in moving from traditional TV ads.
- *Resolution path*: Seek fresh perspective from interactive, direct marketing or game development in the creation of scenario-driven advertising.

- *Symptom*: Uncertain as to value of dynamic video update capabilities.
- *Common gap*: Lack of experience in real-time marketing tactics.
- *Resolution path*: Engage internal or external experts with experience in time-sensitive, supply- or event-driven e-marketing applications.

- *Symptom*: Unclear benefits from trial efforts in enhanced TV advertising.
- *Common gap*: Tactical versus strategic focus.
- *Resolution path*: Gain understanding of potential application areas to identify high-value opportunities and develop trial efforts that take into account degree of change relative to potential value.

If not properly understood and dealt with, such symptoms and related gaps can restrict the advertiser's ability to fully assess and capitalize on the potential value of enhanced TV advertising capabilities. In general, advertisers and their agencies will need to stretch beyond their traditional comfort zones. Marketers will have to rethink the rationale and assumptions associated with traditional TV advertising. To drive greater value, advertisers and their agencies will also need to reconfigure some of the activities involved, as well as embrace competencies and technologies that enable the related work to be performed. As important, the direct involvement of leaders in the marketing organization is needed to set a progressive vision and foster an environment that demands enhanced accountability and a path to higher ROI from video advertising.

## MARKETING IMPACT OF ENHANCED TV ADVERTISING

For the most part, major advertisers remain focused on cost-efficient media scale, and many are quick to dismiss the evolution of enhanced TV advertising capabilities as not-yet-scalable. However, there is no denying that technology is fast changing the manner in which viewers find, access, and consume video content. People now have a much easier time finding specific programs that are increasingly tailored to their needs, wants and passions. Given greater media and audience fragmentation, it is harder than ever before for advertisers to aggregate a mass audience as they could decades ago. Indeed, there will always be mega-events like the *Super Bowl*, and even popular shows such as *American Idol*, but in the future, the vast majority of TV viewing will become far more fragmented and personalized. Advertisers and agencies must recognize that as more people watch TV in an increasingly fragmented fashion, the ability to effectively communicate with highly concentrated audiences becomes ever more critical. By enabling the aggregation of increasingly targeted, customized, and automated executions to deliver greater impact with a cost-efficient scale, enhanced TV advertising capabilities have an important role to play in the evolving marketing mix.

### Early Efforts in Targeted Customized TV Advertising

Over the past few years, some major advertisers have begun to explore the use of targeted customized TV commercials. In one of the very first controlled tests of targeted customized TV advertising, online florist, 1-800-FLOWERS, created a commercial that delivered customized video ads relative to the local cable TV zones in Los Angeles. For this Mother's Day campaign, the advertiser customized the offers based on the average income of each cable zone. Cable zones with average income saw products that ranged from $20 to $30, whereas offers in the more affluent areas ranged from $47 to nearly $500 dollars. To stimulate earlier orders, the campaign also featured an automated countdown of the number of days left until Mother's Day. And to enhance campaign effectiveness measurement, executions included a 10 percent discount for consumers who used a custom execution reference code. Although only a minority of orders referenced these codes, the data provided insight as to what combinations of networks, dayparts, and offers produced stronger results. Forrester Research reported that the response in cable zones that received targeted customized TV ads was double that of the control group.[20]

The 2004 launch of United Airlines' Ted airline in Chicago, serves as a good example of how local video customization can enhance campaign awareness. Relying on a very simple graphical execution, United Airlines used local cable zone TV ad customization to call out individual neighborhoods and suburbs by name to enhance local awareness and support its highly personalized brand position. Viewers living in Arlington Heights saw a version that introduced Ted's Florida route proclaiming that "Your chances of spotting a dolphin in Arlington Heights are pretty slim," while airing simultaneously in Schaumburg was a custom version that led with "Viva Las Schaumburg . . . doesn't quite have the same ring to it," to promote Ted's Las Vegas destination. Across the greater Chicago metro area, more than 20 custom TV ad versions were featured each time a Ted commercial aired. Northwestern University's *Journal of Integrated Marketing Communications* reported that by the end of the Chicago launch campaign, Ted had achieved more than 75 percent brand awareness.[21]

In 2006, Wendy's International used dynamic TV ad customization in a ground-breaking national network execution. Featured in a *New York Times* article, the headline is revealing: *A TV Show's Content Calls the Commercial Plays.* Wendy's customized TV ad executions involved a commercial that featured cute raccoons adventuring into Wendy's for a late night meal. In this case, however, what the raccoons were talking about was what was happening in the play-off football game the viewer was watching. If there was a fumble just before a commercial break, a raccoon said: "Fumble. These guys have hands like feet," while another raccoon replied, "Hey, I've got hands like feet." In the case of a touchdown, the first raccoon stated: "Touchdown. These fans are as rabid as we are," and the second answered, "Hey, I've got my shots." The ads also included other relevant football references, while clearly highlighting the key campaign message that Wendy's is open late.[22] While quantifying the value of creative customization is difficult, it is certainly likely that the ads were made more relevant to football viewers than a typical TV ad execution.

Given that the incremental creative development, production and talent costs were small relative to the cost of the media involved, the TV ad customization effort likely resulted in a substantial return on investment for Wendy's International.

Demonstrations of all of these examples can be found at http://linkname .com.

### Low-Hanging Fruit Based on Ease of Execution

The enhanced TV advertising examples involved simple executions that leverage fairly basic customization with or without addressability. All too often, enhanced TV advertising efforts are seen as requiring extra work, rather than as an opportunity to improve advertising effectiveness. It is important to consider that even though some of the simplest applications of enhanced TV advertising can offer some important business benefits, there is no getting around the fact that they often involve a fair amount of extra work. And more advanced applications may require the advertiser and its agencies to make substantial adjustments involving incremental planning and changes in execution relative to traditional TV commercial development. As the saying goes—no pain, no gain.

*Media Efficiency*    From an ease of implementation perspective, at first glance it may seem that the simplest implementation opportunity involves using existing TV spots in the context of addressable TV ads. For example, an automotive manufacturer could utilize its existing TV commercials for various vehicle types and leverage cable zone addressability on local cable TV to make more efficient use of each ad insertion by featuring the most appropriate brand and vehicle type in each cable zone. Yet, even this basic form of addressability is not widely used today because doing it well requires analysis to determine which brands and vehicle types are best suited for each cable zone. Gaining access to the appropriate data and resources to conduct the analysis has been a gating factor for many advertisers and agencies. Moreover, even when there is a willingness to take on the analysis, there are significant budgetary and political challenges associated with campaigns featuring different brands managed by separate managers. Consequently, most automotive addressable TV ad campaigns have been limited to featuring various vehicle types from the same brand. While such an application offers media efficiency value relative to running the same ad across the whole market, it does not maximize the potential value for addressability. Zip code, household- and even individual-level addressable video advertising all offer great potential for more efficient media use. To capitalize, advertisers have to establish sound analytic competencies to identify suitable niches and effectively assess performance impact. From a creative standpoint, advertisers will have to evolve from reliance on just a few TV spots as doing so is likely to under-deliver relative to using more targeted customized video ads. After all, what is the use of a fine-tuned analysis that identifies segments and subsegments with distinct requirements if ultimately only a handful of TV spots are available to target against the various groups. Clearly, maximizing the value of enhanced TV advertising requires attention to the opportunities to customize and optimize the related messages.

*Message Effectiveness*    An increasingly common use of enhanced TV advertising capabilities involves automated video customization to enhance message effectiveness. Usual applications typically involve simple changes in voice over, graphics, and titling, typically used to create relevant local offers and related call-to-action. For advertisers who rely on a substantial amount of traditional "grab & tag" video versioning services, automated video customization can deliver some time and cost savings. As such, advertisers who already rely on local TV advertising and typically target their promotional offers or localize their call-outs at least at a market level, find it easier to justify the use of more efficient video customization. For example, TV networks use automated video customization to efficiently create program promotion commercials that include a "tune-in" call-out that identifies the time and channel for that program in each specific market or cable zone. You may have noticed that fewer program promotion advertisements instruct viewers to "check your local listings for time and channel."

While cost justification for automated video customization is relatively straightforward when an advertiser already does a substantial amount of versioning, those who are not doing much video versioning may find it harder to justify the incremental costs associated with going from few to many custom versions. Such advertisers should begin by considering the potential value of delivering more customized TV ads. While doing so may be harder to readily quantify, it is possible for relatively small incremental costs in production to have a measurable impact on the return on the related media investment. For example, a major automotive manufacturer decided to use automated video customization to enable greater use of custom regional video content and local market versions more tailored to individual market requirements. While direct economic benefit attribution proved challenging, the regional sales managers and dealer groups involved expressed a strong preference for greater local customization. In cases involving direct response advertising, such as the example from 1-800-FLOWERS, economic value is easier to ascertain.

## Near–Term Applications for Enhanced TV Advertising

As more advertisers and agencies begin to embrace enhanced TV advertising capabilities, it is likely for initial focus to be on applications that minimize the degree of change from current operations while also offering desirable business benefits. When it comes to traditional TV delivery, we can expect to see enhanced TV advertising efforts that emphasize product and offer flexibility and responsiveness more so than changes to the creative messaging. The reason for this is that advertisers and agencies are more set in their ways of using traditional TV ads. Issues such as talent compensation and integration with traffic and billing systems may also deter some innovative uses. Experimentation and adoption associated with emerging delivery channels such as online video and IPTV will likely prove more fertile for innovation because they represent "green-field" opportunities where agencies are more open to trying new things and the talent unions' "new media" compensation agreement already facilitate broader and more varied use of talent online video ads. It is also worth noting that interactive agencies are more likely to embrace innovative uses of online video as they are more accustomed to dealing with technology-driven change and innovation.

***Timely Promotion***   Time-to-market, time-to-respond, and windows of opportunity are generally shrinking due to increased competition and enabling technologies. Television is beginning to undergo a transformation to become a far more facile medium for advertising communications. Automated video customization and dynamic update capabilities create an environment where advertisers can more readily and efficiently adapt their featured products and offers to market conditions. What is the value of having the right offer in-market sooner or the cost of not being able to match a competitive offer on a timely basis? An analysis conducted by a major automotive advertiser revealed that unmatched competitive offers negatively affected their business to the tune of millions of dollars per day. As such, being able to update TV offers in one to two days rather than the more typical three to four days is potentially worth quite a bit.

Direct response television (DRTV) advertisers that conduct business both online and through TV have faced dramatic differences in response timeliness. For example, Dell's online marketing efforts are updated in minutes on an as-needed basis, whereas their direct response TV ads (DRTV) are only updated a couple of times a month. The deployment of automated ad customization and dynamic ad insertion servers by major national broadcast and cable networks enables TV ads that can adapt in real-time to business or program conditions as was the case for the previously highlighted Wendy's TV campaign on FOX. These dynamic ad insertion capabilities should prove useful and valuable to advertisers in general and DRTV advertisers in particular. The latter tend to rely heavily on low cost-per-thousand, run-of-schedule (ROS) media buys where they do not control when the ads will air. However, TV ads that leverage automated customization and dynamic ad insertion are able to automatically adapt to the viewer context such as day-of-week and time-of-day as well as program genre or demographics, even in the context of an ROS media buy.

The combination of addressable TV ads with automated video customization and data-driven content update capabilities makes it possible for major advertisers to become far more adept and timely in managing their local TV advertising efforts especially for campaigns that involve localized and frequently updated promotional content. In some cases, marketers are already using data-driven systems to update their pricing and promotion offers on the Internet. Those same data files can now be used to automate the update of offers on TV ads. With proper planning and set-up efforts, automated systems can also help ensure that proper legal disclaimer information is used relative to the individual market or state requirements where the TV ads air.

*Online Video*   As advertiser demand continues to outpace supply, cost-per-minute rates for online video advertising are currently running two to three times higher than those for traditional broadcast TV. The fact that major advertisers are willing to pay such a cost premium reflects their interest in this nascent video delivery channel. Interest has grown as brand advertisers in particular look to digital media to replace audiences they are losing in traditional media and to add frequency against light TV viewers. Present appeal toward use of online video has less to do with the related enhanced advertising capabilities, but that will change as advertisers gain experience with this new video medium. Online video advertising can be readily designed to take advantage of addressability, interactivity, customization, and dynamicism. So while online video lacks the massive scale of traditional TV advertising, it offers great potential for better measurement and greater accountability. With more and more online publishers incorporating video content on their web sites, the issue of sufficient scale of reach and reasonable cost premiums will likely be addressed by marketplace dynamics.

Online video provides advertisers the ability to customize and target campaigns with a high degree of message localization because a viewer's Web browser identification can be used to ascertain their zip code location. For registered online users, it is even possible to customize and target video ads based on their individual user profile. Customization and targeting for both registered and unregistered users can also be driven by information derived from their web site visit or third-party ad server (such as DART from Double-Click). Advertisers and agencies are just beginning to experiment with geographic addressability and behavioral targeting using online video. Interest is being largely driven by the fact that it is possible to track how viewers engage with their video ads. Examination of such insights can be used to enhance the overall web site experience as well as to better understand that types and versions of video ads work best in terms of various consumer segments, and stages in a prospect or customer buying cycle. For example, a major electronics retailer effectively used targeting based on online behavior to customize the featured product in their video ads relative to what sections of their web site or other web pages a prospect had already visited. The campaign delivered a noteworthy click-through rate 10 times higher than untargeted online video advertising efforts.[23] Such results indicate a great deal of potential for advertisers who can learn to evolve and refine their online video ads to deliver greater viewer relevancy and timeliness.

***Short- and Long-Form Video***    It is important to point out that enhanced TV advertising capabilities are not limited to a traditional 30-second commercial length or any specific length. Preroll online video ads used in conjunction with short-form programming of videos will likely be of shorter duration than traditional TV ads. In the United States, one of the major TV network and interactive program companies has already affirmed that they will only allow a maximum length of 15 seconds for preroll online video ads. Increasingly such short-form video ads will be used to encourage viewers to drill-down or "telescope" to a longer form video communication. The follow-on long-form video can be customized relative to the specific referring ad or viewer context as well as a variety of other potentially available relevant consumer profile information. Such telescoping applications are well suited for online video but are also possible through the use of increasingly popular DVR and VOD service offerings.

The ultimate promise of addressable video advertising is the convergence of engaging video messaging with the precision, customization, and measurability of effective direct marketing and customer relationship management efforts. Will most video communications be eventually customized? Not likely. The adoption, use, and degree of video customization will depend on the value perceived by the viewer and advertiser value derived from the target audience. Consumer-oriented video advertising will likely be customized relative to the context of the video messaging for the target audience as well as related business or market conditions. Targeted, higher-value business-to-business messaging may benefit from even greater video customization. Regardless, what will ultimately determine the types and degree of video customization is the ability for advertisers and their agencies to execute and the related ROI.

It is said that all politics are local yet when it comes to political TV campaigns, they have typically favored those with the deepest pockets who shout out the loudest and those best able to respond promptly and effectively to attack ads. In 2004, Howard Dean's campaign for U.S. president was first to effectively use the Internet to engage and involve individuals through local "meet-ups" and "grass-root" blogs. Dean later became a victim of broadcast mass-media spin when he screamed like a college coach looking to entice his youthful live audience. Several years later, political campaigns have begun to leverage enhanced TV advertising capabilities to more effectively communicate their positions to increasingly fragmented audiences. The ability to address and localize political video messaging down to the neighborhood, zip code, and even individual level, will likely have a profound effect on political advertising and potentially take politics back to more personal discourse.

## Lightning in a Jar—Unlocking the Power of Creativity

Creative advertising concepts can dramatically enhance the value of TV advertising and discussion of the ultimate potential for enhanced TV advertising capabilities would be incomplete without considering the affect of creativity. The Marlboro man remains an icon decades after its TV commercials were discontinued in the United States. Apple Computer's famous Macintosh 1984 TV spot had a profound impact on the brand's perception as a rebellious, more personal computer company that has been long-lasting. It is worth noting that the Macintosh 1984 TV ad, directed by Ridley Scott (who had directed *Aliens* and *Blade Runner*), cost $1.6 million to produce. Media investment behind the commercial amounted to just $500,000 for a single insertion in the 1984 Superbowl. In essence, Steve Jobs invested in the power of the creative idea and brand "buzz" building rather than the conventional approach to simply rely on a heavy dosage of repeat exposures.

The Internet has unleashed some powerful new creative video opportunities. Launched in 2001, the BMW film series was produced specifically for the Web. The short-form films were directed by popular directors who crafted their art within the basic framework of having a central character who helped people through difficult circumstances using deft driving skills in a BMW. Supported with TV spots that mimicked movie trailers, print, and online advertising, the promotional campaign was designed explicitly to drive consumers to the BMW film's web site to enjoy a unique entertainment experience.

The BMW film series registered more than 100 million views. At its peak, an astonishing 94 percent of viewers recommended the films to others; millions of people voluntarily registered to receive BMW information. The BMW films' effort proved that the Internet could be used to effectively deliver a video-driven creative concept to millions of consumers. The effort is credited with launching the marketing technique of branded content, further validating that a heavy-up production investment behind an engaging creative idea can deliver a sound ROI.

As the Internet evolved to empower consumers to take control over how they consume online media, creativity again proved invaluable when Burger King launched The Subservient Chicken, a 2004 viral marketing promotion featuring a person in a chicken costume performing a wide range of actions based on a user's input. The site takes literally the advertising slogan "Get chicken just the way you like it" as it enables instant response to more than three hundred commands. The Subservient Chicken generated more than a million views in its first 24 hours, has since been viewed by tens of millions of young adults, and remains alive and well (see http://www.subservientchicken .com). The Subservient Chicken tapped the interactivity of the Internet to creatively deliver a brand message in a highly customized and engaging way.

Innovative video efforts require a commitment to nontraditional thinking in engaging consumers along with investments in time, talent, and production to execute promising concepts. And perhaps most important, is a willingness to take on associated risks. Evidence of such risks is illustrated by Anheuser-Busch's Bud.TV, a bold attempt to position the Budweiser brand as a video content destination for young male adults. With a reported investment of more than $30 million, Bud.TV hoped to draw millions of monthly viewers, but at its peak attracted less than 250,000 unique monthly visitors. Three months after its launch, the number of visits was too low to be reported by a leading independent web site traffic tracking service. Since then, Anheuser-Busch announced a series of Bud.TV program changes such as a focus on shorter videos, content circulation through major online content hubs and adoption of some social-networking features. These efforts may or may not salvage Bud.TV.

Progressive marketers will embrace using branded video content on the Internet to attract and engage with consumers. Some will succeed while many will fail, for the simple reason that creating a branded content destination which consumers find engaging is difficult. Media conglomerates invest in a portfolio of programs, understanding that the few successes will likely cover the losses. Few marketers can afford to take on becoming media content creators. While development of branded content has a likely role for some marketers, advertising will remain the primary means to efficiently reach large audiences because consumers have a plethora of programming content to choose from. As such, crafting creative video commercials that consumers find engaging remains a critical challenge for advertisers and their agencies.

***Rise of Contextual Relevance***    A research study published in the *Journal of Applied Psychology* in 1999, revealed interesting insights about affecting consumer context.[24] The field study investigated the extent to which stereotypically French and German music could influence supermarket customers' selection of French and German wines. Over a two-week period, French and German music was played on alternate days from an in-store display of French and German wines. Remarkably, 77 percent of sales were French wine on the days that French music days was played and 73 percent of sales were German wine when German music was played. Follow-up responses to a questionnaire suggested that customers were unaware of these effects of music on their product choices. The potential implications for advertisers are clear: Ads can borrow from the program context to be perceived as more relevant and act as a conduit that entices the viewer to engage with the brand message.

A recent definition of "engagement" by the Advertising Research Foundation (ARF) describes it as "turning on a prospect to a brand idea enhanced by the surrounding context." There are plenty of examples of contextual advertisements in print and outdoor media. Magazine ads are often customized to the genre or demographics of key target publications. Some billboard ads use contextual relevance to a location or type of setting. One such example is the BMW airport billboards featuring "airport-mindset," highlights of key product benefit references in contextual terms such as "ready for take-off."

While there have been few instances of contextual ads on TV, efficient video ad customization and other enhanced TV advertising capabilities will make it possible for marketers to leverage contextual video ad messaging. Borrowing from the programming context, vignettes or even storylines of commercials can adapt to the genre or demographics of programs or other viewer factors such as time of day, day of the week, or geography. Contextual video customization can also help advertisers and agencies feature the most relevant product claims and emotional elements to engage viewers at any given place or point in time. Just as the music at the wine store proved to influence the selection of wine, the hope is that greater alignment with program and viewer context can help make video ads more engaging.

Despite some uncertainty over whether contextual video customization and targeting will enhance viewer relevance, it's impossible to ignore how much money Google, Yahoo and other contextual ad networks have made through the text version of such contextual messaging. It is not surprising that online video ads lead the way in exploration of contextual video customization. The more targeted and interactive nature of the Internet makes it possible to adapt video ads relative to what an individual is seeking as well as the context of the web sites they view. Tailoring online video ads based on key search words requests provides alignment with a viewer's focus of interest. Delivery of online video ads that adapt relative to the context of a web site can be used to make the brand message more relevant. Such video customization will evolve to serve cross-channel video advertising applications. And within a few years, it is likely that consumers will begin to see video ads that adapt based on what a viewer recently searched online. Regardless of whether an ad is viewed on TV, DVR, VOD, IPTV, computer, or a portable video device, it could then be customized relative to the search terms of interest borrowing from program or other viewer context to further enhance message relevance.

***Breakthrough Creative***     Historically, the creative agency's role has been to condense key target audience insights and product benefits, add the emotional element that will somehow engage people enough to make them watch the advertisement, and hopefully persuade them to buy. The best creative work delivers executions that engage target consumers while clearly communicating the intended commercial message. Great creative work is often inspired by new business or communication opportunities but is as likely to come from facing particular challenges or constraints. The ancient Greek philosopher Plato claimed that "Necessity is the mother of invention," and that has certainly proven to be the case with advertising. Contextual video ads offer creative agencies the opportunity to extend their creative talents beyond a traditional ad storyline constrained by the standard duration of a commercial, to explore more varied and engaging communications. Borrowing on program or viewer context, creative agencies can now develop storylines that are designed to adapt and make the most of each video ad impression. Such efforts involve substantial mindset changes as they require a fresh approach to creative development, production, postproduction and perhaps even media placement. To enhance chances of success, advertisers will need to take a proactive role in encouraging such contextual creative experimentation by their agencies.

## Journey to the Promised Land

Every journey begins with a single step, but when it comes to exploration of enhanced TV advertising capabilities, missteps abound. The tactically focused advertising workplace is largely consumed with hectic day-to-day operations leaving little time to effectively pursue new opportunities. Even when trial efforts are undertaken, too often these are focused on a given execution or delivery channel without sufficient deliberation or understanding of the broader potential. Such efforts are the equivalent of taking steps in any given direction with little consideration of the merits of the journey. The rationale is often that baby steps are better than no steps, but more often, inadequate preparation or insufficient attention to strategic implications leads to efforts that deliver little in the way of reliable results or useful perspective. Learning to tap enhanced TV advertising capabilities will require marketers and agencies to jointly embark on a journey to untrodden destinations. Proper priorities, planning, and resource allocation will likely differentiate those who gain valuable insights from those that flail and squander efforts.

***Revisiting the Marketing Mix***    In a world of increased consumer, product, and media fragmentation, marketing managers face considerable challenges. However, in allocating their advertising and sales promotion budgets, a Marketing Science Institute research study found that the influence of historical inertia overwhelms all the other factors considered.[25] Simply put, marketing managers rely mostly on the previous year's budget allocation in planning for the subsequent year. Similar observations can be made for TV advertising budget allocation. Historical inertia continues to favor efficient reach over effective messaging. Marketers must recognize that attempts to optimize media budget based solely on costs to reach target audiences fail to recognize the value associated with more refined targeting or tailoring the advertisement to enhance viewer relevance and engagement, and in doing so, improve marketing effectiveness.

To optimize return on investment for video advertising, marketers and their agencies must acknowledge that there is value in delivering more varied and relevant video messaging. To determine the potential value, they must craft experiments that aim to familiarize them with emerging TV advertising capabilities and help identify applications most likely to deliver business value. Advertisers and agencies must seek to better understand the trade-offs between the value of addressability, interactivity, customization or dynamic update capabilities relative to their related incremental costs. The Marketing Science Institute study confirmed that the effects of different budget allocations to advertising, consumer promotion, and trade promotion are complex and interactive. Consequently, the effects and synergies between the various types of enhanced TV advertising capabilities and their influence on overall marketing effectiveness may take time to assess. Marketers should think of enhanced TV advertising capabilities as a set of new tools likely to help improve marketing performance. But as is the case with most tools, the actual value will be determined by how these capabilities are used both in terms of the types of applications and the ability to execute. Early focus should be on figuring out what role these capabilities can play and identifying the most likely execution challenges, including competencies, roles, responsibilities, and funding implications.

***Integrated Marketing***     The concept of integrated marketing communications (IMC) has been around since the early 1990s, placing emphasis on the value of making all aspects of marketing communication including advertising, sales promotion, public relations, and direct marketing work together to amplify overall communications relevance and consistency for each target constituent. Technology-enabled advances such as database and online marketing have made the IMC focus on customer centricity and data-driven insights increasingly practical. Although the concepts and benefits of IMC are well established, its practice has proven challenging to most marketers. A 2007 survey by the U.S. Association of National Advertisers ranked integrated marketing as the top issue senior marketers face, ahead of other important concerns such as accountability and innovation. Part of the problem is that the current structure and competencies of agencies require marketers to deal with serious trade-offs between communications integration and channel expertise.

Despite often being the largest portion of the overall marketing investment for most large consumer marketing organizations, TV advertising remains particularly disjointed from other marketing activities. Enabling the potential of enhanced TV advertising capabilities will require companies to confront and overcome challenges in the re-engineering of video advertising planning, development, management, as well as data-driven targeting and message optimization. To fully capitalize on the potential to leverage video as part of an integrated marketing communications platform, marketers and their agencies will need to map out multichannel "what-if" scenarios around key customer segments. They will also need to customize and align communications with varied consumer segments across a variety of relevant touchpoints and related viewer contexts. And given the increase in complexity and detailed execution involved, marketers and agencies must reengineer their workflow and embrace automation to streamline orchestration of the various moving parts. The good news is that these changes align well with the theory, practice, and rewards of effective integrated marketing.

A good illustration of the potential benefits and challenges for greater integration across marketing communication channels is the case of a major consumer pharmaceutical products company that in 2005 used targeted customized TV ads to enhance local response to its free-standing newspaper insert (FSI) promotion. From prior experience, the advertiser knew that increasing awareness for its FSI coupon via TV ads typically more than doubled response redemption rates. By featuring the FSI promotion only in those local cable TV zones where the brand wanted to enhance its performance, the company validated the ability to focus promotion efforts to increase trial and sales in the targeted areas. Interestingly, while the test was considered a research success, it was not expanded to larger scale due to the related media efficiency concerns associated with using local versus national TV.

Effective integration of video enabled communications is proving to have its own set of challenges and opportunities. Interactive agencies have experience with targeted and interactive efforts but often lack experience with video advertising. Creative agencies have ample experience with TV-related video ad production but often do not have the analytic and measurement competencies to execute online video campaigns that capitalize on the targeting, interactive, and dynamic update capabilities of the Internet. Such challenges make it imperative for marketers to insist on agency partners with suitable competencies and effective collaboration to execute more tightly integrated campaigns that make the most of the various messaging channels. What is ultimately possible is difficult to predict today, but there are some promising areas for greater integration between TV and online video advertising campaigns. For starters, online video offers great potential to better understand what messaging components and executions perform best under various demographic and contextual conditions. Well-conceived experimentation will likely lead to potentially valuable insights that could be used to drive value in related campaign TV ad investments. Many marketers already know how to "test and learn" to optimize online ad offers or promotion. Likewise, proper testing of the various messaging components of online video campaigns will lend themselves to a deeper understanding of what works under diverse market and audience conditions. For instance, a political ad campaign can use online video to learn what issues, endorsements, statistics and call-to-action work best in various market, neighborhood, or program types, to then leverage the distilled insights in fine-tuned TV advertising campaigns. A beer marketer could use online video to learn what messaging components the various segments of its target audience find most engaging under different content circumstances, then apply and leverage the most relevant content and insights in its TV campaigns. Such applications could become largely data-driven, with real-time online video response findings that trigger the most relevant messaging components in related TV advertising.

*Demand Meets Supply*   The reality is that when it comes to leveraging data-driven insights to improve business performance, marketing lags far behind areas such as supply chain management. Some valuable lessons can be learned from closer examination of how supply chain efforts evolved. A *Harvard Business Review* article titled "Localization: The Revolution in Consumer Markets" identifies some important findings.[26] First and foremost, one size does not fit all. Smart consumer-driven companies customize their offerings to local markets. Effective implementation involves combining data analysis with innovative organizational structures that aim to improve responsiveness to local market requirements while maintaining scale efficiencies comparable to centralized supply chain management. A key technique highlighted in the article is the use of clustering based on analysis of data on local buying patterns and market demographics to identify communities exhibiting similarities. Thinking in clusters can then be used to enable meaningful, manageable, modular operations that capture the benefits of customization while keeping things reasonably simple and protecting scale economies. An example cited in the research is Wal-Mart which, over a five-year period, evolved from relying on just five standard diagrams about where products should be placed on the shelves to roughly 200 customized "planograms" that were aligned with individual store-level product mix requirements. Undoubtedly over the past couple of decades technology-enabled innovation has made supply chain management far more sophisticated and increasingly localized. Although managing an undifferentiated product mix across the whole country is certainly easier and very efficient, supply chain optimization has made it clear that the benefits of localization are often worth the increased complexities and effort.

Marketers are just beginning to realize that when it comes to consumer messaging, increased consumer and media fragmentation limits the effectiveness of traditional mass-market advertising. The next decade will likely bring a substantial degree of demand chain innovation, including greater localization of TV and online video advertising that aims to leverage, data-driven, local demand insights to drive more targeted and relevant local video ad messaging. Julie Roehm, the former director of advertising at Wal-Mart proclaimed in *BusinessWeek* magazine that "Recognizing that a one-size-fits-all model is a thing of the past, we have strategically transformed marketing to move from a predominately national approach to a store-by-store, customer-by-customer execution of marketing campaigns."[27] Wal-Mart has already conducted at least one in-market test where featured items promoted in its local cable TV ads varied based on the store location. BMW has been customizing and targeting cable zone level TV ads featuring different vehicle types, models and offers based on sophisticated vehicle affinity models as well as zip code level sales data. As the aforementioned *Harvard Business Review* article concluded, "the greatest benefit of localization is strategic since local customization is difficult for competitors to track, let alone replicate." Well-executed localization strategies can provide durable competitive advantage. That will almost certainly prove to be the case for effective use of enhanced TV advertising such as increasingly customized and targeted video ads.

### *Marketing Communications Portfolio Management and Message Optimization*
Enhanced TV advertising ushers a new world of possibilities for more effective video communications. For starters, these capabilities offer the potential for far greater accountability than mass advertising since they can be used to assess the effectiveness of video communications targeted for specific audiences and business objectives. To tap such potential, marketers and their agencies must build the competencies necessary to thrive in a fast-paced competitive environment where audiences and media vehicles are highly fragmented, and where performance differs by segment, product, offer and message. This transition will require a variety of new skills including a more detailed understanding of the marginal economics of products and customers, especially with regard to marketing activities such as customer acquisition and retention. Effective use of enhanced TV advertising capabilities also requires strong analytic competencies to accurately determine what to test, how it performs, and what the broader potential impact on advertising effectiveness is. Over the long run, advertisers who learn to properly extract and leverage the insights will be better positioned to drive more substantial returns on their related advertising investment.

Some marketers have already begun to use a variety of analytic models for guiding the allocation of marketing resources. In some cases, portfolio models similar to those employed in financial portfolio management are used to help guide allocation of marketing resources across markets, products or consumer segments. Some marketers are using a variety of analytic techniques and services that make use of historical performance to model and simulate marketing mix allocation strategies. Looking ahead, analytic marketing resource allocation techniques will have to evolve to better assess and guide investments aimed at specific segments during various stages of their awareness, familiarity, consideration, and purchase decision cycle. Where possible, it makes sense to differentiate communications based on whether a consumer is a current customer, and if so, relative to the stage or value of relationship with the company or in relation to life stage milestones such as purchasing a home or having kids. Effective practice of customer relationship management (CRM) has validated the worth of such targeted messaging through direct, online, and customer service channels. Within the realm of CRM, direct or online marketing applications, some near real-time message optimization tools have begun to automate related customization and targeting. Despite the fact that TV often represents the largest marketing investment for consumer goods companies, message optimization for video has not been part of the emerging toolkit for advertisers. This will likely change as marketers begin to recognize that enhanced TV advertising capabilities can make their video media investments more accountable, and given effective use, potentially far more valuable.

What will analytic marketing tools and resource allocation models look like going forward? Like the product or segment portfolio and marketing mix modeling efforts that paved the way, message optimization systems are likely to leverage historical usage and performance data to ascertain potential high value opportunities for more customized and targeted video communications. Beyond that, a new breed of message optimization tools will enable more dynamic control with greater targeting and customization flexibility for video delivered across a variety of delivery channels including TV, online video, DVR, VOD, IPTV, and even portable video devices. These systems will make it substantially easier to effectively integrate and coordinate use of customized and targeted video campaigns with related online, direct marketing and CRM efforts. Such tools will evolve to support increasingly automated video customization and targeting for the purpose of maximizing return on investment given a set of established business objectives and predetermined budget, media and messaging constraints. It is also possible that further technology-enabled innovation and experience with enhanced TV advertising capabilities will enable the creation of a new generation of tools that take into consideration the potential risks and rewards of thousands of scenarios. Over time, innovative marketing resource allocation systems will be able to support automated insight generation through simulated and in-market scenario trials, integrated seamlessly with message optimization systems that make it possible to adapt and optimize return on investment based on real-time conditions.

## CONCLUSION

For most marketers, value creation is shifting from a focus on product and media efficiencies largely shaped by economies of scale to emerging means of value creation driven by economies of scope in customer relationships. To navigate through this fundamental shift in marketing, senior executives need to recognize that this is first and foremost an organizational change challenge. The good news is that the organizational and mindset changes needed to succeed in effective use of enhanced TV advertising are well in line with the development of customer-centric marketing efforts. However, marketing practices have only modestly changed to reflect that new reality. There is still enormous opportunity for marketers who master increasingly customer-centric marketing efforts, including the effective use of enhanced TV advertising capabilities. The change in mindsets and practices is significant, but here are five pragmatic steps that companies can pursue:

1. The chief executive suite, and especially chief marketing officers, must recognize the opportunities and challenges they face in becoming far more customer-centric in their marketing initiatives.
2. Senior marketers must establish and strengthen the roles of customer segment managers within the organization.
3. Marketers must validate potential impact through trial initiatives designed to better understand how to leverage emerging capabilities.
4. Marketers and their agencies must develop the competencies and tools to effectively learn from and communicate with increasingly fragmented audiences.
5. Marketers must develop measurement and incentive systems to track and reward performance relative to more targeted customer acquisition, retention, and value maximization efforts.

In summary, enhanced TV advertising capabilities present a brave new world of opportunities for marketers and their agencies. Rather than viewing video communications as static messages aimed at mass audiences, successful marketers will learn to leverage advanced video messaging capabilities to enhance relevance with increasingly fragmented audiences. Embracing enhanced TV advertising capabilities will require a major shift in mindset, execution, and measurement practices. Marketers and agencies that succeed in transforming their organizations will reap economic and strategic benefits relative to those who lag behind or are simply ineffective in their implementation. There is a good opportunity for thoughtful early adapters to gain competitive advantage as they discover, refine, and conquer new destinations that deliver greater levels of effectiveness and accountability for their video-driven marketing efforts.

## NOTES

1. www.tvb.org/mediacomparisons/02_A_Consumers_Continue.asp?mod=R.

2. 2006 North American Consumer Technology Adoption Study, *Forrester Research*.

3. www.web.mac.com/jenmeadows/iWeb/CTU10redev/
   Electronic%20Mass%20Media.html.

4. MAGNA Global, *On-Demand Quarterly*, June 2007.

5. www.forrester.com/Research/Document/0,7211,35326,00.html; www.lyra.com/ PressRoom.nsf/0/19e95b719e3e964a85256ea6004c5d8c?OpenDocument.

6. www.jaffejuice.com/2005/05/a_dissenting_po.html.

7. www.forrester.com/Research/Document/0,7211,40297,00.html.

8. www.news.yahoo.com/s/nm/20070215/tc_nm/mobile3gsm_tv_spectrum_dc_1/.

9. www.forrester.com/Research/Document/0,7211,34538,00.html.

10. www.publications.mediapost.com/index.cfm?fuseaction=Articles .san&s=53168&Nid=27370&p=257661/.

11. Chris Anderson, *The Long Tail* (New York: Hyperion, 2006), p. 29.

12. "The Chaos Scenario," *Advertising Age* (April 2005).

13. www.tvb.org/rcentral/viewertrack/weekly/2006–07/a25–54/a25–54.asp?ms=jan_28– 2007.asp.

14. www.tvb.org/rcentral/mediatrendstrack/media/media.asp?c=1b/.

15. www.minneapolisfed.org/Research/data/us/calc/.

16. "U.S. Digital TV: On-Demand and in High Definition," *eMarketer*, September 1, 2004.

17. Bernstein Investment Research and Management Conference Call on Comcast, May 5, 2006.

18. *Journal of Marketing Research* 17, no. 2 (1980): 173–186.

19. "Boosting Returns on Marketing Investment," *McKinsey Quarterly*, no. 2 (2005).

20. "Visible World Makes TV Ad Targeting Work," *Forrester Research*, March 24, 2003.

21. "Paint the Town Ted," *Journal of Integrated Marketing Communications* (2006): 31.

22. "A TV Show's Content Calls the Commercial Plays," *New York Times*, December 21, 2006.

23. "Things Change, So Let's Shop," *MediaPost's Behavioral Insider* e-mail newsletter, December 8, 2006.

24. Adrian C. North, *Journal of Applied Psychology* 84 (1999): 271–276.

25. "Brand Managers' Perceptions of the Marketing Communications Budget Allocation Process," *Marketing Science Institute Review* (1998): 98–105.

26. "Localization: The Revolution in Consumer Markets," *Harvard Business Review*, April 2006.

27. *BusinessWeek*, November 6, 2006.

# CHAPTER 5

# DEVELOPMENTS IN AUDIENCE MEASUREMENT AND RESEARCH

### JAMES WEBSTER

**M**ost forms of advertiser-supported media depend on an independent third party to verify the size and composition of their audiences. Those estimates become the "currency" used to value media buys. As media around the world become increasingly dependent on advertising revenues, so does this form of audience measurement. At the same time, though, fundamental changes in the media environment and audience behavior are challenging traditional measurement and advertising practices. This chapter highlights the changes that have had the greatest impact on established methods of research, describes the newest developments in audience measurement, and assesses a range of technological, economic, and political factors that will shape audience research in the future.

## CHANGING WORLD OF MEDIA AND MEASUREMENT

Audience measurement practices have evolved largely in response to advertisers. The Audit Bureau of Circulations was created in 1914 to verify the, otherwise inflated, circulation claims of publishers. By the late 1920s, it became apparent that American radio, too, would be an advertiser-supported medium. Unlike print, though, radio left no traces of how many people were in the audience. Radio listeners seemed as immaterial as the airwaves. Without reliable measures of radio's audience, advertisers and broadcasters had nothing to buy and sell.

In 1930, the industry solved the problem by creating the Cooperative Analysis of Broadcasting (CAB). CAB used telephones to ask a sample of listeners what broadcasts they had heard during the day (Beville 1988). Over the years, the techniques for capturing information on media use have changed. In the 1940s, Arthur Nielsen launched a service based on a meter that recorded radio set usage. Not long afterward, written logs called "diaries" were introduced to provide demographic data. Newer versions of both methods are still in use. But the basic model for audience measurement has largely remained unchanged—a third party, independent of the sales transaction, draws a sample of the population to estimate audiences. Those numbers are then published in syndicated ratings reports used by multiple subscribers.

By the beginning of the twenty-first century, though, newer media systems and the demands of advertisers presented audience measurement companies with serious challenges. Three changes in the media environment have been particularly troublesome. First, audiences have been fragmented by the sheer number of media outlets that are available. Second, people have greater control over when media are delivered. Third, people also have greater control over where they use media. Each of these developments and the difficulties they pose for audience measurement set the stage for any discussion of where the entire enterprise is headed.

The problem longest in the making is the sheer proliferation of media outlets. Nowhere has its effect been more evident than in the declining fortunes of broadcast TV networks. Figure 5.1 documents the steady erosion of broadcast audiences in the face of ever-increasing competition. The dark bars show the combined primetime shares of ABC, CBS, and NBC (the Big 3) over a 20-year period beginning with the 1985–1986 TV season. In that year, the Big 3 accounted for almost 70 percent of all the time American households spent watching TV. By the 2004–2005 season, their combined market share had dropped below 30 percent. Over the same span of years, the number of TV channels available to the average household, as indicated by the ascending line, increased fivefold. Recently, Nielsen Media Research announced that the average household had over 100 from which to choose (Nielsen 2007). Filling up those channels were new broadcast networks, superstations, and an avalanche of cable networks, each one claiming a little piece of the pie.

The net result has been audience fragmentation. Notwithstanding occasional hits like *American Idol*, audiences are becoming smaller. Even moderately successful TV programs have audience ratings in the single digits. Cable network ratings are often on the other side of the decimal point. Unless sample sizes keep pace, estimates of such tiny audiences can be swamped by sampling error. And the problem is not unique to TV. The audiences for most web sites are microscopic in comparison.

## Figure 5.1
## Declining Broadcast Network Audience Shares as a Function of Increased Competition

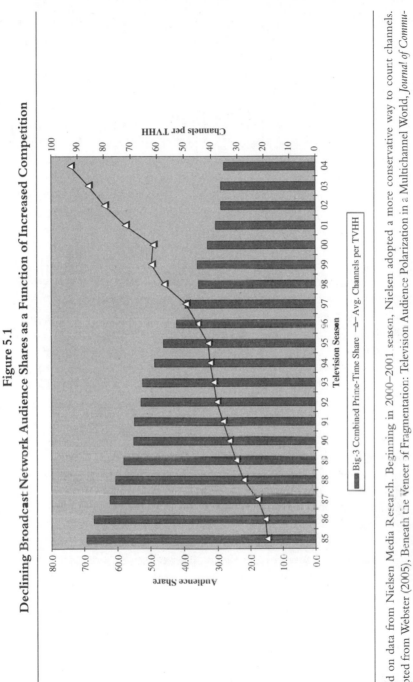

Based on data from Nielsen Media Research. Beginning in 2000–2001 season, Nielsen adopted a more conservative way to court channels. Adapted from Webster (2005), Beneath the Veneer of Fragmentation: Television Audience Polarization in a Multichannel World, *Journal of Communication*, Blackwell Publishing. Used by permission.

The second problem is of more recent vintage. Historically, radio and TV have been *linear* delivery systems, with broadcasters controlling what appeared when. For both the media and advertisers, this mode of delivery was a boon for managing people's exposure to media. Increasingly, though, *nonlinear* media like video-on-demand (VOD), DVRs, and the World Wide Web allow consumers to control when content is delivered. The shifting balance of power presents still more challenges for audience measurement. To begin with, it exacerbates the problem for fragmentation. The "500 channel universe" that John Malone used to talk about seems almost quaint when people have thousands, if not millions, of choices at their fingertips. Without fixed schedules to rely on, it can be difficult to know exactly what programs and/or commercials are actually being delivered. Finally, time-shifting programs and avoiding commercials in the process complicate what used to be a straightforward metric. If exposure is the currency used to transact business, what kind of exposure should we be talking about?

The third problem is related to the second. As media content moves across different technological platforms, consumers control not only when, but where media use occurs. Stories from print media appear online to be read from a workplace computer or a handheld device. Music and radio broadcasts can be downloaded to iPods. Television can be seen on the living room set, over various web sites (with or without ads), on monitors in public places, or viewed on iPods and mobile phones as "mobisodes." All of these points of contact might be occasions for marketers to build a relationship with fans of a particular genre. Unfortunately, most forms of audience measurement have been wedded to a particular medium and its traditional, place-based mode of consumption.

If all these factors weren't enough to strain the existing measurement systems, advertisers, themselves, have introduced new demands. Over the past 20 years, media buyers have insisted on evermore finely grained information about who, exactly, is in the audience. When TV was dominated by the Big 3 networks, Nielsen's household meters provided estimates of how many homes were watching. These were eventually reconciled with diary data to provide broad, if not particularly timely, demographic ratings. By the late 1980s, as cable networks with more targeted appeals began to emerge, advertisers insisted on a faster and more accurate system for estimating the demographic composition of network audiences. In 1987, with Audits of Great Britain threatening to enter the U.S. market, Nielsen installed "people meters" as its standard for national audience measurement (Webster, Phalen, and Lichty 2006).

While people meters can capture and report viewer demographics quickly, the availability of precise, person-specific information pressures the system from a different direction. If, for example, the advertiser is only interested in reaching males eighteen to twenty-four years old, that effectively pares the total ratings sample down to a small subsample. If the advertiser then wants to know how many within that subsample were watching a low-rated cable network or, worse yet, how that audience flowed from one cable network to another, the actual number of people in the sample that fits the bill can become extremely small. Once again, sampling error can overwhelm audience estimates.

In light of all these issues, the features of an ideal measurement system, while difficult to achieve, aren't hard to imagine. It would have two principle characteristics. First, the methods used to capture information on exposure would allow us to track individuals across time and space, noting all media they came in contact with on a second-by-second basis without any effort on their part—even better if those methods unobtrusively measured things like people's levels of engagement or product purchases. Second, such methods would be applied to very large samples or, perhaps, to the entire population. Of course, no measurement systems, not even those on the drawing boards, do all that. And even if some company developed an undeniably "better mousetrap," there is no guarantee the affected industries would adopt it. The following sections review the latest developments in audience measurement, and discuss the economic and political realities that will ultimately shape deployment and adoption.

## NEW DEVELOPMENTS IN AUDIENCE MEASUREMENT

There are three major fronts in the battle to keep track of audiences. The first deals with developing more powerful and flexible meters to monitor media consumption. The second entails harnessing newer technologies that can produce records of their use. The third involves a host of initiatives to quantify exposure to less commonly measured aspects of the media environment.

### Meters

*People meters* are the preferred method of TV audience measurement (TAM) in the United States and much of the world (Webster et al. 2006). In their most elemental form, they record when household sets are on and the channels that are being viewed. Each person in the home is expected to press a button on a set-top box or hand-held device to signal they are watching the set. All that information is retrieved via telephone lines and combined with other data to produce ratings reports as quickly as the following day. Though it's been in use for over 20 years, people meter technology is constantly evolving. The biggest challenges are: (1) knowing what's on the set and (2) who's watching.

Television sets are becoming display devices for a variety of media. Not only do they show linear TV programming, they're used to view DVRs, VOD, DVDs, and play video games. The first thing a meter must do is determine the source of what is being displayed. If it's TV programming, the meter needs to identify what's on the screen from one moment to the next. There are two basic strategies to do that. One approach takes advantage of an identifying electronic code deliberately embedded in the programming. This is sometimes called a *watermark* and is an active method of identification. Not all programming, however, has embedded codes. So an alternative is to have the meter capture a snippet of the programming, often a portion of the audio signal, and match that signature to a library of material. This is called a *passive* method. Most state-of-the-art people meters do both. Meter designers are also working on ways to minimize the amount of hard-wiring that's needed for installation, thus reducing costs and making households more likely to cooperate. In fact, Nielsen Media Research is developing a people meter that could be mailed to cooperating households.

The second challenge is more difficult. Typical people meters depend on the active cooperation of household members for as long as two years. Respondents may suffer from button-pushing fatigue. There are two ways to address the problem. One is to simply remind people that they should be signing in. Set-top units can have built-in displays or, perhaps, even speakers. If the meter knows a set is on or the channel has changed but no one has pressed a button, the unit can send a message in the appropriate language to encourage compliance. Some display units also have motion detectors that can trigger a message. All of these, though, are obtrusive measures that still depend on people's active compliance. An alternative would be to use a technology that alerted the meter to a person's presence without requiring any action from the respondent. Some companies have experimented with electronic tags and digital image recognition systems that can identify people's faces, but no such technologies have actually been deployed.

Even if we assume that people meters can accurately measure what is on and who is watching it, the technology still has drawbacks. First, it is wedded to a particular place. These meters can't follow people around to all the locations where they might encounter TV, not to mention other media. Second, building and deploying the technology are not inexpensive processes. Although Nielsen's mailable people meter might reduce costs, there is almost certainly a point where the market in question will be too small to justify the expense.

Another approach to metering is to make it portable. At this writing, Arbitron, the company responsible for radio measurement in the United States, is beginning to deploy in major markets what they call *portable people meters* (PPM)—small cell-phone-sized devices that people in the sample wear or carry with them during the day. The PPM "listens" for the sound of a radio broadcast that carries identifying codes inaudible to the human ear. If the person is within earshot of a radio, the meter will attribute them to the station's audience. At the end of the day, the respondent places the PPM in a docking station that recharges the device and sends stored information over the telephone. PPMs have built-in motion detectors that alert Arbitron if the meters are not being carried. Figure 5.2 pictures the PPM and its base station.

PPMs have a number of potential advantages. They obviously address the problem of following people around wherever they go. They are also capable of measuring exposure to both radio and TV as long as media within the market embed the necessary codes. In fact, initial testing of the PPM was done

**Figure 5.2**
**Arbitron Portable People Meter™ and Base Station**

Photo courtesy of Arbitron, Inc.

across those media in cooperation with Nielsen. While Nielsen Media Research has, thus far, declined to move forward with PPM measurement for TV ratings, its sister company ACNielsen, is pursuing a joint venture. The so-called Apollo project has 11,000 members of Nielsen's Homescan panel carry PPMs, thus tracking their exposure to advertising as well as shopping and purchasing behaviors. In the future, PPMs might be able to track exposure to print media by seeding them with radio frequency identification (RFID) chips, or outdoor advertising by using GPS technology.

Despite their advantages, PPMs have limitations. They obviously depend on people in the sample to carry them, so they are not a perfectly passive form of measurement. And while they may cost less than traditional people meters to deploy, they are not inexpensive. At present, Arbitron plans to use them in only the top 50 radio markets. The remaining 200-plus local radio markets in the United States will still be measured using paper diaries.

An alternative to PPMs that might increase compliance and reduce costs is to use cell phones to measure media use. This could take advantage of devices that many people already carry. Advanced cell phones can be programmed to take audio "snapshots" at 30-second intervals, capturing either an embedded code or an audio signature, to identify which media a phone user has encountered. The cell phone can also transmit that information to a data collection center where it is processed and turned into a ratings product. The Media Audit, a potential competitor to Arbitron, is developing this technology with a European company named Ipsos. Nielsen Media Research is also working with a company called Integrated Media Measurement Inc. to use cell phones for measuring out-of-home TV viewing.

The Internet is obviously a medium occupying more of people's time and claiming more advertising revenues in the process. One approach to tracking Internet use is to apply the traditional model of drawing a random sample of users, measuring their behavior, and generalizing what you find to the larger population. This strategy is sometimes called a *user-centric* approach. Here, measurement is accomplished by turning the user's own computer into a kind of meter. In fact comScore Media Metrix helped popularize the term *PC Meter*. Companies like comScore and Nielsen//NetRatings have a panel of computer users install software on their machines that ascertains who is using the computer, tracks the various URLs they visit, how long they stay on each page, and so on. Because the cost of metering is relatively low, these companies can recruit very large panels—up to as many as 50,000 people in the United States alone. That's necessary because Internet usage can be extremely fragmented. And even at that, this approach to Internet measurement might estimate the audience for only a few thousand web sites.

Because the Internet is fast becoming an important platform for delivering TV, Nielsen Media Research is planning to integrate Internet measurement into at least some of its national people-meter panel. That would allow the company to track viewers across platforms and develop more precise measures of the reach or repeated use of specific programs. Unfortunately, a good deal of Internet use, especially for online news, occurs in places of business. While companies that measure Web use try to maintain work or college-based panels, it's not always possible to secure the cooperation of the institutions that control those machines.

## Trace-Leaving Technologies

Unlike over-the-air broadcasting, many of the technologies that deliver media today do leave traces of their use. Two, in particular, present interesting possibilities for audience measurement—digital set-top boxes and Internet servers. Both offer relatively unobtrusive ways to track behavior that can be extended to very large samples or entire populations of users. The latter advantage, in particular, would go a long way toward addressing the problems caused by audience fragmentation.

More and more TV is coming into homes over broadband digital networks. Television sets receiving those signals are typically managed via set-top boxes. The boxes are capable of monitoring any state change, such as when the box goes on or off, or when the channel is changed, and sending that information back "up-stream" to the cable company's central hub. Other related technologies like VOD or DVRs can offer the same kind of intelligence. TiVo, TNS, and Nielsen are all trying to develop the measurement potential of set-top boxes. Conceptually, these devices are rather like the household meters that have been in use since the 1940s (Webster et al. 2006). In theory, they can keep a precise, second-by-second record of set activity. But by themselves, they offer no way of knowing what's on or who is watching. The first problem can be addressed with scheduling information, though it can be hard to account for last-minute schedule changes or what commercial airs when. The second problem is thornier. Associating household-level demographics with set-top data can violate privacy laws. In an effort to create a privacy compliance system, a company called erinMedia has tried to estimate audience composition by combining the demographic data from zip codes with the set-top box data within those areas. To date, there has been no independent verification of the accuracy of those estimates.

Even if one managed to secure the cooperation of all the services providing TV via set-top boxes, a fair amount of viewing behavior would go unmeasured. Not all households subscribe to digital cable or satellite service and, even in those that do, not all sets are hooked up to digital boxes. In fact, as more broadcast TV goes digital, there's evidence that some people will save themselves the cost of cable subscription and go back to watching HDTV over-the-air (Mohl 2007). Furthermore, set-top boxes are, by their very nature, wedded to TV viewing that happens on fixed TV sets. As we've already noted, TV is moving to different platforms, some of which are mobile. The question will be, can you safely infer all of this off-the-record viewing with set-top data? Probably not with the kind of precision advertisers seem to want as their currency in the national marketplace. It is more likely that this approach to measurement will gain traction where other state-of-the-art approaches aren't viable. For example, it could be useful in smaller TV markets or in quantifying the audience for local cable advertising.

Estimating the traffic on web sites by using servers raises some of the same issues. The Internet is, essentially, a network of computer networks. Any visit to a web page triggers a record of the event on the affected servers. Monitoring server traffic, an approach sometimes dubbed "server-centric" measurement, provides a census of web site use. While knowing what is served is not a problem, knowing who's being served is. In their unadulterated form the "hits" a server gets can be difficult to decipher. Placing identifying bits of code, called "cookies," on a visitor's machine can mark repeat customers or facilitate tracking individuals across web sites. If visitors have static IP addresses, it may be possible to infer repeat customers and, perhaps, something about where they are physically located. Of course, if visitors are willing to divulge information about themselves, or if server-side data can be married to a matched panel of respondents, then more precise estimates of audience composition are possible.

Both set-top boxes and the Internet provide technologies that can address commercial messages to specific households or machines. Google has made enormous amounts of money with targeted, search-driven advertising. Recently they announced a deal with satellite-TV operator EchoStar to sell TV spots through an online auction system. As it's described in the press, Google will " . . . tell advertisers how many TV set-top boxes were tuned in to each commercial they ran, and charge based only on the number of set-top boxes where the commercial played" (Delany 2007). Clearly, this moves Google in the direction of audience measurement, though just how they will gather demographic information, or what intelligence might be used to address the advertising remains unclear. Nielsen has certainly taken note. Their CFO is quoted as saying "People want to get into this space because it's big. Television advertising is about $70 billion—many times bigger than Internet. So you can understand, at least, Google's motivation in this case" (Mandese 2007). Whether this plays out as a competition or an occasion for collaboration remains to be seen.

## Nontraditional Media and Measurement

While more money is spent on TV than any other medium, the growing power of viewers to skip ads altogether has encouraged advertisers to look for alternatives. To oversimplify a bit, there are two strategies. One breathes new life into old media, the other harnesses new media. In either event, advertisers need audience measurement to evaluate media performance. A few of these many initiatives are briefly mentioned here.

Some efforts simply apply conventional telephone survey research to established media in order to provide new, more precise metrics. In 2005, Knowledge Networks/SRI launched a service to generate ratings-like data for the yellow pages. Cinema goers are an increasingly attractive target for advertisers, especially in the United States, so Arbitron and Nielsen have offered sample-based reports on those audiences. Placing products in movies is a long established practice. But with more TV viewers skipping ads, it's becoming common in TV as well. IAG and Nielsen offer syndicated services that quantify the value of those placements. The latter can also produce audience ratings for the minutes when a particular brand or sports sponsorship appears. Other efforts apply more innovative forms of measurement to old media. Nielsen Outdoor has members of a random sample carry GPS tracking devices called *Npods* that determine when and where they encounter outdoor ads on billboards or public transportation. This allows Nielsen to generate statistics like reach and frequency across various demographic categories.

In addition to the Web, the new media that have generated the most interest among advertisers are video games. They occupy an increasing share of time spent with media, especially for the elusive young male demographic. Games can carry the equivalent of product placements. For those that are played offline, the insertion of the ad is a one-shot proposition. More games, though, are now being played online. This allows companies like Massive, Inc. to serve different ads into different games, or target the ads to specific times or geographic locations. Like any advertising medium, though, the system needs independent third party measurement to authenticate exposure. Recall that state-of-the-art people meters must first determine the source of what's being displayed on the TV screen. If a console game is in use, the meter can identify the audio signature of the game, which provides a basis for audience measurement. Nielsen recently launched such a service called "GamePlay Metrics" that simply exploits its national people-meter sample.

It sometimes seems that major audience measurement companies and/or newcomers to the business are introducing new techniques and services all the time. To date, though, no one has created that ideal system that does it all. In 2006, Nielsen Media Research did announce an "Anytime Anywhere Media Measurement" (A2/M2) initiative to "follow the video" wherever consumption occurred (Nielsen 2006). To do that, it is using its people-meter sample as a springboard to collect information across other platforms like video games or the Internet. However, there's a limit to how much you can expect members of any given sample to do. So you are typically left with multiple independent samples providing only pieces of the puzzle. This problem is exacerbated when you want information on other media like print or outdoor, or other behaviors like product purchases. One solution is to graft data from one sample onto another sample by exploiting variables common to both, creating a unified database. This is called "data fusion" (e.g., Gilula, McCulloch, and Rossi 2006). While it offers a useful expedient, it is never as precise as affirmatively measuring the same individuals on all variables of interest.

## POLITICAL ECONOMY OF AUDIENCE MEASUREMENT

The foregoing discussion might make it seem that settling on a system of measurement was simply a matter of applying objective criteria and picking the best one. Unfortunately, building a better mousetrap isn't enough. While the quality of audience metrics is certainly a concern, that's not the only factor that comes into play. First, audience measurement companies are profit-making enterprises, so the systems that are developed and the ways in which they are deployed are powerfully affected by the economics of business. Second, many decisions about audience measurement have no objectively right or wrong answer. Rather, they reflect a consensus among those who are using measurement services. Third, with millions of dollars hanging in the balance, the users of audience measurement might well engage in political maneuvering to advance their own interests. It is no small matter to tinker with the industry's currency.

### Economics of Measurement

Syndicated audience ratings reports are, like many forms of information, characterized by high "first copy" costs, and very low marginal costs. The machinery needed for state-of-the-art audience measurement is expensive. And those costs must be sunk before even one report is produced. Once the ratings have been generated, however, they can be widely distributed without diminishing the supply. They are what economists call a "public good." These characteristics give syndicators a good deal of flexibility in pricing to attract new business. Charging customers for customized reports or privileged access to the database can have high profit margins. Ultimately, the prices that are charged may have more to do with a customer's ability and/or willingness to pay than the actual costs of supplying the product. The economics of measurement also make it difficult for competitors to enter the market. They must incur the first copy costs with uncertain prospects for dislodging the incumbent. This is compounded by the fact that the data provided by the incumbent is often deeply engrained in the buying and selling systems of the industry. So the customers themselves might resist the costs of switching to a new regime of measurement.

The traditional method of estimating audiences from samples also presents an economic puzzle. In the increasingly fragmented media environment, relative sampling error can easily swamp estimates based on small samples. The solution is to increase sample sizes. But doing so comes at a price. All other things being equal, cutting sampling error in half requires quadrupling sample size. Since each additional respondent generally costs the same, you rapidly reach a point of diminishing returns. One way to improve the economics is to have your samples do double duty. In 2004, Nielsen began introducing people meters in larger local markets, replacing the older combination of household meters and diaries. While local people meters (LPM) are widely regarded as a "better" form of measurement, Nielsen's motivation wasn't just delivering more timely demographics to local stations. Before introducing LPMs, Nielsen had estimated national TV audiences with a sample of roughly 5,000 households. By using the same people meter technology in the top 60 U.S. markets, Nielsen can fold those markets into the national sample and eventually bring it up to 17,000 households (Bachman 2007). Even with this strategy, though, the remaining 150 local market areas, which represent less than 30 percent of all U.S. TV households, are simply too small to justify the expense. While Nielsen has promised to make all local measurement electronic by 2011, it remains to be seen how that will be accomplished.

Another way to improve the economics is to have the measurement technology itself do double duty. If you can design a people meter to measure not only TV viewing but also video game use, you create another revenue stream that might justify larger samples. Similarly, one of the appeals of PPMs is that they can measure multiple media. If one technology can capture both radio and TV usage, it could be introduced into smaller markets more profitably than would be the case if it measured just one or the other.

## Objective versus Subjective Decisions

One of the virtues of discussing sampling error is that there are, at least, objective standards to decide what results in better measurement. Bigger samples have less sampling error, and less sampling error is a good thing. Not all questions of audience measurement are so cut and dry. Many practices within the affected industries are the result of a consensus about how business is to be conducted, but they are not self-evidently better than the alternatives.

Such subjective decisions can have profound consequences. At this writing, the most noteworthy example is deciding what constitutes exposure to TV and, in turn, the nature of the industry's currency. In the United States, the "upfront" market, which occurs in late spring, is the occasion for national advertisers to buy time in the upcoming TV season that begins in the fall. The networks typically guarantee what audiences will be delivered to advertisers. For years, the agreed-on measure of what constituted a delivered audience was a TV program's ratings. But the rapid penetration of DVRs, which allow people to defer viewing and/or skip commercials, along with the ability of people meters to measure audiences on a second-by-second basis, has dissolved that consensus. Advertisers have always been less interested in who sees a given program than who sees their commercials. As a result, for the 2007 upfront negotiations, Nielsen released "commercial ratings" based on the average commercial minute in the program. Many advertisers, though, would like them to go further and provide ratings for specific commercials and brands. Moreover, there is a question about when that viewing must occur in order to be counted against the guarantee. There is no one right answer, so Nielsen actually released six different streams of data. These included one for "live" viewing only, one for live plus same day, live plus one day, and so on for a week. It's for the buyers and sellers to come to an agreement on which metrics will be used.

## Politics of Measurement

By one recent estimate, a single prime-time ratings point on one of the Big 3 U.S. networks was worth $400 million dollars a year (Mandese 2006). Any change in how ratings are estimated, then, can add or detract from the bottom line. The realization that ratings are the life's blood of electronic media is not new. In the 1960s, the U.S. Congress held hearings on the accuracy of ratings, which resulted in the creation of the Broadcast Rating Council to promote industry self-regulation (Beville 1988). The Media Rating Council (MRC), its successor, still audits and accredits ratings services in the United States. Its seal of approval is an important, though not legally mandated, prerequisite for launching a new rating service.

With so much riding on ratings data, the affected parties are not above playing politics with the process. In 2004, as Nielsen began introducing LPMs into major markets, a political firestorm erupted. A public interest group, called "Don't Count Us Out," (DCUO) charged that the people meters severely undercounted minority viewers and would, therefore, jeopardize programming aimed at those audiences. While Nielsen did uncover problems with the "fault rates" in minority households (i.e., temporary meter outages), it became apparent that one of Nielsen's own clients was vigorously stoking the flames. News Corporation, the owner of Fox TV stations, believed that LPMs would leave their stations with lower ratings than those produced under the old system. To slow or stop the introduction of LPMs, they spent nearly $2 million bankrolling DCUO, organizing news conferences, running inflammatory ads, and operating telephone banks (Hernandez and Elliot 2004). Hillary Clinton and Al Sharpton weighed in, prompting the U.S. Congress to once again hold hearings and even propose legislation that would have required MRC accreditation.

While that legislation eventually failed, the story of LPMs offers a cautionary tale. Introducing people meters into local measurement was hardly revolutionary. They had been the standard in national measurement for nearly two decades. They were widely regarded as superior to the older system that relied on diaries, and whatever biases they did have were well understood by media researchers. Yet, even this measured change caused Nielsen considerable grief (Barnes 2004). One can hardly imagine the kind of reaction more radical changes might provoke. The future of audience measurement, then, isn't determined just by technical innovation, it also depends on whether powerful clients with diverse interests will adopt those methods.

# REFERENCES

Bachman, K. 2007. Nielsen to use same people meter model for LPM, national samples. *Mediaweek*, March 26.

Barnes, B. 2004. For Nielsen, fixing old ratings system causes new static. *Wall Street Journal*, September 16.

Beville, H. M. 1988. *Audience ratings: Radio, television, cable* (Rev. ed). Hillsdale, NJ: Erlbaum.

Delaney, K. J. 2007. Google furthers TV push with dish deal. *Wall Street Journal*, April 3.

Gilula, Z., R. E. McCulloch, and P. E. Rossi. 2006. A direct approach to data fusion. *Journal of Marketing Research* 63: 1–22.

Hernandez, R., and S. Elliot. 2004. Advertising: The odd couple versus Nielsen. *New York Times*, June 14.

Mandese, J. 2006. Prime-time rating points valued at nearly $400 million. *MediaPost*, October 11.

Mandese, J. 2007. Google highlights Nielsen earnings call. *MediaPost*, April 17.

Mohl, B. 2007. Want HDTV without paying the cable bills? *Boston Globe*, February 25.

Nielsen Media Research. 2006. *Anytime anywhere media measurement.* News Release, June 14.

Nielsen Media Research. 2007. *Average U.S. home now receives a record 104.2 TV channels.* News Release, March 19.

Webster, J. G. 2005. Beneath the veneer of fragmentation: Television audience polarization in a multichannel world. *Journal of Communication* 55 (2): 366–382.

Webster, J. G., P. F. Phalen, and L. W. Lichty. 2006. *Ratings analysis: The theory and practice of audience research.* 3rd ed . Mahwah, NJ: Erlbaum.

# CHAPTER 6

# RETHINKING MESSAGE STRATEGIES: THE DIFFERENCE BETWEEN THIN AND THICK SLICING

ANGELA LEE

You may remember seeing the advertisement that shows a gorilla stomping on a suitcase and throwing it around in the backstairs as the hotel guest takes the front elevator down to the lobby. But when the elevator door opens and the hotel guest steps out, he is met by the ever-polite and smartly dressed porter with the same piece of luggage, untarnished. This advertisement uses humor to capture consumers' attention and to illustrate how strong the suitcase is. Many who saw the advertisement agreed that the advertisement offered compelling evidence for Samsonite's durability—all to the dismay of American Tourister the sponsor of the advertisement.[1] This example clearly illustrates that there is more to understanding advertising effectiveness than meets the eye. Consumers may remember the advertisement and be persuaded, but the campaign could hardly be considered successful if it benefits the competitor. How then should advertisers think about creating effective campaigns?

To understand how consumers will react to advertising, two types of consumer insight are needed. One type of insight pertains to message content: What knowledge do consumers have about a brand and its category, and what are their beliefs about each? This insight is brand and category specific. Another type of insight pertains to how consumers make decisions when they are exposed to advertising. Such insight is applicable across products and categories. This chapter focuses on the latter—insight about how consumers process advertising messages and make decisions. In particular, a distinction is made between how consumers make decisions based on thick slices of information that involve conscious processing and how they make decisions based on thin slices of information that involve unconscious processing.

The conventional wisdom in advertising copy development is that an effective message is one that captures attention and encourages elaboration of the message. This gold standard in advertising copy strategies is based on the assumption that when people pay attention to a message and think about its content, they will understand the arguments presented in the message and come to appreciate the benefits advocated in the appeal. Comprehension followed by agreement with the message is what makes it effective.

However, with the ever-increasing advertising clutter in the environment and consumers tuning out as the result of information overload, the traditional approach of advertising copy strategy that relies on thick-slicing and conscious, deliberative processing of rich, contextual information is now augmented by a newer approach that leverages thin-slicing and unconscious, automatic processing of briefly exposed information.

What exactly is unconscious processing and how does it differ from conscious processing? When consumers engage in conscious processing of the advertising message, they are aware of the advertisement. They are paying attention and thinking about the message, and they are aware of how they are thinking about it. When consumers engage in unconscious processing of the message, however, they may not be aware of the advertisement. In some cases, consumers may be aware of the message but they are simply not paying attention to it. Processing of the advertisement takes place at an unconscious level and consumers are unaware that they are processing the message. In other cases, consumers may be completely unaware of the advertisement, yet processing takes place at an unconscious level. Thus, unconscious processing of the message can occur regardless of whether consumers are aware of having seen an advertisement.

This chapter provides an overview of the different advertising message strategies that leverage consumers' conscious versus unconscious decision-making processes and describes the different measures available to assess advertising effectiveness when consumers engage in conscious versus unconscious processing. First, we examine conscious message strategies briefly because they have been discussed in detail elsewhere.[2] Then we consider emerging strategies that are explicitly directed at the unconscious decision maker in greater detail.

# TRADITIONAL APPROACHES TO EFFECTIVE COMMUNICATION

While the ultimate goal of the advertiser is to promote brand choice and purchase behaviors, any advertising message should adopt a more specific objective that reflects the steps of the conscious decision maker—from building brand awareness and forming favorable evaluations to developing brand loyalty and making repeat purchases. To create an effective advertisement, message strategies have traditionally relied on a deliberative decision-making model that is based on content. That is, advertisements are designed to prompt and hence benefit from careful, conscious consideration of the advertising message.

To cut through the clutter, an advertisement needs to catch the consumers' attention. And to win them over, the advertisement has to draw them into the message and convince them of the benefits. Here we discuss some of the more commonly used message strategies that advertisers use to persuade consumers. Some of these strategies may also have implications for consumers who are processing the message unconsciously.

## Strong Arguments

A strong message is one that delivers unique brand benefits that are valued by consumers. Values are created when the message addresses concerns important to the consumers. At the same time, the claims made in the message should be perceived as credible; that is, consumers should have reasons to believe that the brand can deliver on these benefits. Credibility results from the presentation of compelling arguments that consider both pros and cons, or it may be the result of product demonstrations. Two-sided arguments are particularly effective when consumers are initially negative toward the product. That is, a message that directly speaks to a perceived weakness voiced by consumers and then offers strong arguments to refute that belief will be especially powerful. For example, many men consider body wash effeminate; to overcome this unfavorable attitude, Zest body wash used a macho football player who announced that men think body washes are for ladies, and went on to tell why Zest was meant for men.

Product demonstrations are another way to dispel initial negative attitudes. For example, if consumer's perception is that a national brand of diapers superior to the store brand in absorbency, then a demonstration showing greater absorbency of the store brand over the national brand leaves no ambiguity about the superior quality of the store brand. Other message strategies to enhance the credibility of the message include the use of an expert spokesperson or testimonials from reputable sources.

## Multiple Iterations of an Important Idea

A strategy made popular by the Leo Burnett advertising agency that reinforces consumers' beliefs and helps them remember the merits of a brand is to provide them with a variety of reasons to believe that a brand possesses a specific benefit. This strategy could be executed within one message, or over multiple messages. For example, one "big idea" in the airline industry might be convenience. And convenience might be conveyed by United Airlines featuring its online check-in, curbside check-in, and the number of scheduled flights across the country either in a single advertisement, or across different advertisements. The different reasons provide a rich context for the consumers to think about and be convinced of a primary benefit.

## Story Telling

An interesting story is always a good strategy to captivate attention and make connection with the audience. Advertisers can use a series of episodes to first present a problem or a goal; the story develops and the situation becomes more complex; and finally an outcome is revealed. This approach attempts to attract consumers' attention and persuade them by dramatizing the benefits of a brand in a setting that consumers might experience. For example, Thai Insurance CM tells a series of moving stories with a common theme that we may not have much time to spend with our loved ones. In one advertisement, an expectant mother asked to have a Caesarean section before the baby's due date—so that the baby could be held by his father who was dying from an inoperable brain tumor but hanging on just for that moment. That there is so much that we would like to do, yet time is running out is clearly communicated in the story. The irony is that although the drama captures people's attention, it runs the danger of the audience becoming so absorbed in the story that they fail to link the benefit to the brand. A good strategy to circumvent this is to embed the brand into the storyline to strengthen the brand link.

## Message Source

For some brands, the reason to believe that they can deliver on the advertised benefits may simply reside in the equity associated with those brands. For example, Apple's iPhone was the most desirable cellular phone months before it became available on the market. But for many brands, using a spokesperson could be an effective means of enhancing the impact of an appeal. Spokespeople can enhance message impact in two ways:

1. Well-known spokespeople can serve as icons that attract attention to the advertisement. This helps conscious processing.
2. In addition, well-known spokespeople can help build brands by imparting traits and abilities to personify a brand's benefits.

These transfers of personality traits and personal achievements often happen at an unconscious level and do not necessarily require deliberate processing on the part of consumers. For example, the athletic prowess and passion of Tiger Woods and Michael Jordan make an important statement about the sense of accomplishments that Nike wants to inspire; and world-champion cyclist Lance Armstrong's endurance and speed effectively personify the benefits that the U.S. Postal Service wishes to convey. By using a celebrity spokesperson it is important that the image or personality of the celebrity match the image of the brand if the endorsement is to be perceived as credible. Supermodel Gisele Bündchen, for example, would be an effective spokesperson for Victoria's Secret, but probably not for office machines, construction equipment, or cleaning supplies.

Although spokespeople can enhance attention to a message and personify the brand's benefit, their use is often tempered by several concerns. When popular spokespeople advertise for a variety of products (e.g., Tiger Woods was a spokesperson not only for Nike, but also Buick and American Express), their impact on each of the brands may be diluted. In addition, if spokespeople run afoul of the law or engage in tasteless behavior, the firm might be forced to drop the spokesperson (or risk tarnishing their brands through association), thus losing continuity in the campaign. The same consequence emerges if a spokesperson dies. Although well-known spokespeople could be very effective in attracting attention regardless of the product category, a mismatch between their persona and the advertised product will likely undermine the persuasiveness of the message.

**Incongruity**

Incongruity is often the key to attracting attention. This may take the form of something totally new and unfamiliar. Or it may take the form of a disparity between what consumers know and what the advertising is telling them. Humor typically involves some incongruity and is an effective strategy to gain attention. Not only does a fun advertisement capture the attention of the viewer, it often generates positive word-of-mouth that results in an even larger share of eyeballs through media such as the Ad Forum or YouTube. However, you should be careful when using humor in advertising: people may remember the joke at the expense of recall of the brand. Hence a strong brand link is critical when humor is used. A good strategy would be to use humor to deliver the benefit of the brand.

At an unconscious level, the good mood induced by humor facilitates processing of the message. Specifically, good mood helps consumers make linkages between disparate pieces of information. From that perspective, metaphors and parodies are most effective when the message also introduces humor.

## MEASURING EFFECTS OF CONSCIOUS PROCESSING

All the strategies discussed so far focus primarily on situations when consumers are consciously processing the advertising message, and any benefits via unconscious processing are incidental. The basic idea is to attract attention, prompt elaboration, and promote acceptance of the arguments conveyed in the message. To assess whether these advertising messages are effective in attracting and retaining attention and succeeding in persuading the consumers, advertisers can rely on measures such as awareness, recall of the content of the message, brand attitude, purchase intent, and actual behavior.

### Awareness

Sometimes the objective of the advertising campaign is to enhance brand recognition and inclusion in the consideration or choice set. Two measures are useful for these purposes. One is brand awareness. It entails asking people to indicate the category membership of a brand. For example, consumers might be asked to indicate the category to which Pantene belongs. Brand awareness would be demonstrated by the response "a shampoo." When brand awareness is low, the appropriate media strategy is reach, which involves efforts to expose as many target members as possible to a message at least once.

Top-of-mind awareness is another measure of awareness that has diagnostic value. To assess the top-of-mind awareness of a brand of shampoo, consumers would be asked to name as many brands of shampoo as they could. The number of times a particular brand is mentioned, as well as the order in which the brand is listed, can be used as indicators of how readily that brand comes to mind. When top-of-mind awareness is low, the appropriate media strategy is to aim for frequency rather than reach; this entails exposing target members to a campaign multiple times, even if it means reaching fewer target members.

## Brand Knowledge

Knowledge of the information in the message is an indicator that the consumer has paid attention to the message. However, capturing brand knowledge (e.g., Please tell us what you know about Heineken.) is different from assessing memory for the advertisement (e.g., Do you remember seeing an ad for Heineken? If so, please tell us everything you could remember about the ad.). People make brand choice and purchase decisions on the basis of what they know about the brand rather than on whether or not they remember seeing the ad. In fact, when consumers can trace the source of their brand knowledge to an advertisement, they may even discount the credibility of the information. As a result, consumers tend to like the brand more if they do not remember seeing the advertisement. Hence it is more appropriate to assess what consumers know about the brand (i.e., what they have learned from the advertisement) rather than what they remember from the advertisement. And if the objective of the advertiser is to increase brand knowledge, the media strategy should aim to achieve reach rather than frequency.

## Brand Attitude and Purchase Intent

The ultimate goal of an advertising message is to influence consumers' behavior. Whereas information recall measures the ability of the message to inform, brand attitude and purchase intent measure the ability of the message to persuade. In assessing the effectiveness of a message, brand evaluation ratings (e.g., Please rate X using a scale from 1 to 7 with 1 = very unfavorable and 7 = very favorable) and purchase intent scores (e.g., Please indicate the likelihood of your purchasing X when it becomes available using 1 = definitely will not buy, 2 = most likely will not buy, 3 = not sure, 4 = most likely will buy, and 5 = definitely will buy) by those consumers who have been exposed to the advertising message are compared with ratings by those who have not been exposed to the message. Sometimes the same consumers may be asked to evaluate the brand and indicate their purchase intent *before* as well as *after* they are exposed to the message. The caveat in using the latter approach is that consumers may be alerted to the purpose of the measures in which case their responses may be colored by say, their desire to be helpful and not disappoint the researcher (in which case their *after* responses may be overly positive) or their motivation to show that they are not easily persuaded by advertising (in which case their *after* responses may be more negative). Thus, before-after measures are best used in situations where the task is to compare the impact of different ads because message recipients' motivations to be helpful or exhibit resistance to persuasion would be similar across the different ads and therefore not explain unique performance.

## Behavioral Measures

A key measure of advertising effectiveness is the actual purchase behavior or any other action as advocated by the advertisement (e.g., click rates, reduced tobacco or alcohol consumption). Consumers' brand choices, for example, could be observed in a simulated test market study that allows the advertiser to compare the effects of different advertising messages on sales. For most consumer packaged goods, scanner data that provide up-to-date information on consumers' actual purchase behavior are available. However, the external validity from using actual field data comes at the expense of the advertiser's ability to unambiguously attribute sales to advertising. Different marketing mix strategies may be affecting brand choice at any one time, not to mention external influences from competitors, channel members, government regulations, economic conditions and consumption trends. Controlling for these different factors using quantitative modeling techniques can more accurately assess the effectiveness of the advertising message.

Developing effective advertising and marketing strategy is facilitated by considering the indicators we have discussed in concert. To explain a brand's sales performance, you might first examine brand awareness. Low brand awareness may be remedied by an improved selection of media and vehicles, as well as by an increase in the advertising budget. And as noted earlier, low top-of-mind awareness may be enhanced by increasing advertising frequency. If awareness is high, but attitude and purchase intention are weak, the remedy calls for a focus on the brand's positioning and the creative execution of the position. Strong brand awareness, attitude, and purchase intention but weak sales are likely attributable to a problem in pricing or distribution. Finally, substantial trial but low repeat purchase points to weakness in product quality. Thus, examining the relationship among indicators of conscious processing provides a means of attributing performance to specific elements of the marketing mix: advertising, price, distribution or product. As such, it offers a starting point for enhancing brand performance.

# ADVERTISING DIRECTED AT UNCONSCIOUS PROCESSING

While traditional approaches to media message strategies focus primarily on conscious processing of advertising messages, most decisions made by consumers on a daily basis do not rely on deliberate processing of information. Malcolm Gladwell in his recent bestseller *Blink* provides a summary of some recent research that indicates the prevalence and importance of unconscious decision making. Speed-dating and thin-slicing suggest that people make fairly important decisions often quickly and with little information. And thin-slicing aptly describes how consumers process most advertising messages and make purchase decisions on a daily basis—based on quick, unconscious assessments of little information without much conscious deliberation. An amazing finding in recent research is that decisions based on six seconds worth of thin slices may not be very different from decisions based on thick slices. How then do consumers make these unconscious decisions? And how can advertisers design advertisements to facilitate decision making at the unconscious level?

When consumers are not actively processing the information in the message, their product judgments and purchase decisions are likely to rely on their feelings about the advertisement or the brand rather than on the content of the advertising message. Positive feelings toward the brand may come about as the result of conditioning and associations or the ease of information processing, also known as processing fluency. And different message strategies that leverage the effects of associations and processing fluency can be used to enhance brand value.

### Value-by-Association Message Strategies

Consumers may learn to like a product if it is associated with something they like every time they see it. For example, consumers can be "conditioned" to think that a computer has a faster processor when it is shown with a running Scooby-Doo in the advertisement as compared to a walking Scooby-Doo, or that a mouthwash has a sharper taste when it is packaged in an angular bottle with sharp edges rather than a rounded bottle with curvy sides. Similarly, a beverage may be perceived as energizing or relaxing depending on whether an icon of a sun or a moon is displayed in the corner of the advertisement, even though consumers pay very little attention to the advertisement and may even deny having seen the sun or the moon in the advertisement. In brief, consumers often form impressions of products based on brief exposures to advertising messages without much awareness of the details in the message.

And messages that contain not much more than just iconic cues may be more effective than messages that present a substantial amount of information about the product. It is through a subtle transfer of meanings or positive feelings from the advertising context to the brand that consumers form favorable impressions of the brand.

To leverage this transfer of meanings and feelings, advertising can incorporate elements that induce positive associations to the brand, and at the same time avoid elements that provoke negative associations. Elements that are instrumental in conveying meaning are not limited to objects or characters (real or fictitious). Movements, background music, color, and language can all be used to facilitate meaning transfer. For example, in an advertisement for Tampax, a woman dressed all in white is shown leaving her home, getting on a bus, and walking to her office. The use of color implies confidence in the product; and the movement toward her goal (i.e., to get to the office) implies she will not be slowed down by her monthly cycle.

In a recent advertisement for Harley Davidson, some black sheep were shown breaking away from their herds and making their way to Sturgis, South Dakota (where the world famous bikers rally is held), to the music of Guns and Roses (GNR) singing "Paradise City." Black sheep, breaking away, Axl Rose and GNR—are all symbols of the aspirations of many Harley buyers who want to distance themselves from their lives as lawyers and accountants. And the choice of a song from the 1980s is likely to resonate with the Harley biker whose average age is 46.

## Processing Fluency Message Strategies

Consumers may also rely on how easy or difficult it is to process the message or the brand (rather than the content of the message) to evaluate the product and to make purchase decisions, especially when they are not motivated to process information carefully. When considering how processing fluency can influence product judgment and brand choice, it is useful to distinguish between four different types of processing fluency that advertisers could leverage: perceptual fluency, conceptual fluency, regulatory goal fluency, and retrieval fluency.

*Perceptual Fluency*    *Perceptual fluency* refers to the ease with which consumers can recognize or identify the brand. Perceptual fluency plays an important role in stimulus-based choice situations where consumers make their purchase decisions with all the different options available to them in the physical environment, as in a supermarket. When consumers are not highly involved in the shopping experience (as with most trips to the supermarket), they may rely on how eye-catching something is to make a purchase decision. And perceptual fluency is what makes a brand stand out among its competitors on the shelf.

How can a brand's perceptual fluency be enhanced? Repeated exposures to the brand have consistently been shown to increase perceptual fluency and liking—a phenomenon referred to as the "mere exposure" effect. By simply being exposed to the brand (or its image), consumers become more favorable toward the brand even when they are not aware of having seen it before.

An advertising message designed to enhance a brand's perceptual fluency should present the image of the product as close to how the actual product appears to the consumers at the time of purchase as possible. For example, if the product is placed on the shelf in the store in its packaging, then the product image in the advertising message should show the packaging, as viewed from the same angle as the shopper would observe it in the store. The greater the overlap between the image in the advertisement and the image in the store is, the more familiar the store product feels to the shopper, and the easier it is to process. Hence, the product shot in the advertisement should ideally be unencumbered by other information so that the visual image matches as much as possible the image that consumers see at the time of purchase to maximize the perceptual fluency effect. And with consumers zapping through advertisements using Tivo or while watching DVDs, it pays for advertisers to fixate the brand name or logo or some other image of the product in the same position across multiple frames so that the image will remain on the screen for a prolonged period to enhance perceptual fluency.

**Conceptual Fluency**    *Conceptual fluency* refers to the ease with which something (e.g., brand name, usage occasions, product information) comes to mind and its meaning is grasped. In memory-based choice situations where consumers have to retrieve the different options from memory, a brand that enjoys high top-of-mind awareness has a higher probability of being included in the choice set. Conceptual fluency also enhances evaluations. People like familiar things, and brands that come to mind more readily are often preferred. Ever had the experience of not liking a song when you first heard it, but after hearing it played on the radio for a week, you started humming along when it comes on? Not only do brands that come to mind more readily enjoy more positive evaluations, product statements that are conceptually fluent are also considered to be truer.

One sure way to facilitate the retrieval of brand information is to encourage elaboration of the message, which requires the conscious processing that we discussed earlier. Nonetheless, there are message strategies that enhance conceptual fluency even when consumers are not paying attention.

While most people would agree that jingles are easier to remember than simple statements that share the same meaning, they may be surprised to find that taglines that rhyme are more persuasive than those that don't rhyme. Research shows that poetic aphorisms that rhyme are judged to be more believable than modified versions that retain the meaning but not the rhyming form.[3] For example, "what sobriety conceals, alcohol reveals" is thought to be a more accurate description of human behavior than "what sobriety conceals, alcohol unmasks"; and "woes unite foes" rings truer than "woes unite enemies." Thus, advertisers can use rhymes and jingles in the message to enhance conceptual fluency, strengthen the credibility of the message, and generate more favorable attitudes toward the brand—all without the conscious awareness on the part of the consumer. Using rhymes is particularly effective when the taglines explicitly link the benefits to the brand—a hard-sell strategy. Examples of some effective taglines include "Bounty—the quicker picker-upper" and "Nothing sucks like Electrolux."

***Processing Fluency***    Using contexts that prompt automatic activation of the product is one way to enhance the *processing fluency* of the message. When consumers encounter a particular context (e.g., a summer pool party), certain products may automatically come to mind (e.g., hamburgers, ketchup, barbeque sauce); the activation of these products in memory in turn makes the message about these products easier to process and enhances consumers' evaluation of these products.

Another message strategy that advertisers can use to enhance processing fluency of the brand is to use a spokesperson whose image or personality matches that of the brand. The idea behind this strategy is that if the spokesperson's personality traits are consistent with the attributes and values represented by the brand, being exposed to the spokesperson will automatically activate these attributes and values in memory, which in turn makes the message about the brand easier to process.

***Regulatory Goal Fluency***    Consumers can more easily process a message that is consistent (versus inconsistent) with their self-regulatory goal. People's attention, attitudes, and behaviors are guided by two fundamental motivational systems: a promotion system that services the need for growth and nurturance, and a prevention system that services the need for safety and security.[4] People with a dominant promotion goal regulate their attention and behaviors toward fulfilling their hopes and aspirations and are sensitive to the presence and absence of positive outcomes, whereas those with a dominant prevention goal regulate their attention and behaviors toward fulfilling their duties and obligations and are sensitive to the presence and absence of negative outcomes. In essence, people's regulatory goal functions as an unconscious filter when they process product information, especially when they are not motivated to process the message. For consumers with a promotion goal, messages that address promotion concerns (e.g., growth and achievements) and exhibit characteristics of the promotion system are easier to process and understand than messages that address prevention concerns (e.g., safety and security) and exhibit characteristics of the prevention system. And the opposite applies for consumers with a prevention goal.

To appeal to consumers with a promotion goal, an advertisement can focus on the fulfillment of hopes and aspirations, highlight desirable outcomes, describe long-term goals and speak of the future, use language that is more abstract (such as adjectives), emphasize why people do certain things, or convey feelings of joy and excitement or disappointment and sadness. And to appeal to consumers with a prevention goal, the message can focus on the fulfillment of duties and obligations, highlight undesirable outcomes; solve immediate problems and speak of the present, use language that is more concrete (such as action verbs), emphasize how people do certain things, and convey feelings of fear and anxiety or contentment and peacefulness. To the consumers, a "regulatory fit" message is more fluent and therefore more persuasive than a "regulatory nonfit" message.

Broadly speaking, there are two ways to develop regulatory fit messages. First, a fit message may be created by developing an appeal that caters to the target's promotion or prevention goal. And in developing the message, the advertiser would need to know whether their target consumers are promotion or prevention oriented. Research has shown that Americans are more likely to have a dominant promotion goal, whereas East Asians such as Japanese, Koreans, and Chinese in Hong Kong are more likely to have a dominant prevention goal. Young people are more likely to be promotion oriented and the elderly are more likely to be prevention oriented. But within each culture and within each age group, there will be some people who are more promotion or prevention oriented than others. And within the individual consumer, there are times and situations when they will be oriented toward a promotion goal, and times and situations when they will be oriented toward a prevention goal. For example, while Americans are likely to be guided by a promotion goal, they may temporarily become prevention oriented when they are prompted to think that they are part of a team or are reminded of their family.[5] Further, different product categories may be differentially suited to using promotion or prevention appeals. For example, buyers of home security systems are likely to be prevention-oriented, whereas buyers of sports cars are promotion-oriented. And financial investors tend to be promotion-oriented when they think about stocks but become prevention-oriented when they think about bonds.[6]

Another way to create a regulatory fit message is to match different elements within the message so that they are consistent with the promotion or prevention system based on the characteristics described earlier. For example, a message can explicitly put its audience in a promotion or prevention mindset by reminding them of certain cultural values or prompting them to adopt a specific self-view. The idea is that a collectivistic or interdependent mindset prompts people to be prevention-oriented, whereas an individualistic or independent mindset stimulates a promotion orientation. Then the rest of the message could highlight benefits that fit the particular mindset—a promotion mindset is matched with promotion benefits, and a prevention mindset is matched with prevention benefits. For example, an advertisement for Welch's Grape Juice can use a tagline that says "Give your *family* a chance at great taste!" and then elaborate on the antioxidants and flavonoids that reduce the risk of cancer and heart disease. Compare this strategy to another advertisement with the tagline "Give *yourself* a chance at great taste!" and elaborates on the vitamin C and iron that contributes to greater energy. In both cases, the benefits match the self-view highlighted in the message, creating an experience of regulatory fit that enhances persuasion.[7]

Consider another illustration of regulatory fit that relies on a match between the frame of the message (e.g., gain versus loss) and the benefits (energizing versus preventing clogged arteries). Promotion messages are more effective when they are presented in a gain frame that highlights desirable outcomes than in a loss frame that highlights undesirable outcomes. For example, an advertisement that positions Welch's grape juice as an energizing beverage is more persuasive when its tagline says "Get energized—Drink Welch's Grape Juice!" than when it says "Don't miss out on getting energized—Drink Welch's Grape Juice!"[8] Conversely, prevention messages are more effective when they are presented in a loss frame that highlights undesirable outcomes than in a gain frame that highlights desirable outcomes. Thus, the tagline "Don't miss out on preventing clogged arteries—Drink Welch's Grape Juice!" is more persuasive than one that says "Prevent clogged arteries—Drink Welch's Grape Juice!"

Fit messages may also be created by matching temporal construal (e.g., distant versus near future) with level of abstraction (e.g., why versus how). For example, an advertisement for an elliptical cross trainer could prompt people to think about their health *in the future* and *why* they should exercise using the machine (i.e., a promotion fit message), or the advertisement could remind people to think about their health *now* and *how* they could exercise using the machine (i.e., a prevention fit message).

The strategy of matching different elements within the message to be consistent with the consumers' promotion or prevention goal is particularly useful when the advertiser does not know whether its target audience is promotion- or prevention-oriented; or if their target audience includes both promotion- and prevention-oriented consumers. Another message strategy is to highlight both promotion and prevention benefits within a single message so that the advertisement may appeal to consumers with either a promotion or a prevention goal. This seems to work particularly well when consumers are not motivated to pay attention—they use their regulatory goal to filter out less relevant information.[9] This does not mean that there is no advantage of knowing who their consumers are; as a promotion fit message is most effective when the recipients have a dominant promotion goal, and a prevention fit message is most effective when the recipients have a dominant prevention goal. But such information is not always available.

There is one caveat when leveraging regulatory goal fluency effects: regulatory goal fluency effects work both ways in that fluent processing arising from regulatory fit accentuates the reaction of consumers toward the message. If their initial reaction toward the message is positive, then the ease of processing the message makes their attitude more positive. However, if their initial reaction is negative, then their attitude becomes even more negative with a fluent message. Thus, it is important that the advertisement prompts a favorable first impression as well as produces a positive attitude when scrutinized.

*Retrieval Fluency*   A fourth type of processing fluency has to do with the ease (or difficulty) with which consumers generate certain thoughts or retrieve information from memory, and the inference they make regarding this retrieval ease. Persuasive messages can be created by using taglines that prompt easy retrieval of information that benefits the brand. For example, consider an ad that asks the consumer "Can you think of one reason to drive a BMW?" and compare that to an ad that asks "Can you think of 10 reasons to drive a BMW?" Surely having 10 reasons to drive a BMW should be more persuasive than having just one reason to drive the car. However, consumers may rely on how easy or difficult it is to generate reasons as the basis to evaluate how desirable a BMW is; and most consumers find it easier to generate one reason than 10 reasons. The consumer who saw the 10 reasons tagline may think: "Gee! I can't think of 10 reasons why I should drive a BMW, it must not be as good a car as I originally thought" and downgraded his evaluation of BMW.[10] By the same token, such metacognitive reasoning of making inferences based on one's knowledge of how one thinks can be applied to reverse the effect. For example, the consumer who is asked to generate 10 reasons why one should *not* drive a BMW may find it difficult to do so and hence upgrade his evaluation of the car.

Many of the executions that advertisers could use to leverage the effects of processing fluency have in fact been used in advertising. However, they have always been treated as minor details or gimmicks in the execution of some larger strategy, rather than as message strategies in their own right. As message strategies, these executions have important implications for copy design as well as for copy testing and measurement of advertising effectiveness.

## MEASURING EFFECTS OF UNCONSCIOUS PROCESSING

Along with recognizing the prevalence of thin slicing and unconscious processing is the need for measurements that assess the effectiveness of unconscious message strategies. Unconscious processing is what people engage in when they are not consciously deliberating or thinking about the arguments in the message. While unconscious processing of an advertisement can take place without consumers being aware of the advertisement, unconscious processing does not require the absence of advertising awareness. In fact, unconscious processing of some aspects of the advertisement may be happening at the same time when consumers are consciously processing other aspects of the advertisement; or it may be happening when consumers are totally unaware of the advertisement. How then can advertisers measure the effects of unconscious processing?

Given that an important goal of an advertising message is to enhance brand evaluation and promote brand choice, then any message, irrespective of how it is being processed, should satisfy the criteria of enhancing brand attitude and increasing brand choice. Thus, many of the traditional measures described earlier such as top-of-mind awareness, brand attitudes and purchase intent could be used to assess the effectiveness of the message, even if consumers are not paying attention or are unaware that they have been exposed to the message.

However, there are times when consumers are unable to articulate what they know or how they feel about the brand, or they are unwilling to do so. For example, if asked "How often do you eat ice cream?" someone who eats ice cream five times a week may report eating ice cream twice a week because they did not want to admit to eating ice cream that often. But they may also report eating ice cream twice a week because they honestly believe they don't eat ice cream more often than that. In these situations, measures other than self-reports are needed to capture consumers' beliefs and attitudes; and some of these measures can also be used to assess the unconscious effects of advertising.

## Projective Techniques

These devices use ambiguous stimuli to elicit responses from the consumers to get at their inner feelings. One projective technique requires consumers to make associations. For example, consumers may be presented with a list of words (or pictures) and are asked to indicate the first word that comes to mind when they see each word. Or they may be asked to come up with a person or a personality type in response to a brand name. Sometimes consumers are asked to complete a story, or fill in the thought balloons of some characters in a drawing. Projective techniques are particularly useful in understanding brand image, key benefits, and usage occasions. The Zaltman Metaphor Elicitation Technique (ZMET) is an example of a projective tool that involves first asking consumers to describe their thoughts and feelings about buying or using certain products by selecting pictures and photographs to form collages, followed by an intensive debriefing session with a trained interviewer-cum-therapist to discuss the meanings behind the pictures in an effort to uncover their inner feelings toward the product.[11] For example, a woman asked to express her thoughts about pantyhose selected a picture of an ice-cream sundae spilled on the ground to express the embarrassment caused by runs in her stockings. A comparison of consumers' inner feelings before and after being exposed to an advertisement can provide clues to how the advertisement may have altered their beliefs and feelings toward the brand.

*Perceptual Identification Task*    For this task, respondents are seated in front of a computer and asked to identify words or pictures that are presented very quickly (e.g., 25 msec) on the computer screen. The accuracy of identification provides a measure of accessibility of certain words or concepts in memory. Accurate identification of a brand name may be used to measure the perceptual fluency of the brand name, or to assess the top-of-mind awareness the brand enjoys. Identification of words or concepts taken from an advertising message may also be used as an indicator of the processing fluency of the message.

*Response Times*   How quickly a person responds is typically measured in milliseconds using a computer. Response times are useful in assessing the accessibility and processing fluency of different concepts in memory. Because response times can capture consumers' automatic reaction to brands and concepts, this measure can be used to assess advertising effectiveness regardless of whether consumers are aware or unaware of their exposure to the advertisement. By observing how fast a consumer can identify a brand name, the top-of-mind awareness of a brand can be determined. By timing how long it takes someone to read a message, the processing fluency of the message can be assessed. And by measuring how quickly consumers can respond to a question about a brand, the accessibility of their attitude toward the brand is known.

## Implicit Association Test

This test is a response time measure developed to understand the root of people's unconscious thinking and feeling and can be used to measure consumers' attitudes toward different products. The Implicit Association Test (IAT)[12] is based on the premise that people organize attitudes, stereotypes, and self-concepts as networks of associations in memory based on valence. For example, flowers are more likely to be associated with positive words such as "happy" than negative words such as "vomit," whereas the opposite is likely for insects. When taking the IAT, people respond to two categories of words. The first category consists of pleasant words (e.g., happy, peace) and the second category consists of unpleasant words (e.g., ugly, vomit). People respond by pressing one key when they see a pleasant word and another key when they see an unpleasant word. In addition, people also respond to two target sets containing the words of interest. For example, one set may be dessert-related words and the other set vegetable-related words. The results may show that people respond faster to the dessert words using the same key as the pleasant words than the same key as the unpleasant words; and they respond faster to the vegetable-related words using the same key as the unpleasant words than the same key as the pleasant words. The difference in response time between the two blocks of trials is used as a measure of people's implicit attitudes toward dessert and vegetables.

The IAT is not limited to measuring positive versus negative implicit attitudes. The test can also be used to measure brand image by pairing brand names (e.g., Apple versus IBM) with brand personality traits (e.g., sincere versus trendy), or brand loyalty by pairing brand-related words with self-concepts (e.g., respondents' own name versus other people's names). Comparing consumers' IAT score before and after exposure to the advertising message would provide the advertisers with a measure of advertising effectiveness even when consumers are not paying attention.

## CONCLUSION

Consumers typically do not pay much attention to things around them, nor do they process advertising messages with great care. But there are times when they would be interested in learning more about a brand or a product category, such as when they are in the market for the product. But even then, an advertisement will remain in the background unless it succeeds in capturing their attention and effectively communicates the benefits of the brand. Returning to the gorilla and the suitcase advertisement mentioned earlier, while humor made the advertisement memorable, and the gorilla stomping on the suitcase effectively communicates the durability of the suitcase, the advertisement failed to establish a link between the benefits and the advertised brand. As a result, consumers attributed the benefits portrayed in the advertisement to the leading brand in the category. To be effective, humor should be used to link the benefit of the product to the brand name. For example, the gorilla could be shown biting and chewing the part of the luggage that bears the brand name but failed to make any headway.

But capturing attention and making compelling arguments are not the only strategies that advertisers could use to reach out to their target consumers. There are message strategies that advertisers could use to target those consumers who are not paying attention to the advertising message. Two different categories of strategies that advertisers could use to reach out to their target audience are described in this chapter. One set of strategies targets those consumers who are aware of the message, who process the message consciously. Another set of strategies targets those consumers who process the message unconsciously, who may or may not be aware of their exposure to the message. Whereas the conscious message strategies focus on capturing attention and offering compelling arguments, the unconscious message strategies focus on making the message easier to process and creating positive associations. And message strategies that aim to persuade the consumers through the use of subtle cues may prove to be the more effective strategies in times of thin slicing.

## NOTES

1. This was before Samsonite acquired American Tourister.
2. Brian Sternthal and Angela Y. Lee. "Building Brands through Effective Advertising," in *Kellogg on Branding,* ed. Alice M. Tybout and Tim Caulkins (Hoboken, NJ: Wiley, 2005), 129–149.

3. M. S. McGlone and J. Tofighbakhsh. "Birds of a Feather Flock Conjointly(?): Rhyme as Reason in Aphorisms," *Psychological Science* 11, no. 5 (2000): 424–428.

4. Tory E. Higgins. "Beyond Pleasure and Pain," *American Psychologist* (November 1997): 1280–1300.

5. Jennifer L Aaker and Angela Y. Lee. I Seek Pleasures and We Avoid Pains: The Role of Self Regulatory Goals in Information Processing and Persuasion. *Journal of Consumer Research* 28 (2001): 33–49.

6. Rongrong Zhou and Michel Tuan Pham. "Promotion and Prevention across Mental Accounts: When Financial Products Dictate Consumers' Investment Goals," *Journal of Consumer Research* 31 (2004): 125–135.

7. See note 5.

8. Angela Y. Lee and Jennifer L. Aaker. "Bringing the Frame into Focus: The Influence of Regulatory Fit on Processing Fluency and Persuasion," *Journal of Personality and Social Psychology* 86 (2004): 205–218.

9. Jing Wang and Angela Y. Lee. "The Role of Regulatory Focus in Preference Construction, *Journal of Marketing Research* 43, no. 1 (2006): 28–38.

10. Michaela Wänke, Gerd Bohner, and Andreas Jurkowitsch. "There Are Many Reasons to Drive a BMW: Does Imagined Ease of Argument Generation Influence Attitudes? *Journal of Consumer Research* 24 (1997): 170–177.

11. Gerald Zaltman. *How Customers Think: Essential Insights in the Mind of the Market* (Boston: Harvard Business School Press, 2003).

12. Frédéric F. Brunel, Brian C. Tietje, and Anthony G. Greenwald. "Is the Implicit Association Test a Valid and Valuable Measure of Implicit Consumer Social Cognition? *Journal of Consumer Psychology* 14, no. 4 (2004): 385–404.

# CHAPTER 7

# MANAGING THE UNTHINKABLE: WHAT TO DO WHEN A SCANDAL HITS YOUR BRAND

MICHELLE ROEHM and ALICE M. TYBOUT

**T**he specter of scandal looms large over the modern marketplace. With recent targets ranging from telecommunications firms to collegiate sports teams and from lifestyle gurus to pharmaceutical companies, no sector remains untouched. As a result, effective scandal management has become an essential component of the successful businessperson's toolkit.

The goal of this chapter is to assist managers by providing a framework for:

1. identifying situations in which an event may develop into a scandal that damages a brand and
2. developing an effective strategic and tactical response when a brand scandal occurs.

Our scandal management framework is comprised of four steps:

1. Assess the likelihood that your brand will be affected.
2. Issue an immediate acknowledgment.
3. Choose a strategic approach.
4. Design a specific response.

In discussing each step, we offer diagnostic questions to help the manager select the most appropriate course of action and illustrate effective versus ineffective responses by drawing on a number of real-world scandals.

## WHAT IS A SCANDAL?

Before discussing how to respond to a scandal, it is important to understand what we mean by the term *scandal:* A scandal occurs when a negatively perceived event or action gains notoriety with some relevant audience.

In this definition, the phrase "negatively perceived event or action" implies that scandals emerge from specific unfavorable occurrences. "Gains notoriety" indicates that scandals come about when information becomes public, thus, negative activities that remain secret do not qualify. "With some relevant audience" reflects the idea that scandals require spectators and that it is within their minds that the scandal develops and resides. Finally, it is worth noting that the audience in our definition could refer to a broad group (e.g., people in the United States in general) or a narrow one (e.g., people in a specific location where an incident occurred).

Our definition suggests that scandals may arise from a range of transgressions that violate some standard of behavior. For example, an alleged event or action might be viewed disapprovingly—and therefore become the basis of a scandal—because it breaks specific laws (e.g., the members the Duke Lacrosse team being accused of a crime such as rape, Martha Stewart allegedly circumventing insider trading rules) or because it simply defies conventional expectations in some unfavorable way (e.g., a finger appearing in a bowl of chili at Wendy's).

Last, it's important to note that scandals may take hold regardless of whether the central accusations are true or false. Consider the following examples:

- Top executives at WorldCom were charged with numerous counts of financial mismanagement. These charges were supported by evidence of over-reporting $11 billion in assets, and the result was stiff fines for several senior executives and a lengthy jail sentence for the former CEO, Bernie Ebbers.
- Wendy's fast-food outlet was charged with serving a customer a bowl of chili that included a severed finger. This charge was ultimately revealed to be a hoax concocted by the customer who filed the complaint.
- Three members of the Duke University lacrosse team were accused of raping a woman at a party. After much publicity and public debate, these charges were dropped by the Attorney General of North Carolina, who questioned both the evidence supporting the case and the judgment of the district attorney who filed the charges.

In each instance, a scandal occurred even though in the latter two cases the charges were ultimately judged to be false. Thus, according to our definition, scandals may be created even by unproven accusations or unsubstantiated rumors.

## FRAMEWORK FOR MANAGING A SCANDAL

### Step 1: Assess the Likelihood That Your Brand Will Be Affected

When a potentially scandalous event occurs, it is tempting to react immediately and try to "jump out ahead of the news." But before taking action, we strongly recommend pausing—albeit briefly—to assess the likelihood that your brand will be affected by the scandal. This preliminary assessment is necessary because if a scandal has not already become associated with your brand, issuing a preemptive denial may be damaging in that the denial may be perceived as "protesting too much," and thereby raise the very suspicion you sought to alleviate (Roehm and Tybout 2006).

As an example, consider the Perrier benzene scare, and imagine yourself as a marketer for a competing brand of bottled water at the time that scandal broke. A natural inclination might have been to quickly release a statement assuring the public that your bottled water did not suffer from the same contamination problem as the Perrier product. However, if consumers had not already inferred that other bottled waters might contain the same poisonous substance, a proactive denial might be interpreted as the action of a guilty party. Ironically, the audience may be left with *new* doubts about the safety of your product, when your intention was to quell exactly these kinds of concerns.

To avoid such backfires, it is important to evaluate the likelihood that any particular transgression will attach itself to your brand. Scandal associations may be formed through two routes. The first and more obvious occurs when a scandal is attached to a *perpetrating* brand (the brand initially accused of a scandalous action). For example, when WorldCom executives engaged in questionable accounting practices, a link between accounting fraud and the WorldCom brand was created in many consumers' minds. The second route is less apparent but equally important: Sometimes a focal brand may become tainted by the wrongdoings of another brand. When the WorldCom scandal broke, trust ratings for other telecommunications companies also fell, and investors became skittish about the industry in general. This skittishness presumably reflected the assumption that other telecom companies might also have engaged in accounting fraud. We call this effect *scandal spillover,* and a brand that may become tarnished in this way is a *spillover brand.*

Next we discuss three key questions that should be asked when assessing the likelihood that your brand will be impacted by a scandal.

***Perpetrating Brands***     To diagnose the potential for scandal linkage to a perpetrating brand, an important first question to ask is: *Will the potentially scandalous incident gain significant attention?* When a negative event is mundane or lacks shock value, it may stand little chance of garnering attention. News that a rock star trashed a hotel may, for example, gain little notice, because this sort of behavior is de rigueur in that world. Such incidents may thus wind up as insignificant blips on peoples' radar screen and have few, if any, long-term ramifications.

By contrast, other negative occurrences mesmerize the public, providing plenty of opportunity to mentally link the action with a proximal brand. Events that fall into this latter category tend to be those that are surprising, vivid, and/or have significant emotional impact.

Consider, for instance, the Duke lacrosse scandal, in which players on the team were accused of raping a young woman at a party. This incident plays to all three of these dimensions. First, there was the unexpected juxtaposition of an appalling crime with the image of clean-cut college athletes. In addition, the offense lends itself to a vivid mental picture that is easy to construct and difficult to set aside. Finally, speculation that such heinous victimization might have been racially motivated stirs up strong emotions such as outrage and disgust. As a result, the event received extensive press coverage, which is summarized in a 24-page entry on Wikipedia.

Is doom assured when a misdeed meets these criteria? Not necessarily. Even when consumers' attention is captured, it is still possible that they may not blame a perpetrating brand for a given wrongdoing. Whether the brand is blamed will depend on two countervailing forces. One is a natural tendency for human beings to assign blame when harm has been done (Alicke 2000). More specifically, there is a tendency to locate fault with the party who appears to have produced the harm (e.g., a brand), rather than attributing it to situational or contextual factors (Jones and Harris 1967). For example, when an *E. coli* breakout was traced to food consumed at Jack-in-the-Box restaurants, consumers quickly assigned blame to the fast-food franchise rather than railing against loose and regulatory policies and practices that govern the handling of meat by restaurants.

By contrast, a second natural inclination is to defend those brands to which we feel truly committed. Committed individuals are those who have publicly expressed loyalty to a brand and who tend to act in ways that reinforce this loyalty. Recent research suggests that people who are committed to a brand tend to discount and even counter-argue negative information about it (Ahluwalia, Burnkrant, and Unnava 2000).

Both the Wendy's and Duke lacrosse scandals provide examples of this phenomenon. Loyal Wendy's customers rejected the assertion that Wendy's lax practices had allowed a finger to make its way into a bowl of chili. To show their support, a number of customers visited the restaurant and pointedly ordered chili. A parallel reaction arose among loyal Duke alumni. As a vote of confidence in the university, donations during the year in which the scandal took place set a record of $341 million, and a substantial portion of the giving occurred during the time period in which the rape scandal was hotly debated in the press. Further, sales of Duke University apparel, particularly Duke lacrosse T-shirts, tripled following the incident.

These observations suggest that before reacting to a possible scandal, a second crucial question should be posed: *Is the audience for the scandal information committed to my brand?* If the audience is committed to your brand, then reacting strongly in response to a brand scandal may be unnecessary and could even backfire. Those committed to your brand are likely to defend rather than blame the brand and company-issued denials may only undermine the resolve of such loyalists by inviting suspicion. If, however, the audience has little commitment to your brand, then the brand is likely to be blamed and a response is needed.

An additional factor that may work in favor of a perpetrating brand in the aftermath of a scandal is spillover to other brands. Research we have conducted in at least two different industry settings (fast food, athletic shoes) indicates that perpetrating brands benefit when consumers infer that other brands may also have engaged in the scandal behavior. For example, in one study, we exposed participants to a hypothetical scandal involving Nike and found that final ratings of Nike were higher in conditions where participants inferred that Reebok might also be guilty of the scandalous behavior than in conditions where such spillover did not occur. We propose that spillover causes people to reason that they might have been unfairly harsh on the perpetrating brand if other brands are guilty of the same transgression. As a result, they may "correct" their attitudes toward the perpetrating brand by adjusting them to be more favorable. Thus, the final question to ask when assessing the likely damage to the perpetrating brand is: *Will the scandal be likely to spillover to other brands?* We discuss next the factors that affect the likelihood that spillover will occur and, thereby, offer a reprieve for the initially scandalized brand.

## SPILLOVER BRANDS

In evaluating the likelihood that your brand may be affected by another brand's scandal, the likelihood that audience members will devote attention to the malfeasance is again relevant. In addition, an important follow-up question is: *Is my brand similar to the perpetrating brand on the scandal attribute?*

Similar brands, such as direct competitors, are most at risk for "spillover" or guilt by association. An important caveat, however, is that the *type* of similarity determines whether a competitor will actually be tainted by a perpetrating brand's scandal. For spillover to occur, the focal brand must be similar to the perpetrating brand *on the attribute that is involved in the scandal.*

The results of an experiment we conducted illustrate the role of similarity in spillover effects. We examined three fast-food restaurants: Burger King, Dairy Queen, and Hardee's. The perpetrating brand and the topic of the scandal were varied such that the scandal involved either Burger King or Dairy Queen and pertained to either hamburgers or ice cream. Hardee's served as the focal brand for which spillover was assessed. Although the three firms are viewed as highly similar overall, the basis for their similarity varies. Burger King and Hardee's are perceived as similar in terms of their hamburger offerings, but not in terms of their desserts, such as ice cream. In contrast, Dairy Queen and Hardee's are viewed as similar in terms of their ice-cream desserts, but not in terms of their hamburgers. As a result, both a Burger King scandal related to hamburgers and a Dairy Queen scandal related to ice cream spilled over to Hardee's. However, no spillover was found for either the Burger King ice-cream scandal or the Dairy Queen hamburger scandal (Experiment 1, Roehm and Tybout 2006). These findings suggest that spillover is most likely to occur for competitors who are similar to the perpetrating brand on the scandal attribute.

If, after considering the foregoing questions, you conclude that a scandal is likely to become associated with your brand, we recommend that an immediate acknowledgment of the situation be issued (step 2). But if you believe that the scandal is unlikely to implicate your brand, then you should make no official mention of the scandal. In fact, as noted earlier, if your brand is unlikely to be affected, making any statement about the scandal—even a direct denial of any involvement—may be misinterpreted as implying guilt, for why else would you be raising the scandal issue?

### Step 2: Issue an Immediate Acknowledgment

The goal of the immediate acknowledgment is to convey responsiveness and concern for any victims of the scandal event and to avoid the appearance that the brand has something to hide. If the scandal event poses an ongoing danger (i.e., cyanide in Tylenol, E. coli in Jack-in-the-Box hamburgers), the initial response also may include announcing the withdrawal of the product from the market while the investigation proceeds.

We recommend that the immediate acknowledgment include the following:

- An expression of concern for any parties harmed by the scandal event,
- An outline of the steps that are being taken to investigate and/or remedy the problem,
- Identification of a person in charge of the investigation and an outline of the time table for providing progress reports, and
- If appropriate, a summary of any immediate actions taken or underway to ensure no further harm occurs.

Why is immediate response necessary? When responding to scandals, managers often use how Tylenol handled its cyanide scandal as a model. Many people believe that the infamous tampering incidents did not permanently damage the Tylenol brand because the company took swift and decisive action along the lines specified here. By contrast, other brands have been damaged by their slow response to a scandal event. For example, Jack-in-the-Box took several days before issuing an initial press release regarding an *E. coli* outbreak linked to its hamburgers and the brand has never fully recovered. Similarly, Martha Stewart's nearly three weeks of silence following reports that she was being investigated regarding the sale of several thousand shares of Imclone stock, likely contributed to the public sentiment against her. To make matters worse, in her first public reaction, Stewart appeared to be less than forthcoming, as she dodged a surprise series of questions while making a regularly scheduled appearance on CBS's *The Early Show.*

Just as important as what should be included in the immediate acknowledgment is what should be left out. The marketplace is littered with examples of brands that have eroded much-needed credibility by making statements that were subsequently changed or reversed. Consider the handling of the Perrier benzene scandal. Perrier's initial explanation attributed the problem to mistaken actions of an employee in a North American bottling plant. However, when benzene was discovered in bottles of Perrier manufactured outside the United States, the company was forced to retract the original story, and instead explain that the benzene came from carbon dioxide, an ingredient in Perrier that provides its bubbles. The bumbling of the explanation and the resulting toll taken on the brand's credibility may help to explain why, over a decade later, Perrier's revenues remained 40 percent below their peak.

To avoid such problems, we believe that strongly worded statements—such as apologies, denials, announcements of victim compensation—should be deferred to a follow-up response stage (Step 3). By that time, a more comprehensive understanding of what caused the problem should be available and statements can be made with greater confidence that they will not require later retraction.

After issuing an immediate acknowledgment, the emphasis should be on conducting a thorough investigation to get to the root of the scandal. An accurate and truthful depiction of the events is essential to formulating a comprehensive and strategic response, which is the focus of our Step 3.

## Step 3: Choose a Strategic Approach

After you have conducted research into the scandal, your brand's follow-up response will depend on whether the allegations are found to be true or false.

***When the Allegations Are False***   When the allegations against a brand are false, a strong denial is in order. Recent experimental research indicates that denials can prompt the audience to correct misperceptions about a brand's involvement in a scandal (Roehm and Tybout 2006). Accordingly, once internal and police investigations indicated that the Wendy's chili incident was a ruse concocted by a scheming customer, the company publicized this information, highlighting the fact that there was no evidence of any wrongdoing on the part of the company. This assertion of the brand's innocence encouraged customers who might initially have believed Wendy's was guilty of negligence to correct their misperceptions. In a similar vein, once the three members of the Duke lacrosse team were declared innocent, the players and the university publicized this verdict. The university also sought and gained reinstatement of the team for the 2007 season, allowing it to reach the NCAA finals.

***When the Allegations Are True***   When misdeeds are confirmed, a brand's response may involve an apology, victim compensation, and/or punishment for those responsible. An *apology* is defined as a statement that acknowledges both responsibility and regret for a violation (Kim, Ferrin, Cooper, Dirks 2004). Indeed, both of these core components are evident in the two apologies issued by Mel Gibson in the wake of his recent drunken anti-Semitic tirade (see the Appendix).

*Compensation* involves some form of payment or other action that helps to restore victims to pretransgression status (Darley and Pittman 2003). For example, Jack-in-the-Box might be asked to pay medical bills for those who got *E. coli* infections from eating at the chain's restaurants.

*Punishment* delivers retribution and is an important mechanism for protecting the moral and behavioral codes that structure society (Darley and Pittman 2003; Trevino 1992). Thus, in sending Martha Stewart and WorldCom executives to jail, the laws that were broken were reinforced. Conversely, if punishment had not occurred in those cases, it would call into question the utility and relevancy of the legal system (e.g., if insider trading goes unchecked, was it really that wrong to begin with?). Such ambiguity threatens the maintenance of a safe and civilized living environment, and because of this, people react negatively when punishment is perceived to be warranted but not carried out.

Calibrating the proper degree of emphasis on an apology, compensation, and punishment necessitates consideration of the following question: How intentional is the scandalous event perceived to be? A scandal may be the result of actions that are purely accidental (no harm was meant and there was no understanding that a specific action would produce harm), negligent (harm was not purposely inflicted, but there was a failure to avoid it) or intentional (the action was known to be harmful and was pursued anyway). The intentionality of the actions will influence whether an apology, compensation, and/or punishment is expected by audience members (Darley and Pittman 2003).

*Accidental*   If the negative event plaguing your brand was truly accidental, audience members may not perceive punishment or compensation to be necessary. Instead, all that is needed is an earnest apology for having created a negative (though unintended) outcome. For example, following the accidental shooting of Harry Whittington during a quail-hunting party, Vice President Dick Cheney publicly took responsibility and expressed his regret. In a Fox News interview, Cheney said "Ultimately, I am the guy who pulled the trigger and fired the round that hit Harry. . . . You can talk about all the other conditions that existed at the time, but that's the bottom line. . . . And, it was, I'd have to say, one of the worst days of my life at that moment."

*Negligent*   If the scandal event is the result of negligence, a perceived need for punishment is also unlikely, because the associated motives were innocuous. However, compensation may be necessary to return to a state of "fair" distribution of assets.

Just what does "fair" mean? Perceived fairness varies as a function of the context (Deutsch 1976). If the venue of your scandal is *economic*, compensation will be viewed as necessary if the *rewards* consumers received were not commensurate with their inputs. Trend Micro, a company specializing in network antivirus and Internet content security, operates in the economic context of the software marketplace. In April of 2005, disaster struck when an automatic update to the company's antivirus software caused a conflict with the operating systems on 150,000 customers' computers, rendering them inoperable. Restated another way, the affected customers did not receive the rewards of adequate software performance that their input purchase dollars should have guaranteed. Fortunately, the company responded in an appropriate manner, contritely accepting responsibility and fully compensating customers for the damage it had created to the tune of $9 million.

If the context is *social* rather than economic, outcomes will be perceived as unfair if equal treatment was disrupted of involved parties. Scandals that have plagued professional baseball—a sport that provides a source of social interaction and leisure-time fun for its fans—bear out this point. Relatively sudden growth in body size and batting power has provoked suspicions that star players such as Mark McGwire, Sammy Sosa, and Barry Bonds used steroids as they vied to challenge records for most home runs in a season, most home runs overall, and so forth. Steroid use is considered unfair because the athletes who originally set the records did not have access to the same performance-enhancing drugs.

Major League Baseball officials are widely held to have been negligent in turning a blind eye to the steroid problem because no testing policy was instituted until the 2003 season, long after concerns were initially raised. Moreover, many audience members believe that covert use continues among certain players, unchecked by testing procedures that remain too lax. A 2005 poll by *USA Today,* CNN, and Gallup revealed that 82 percent of fans surveyed believe that compensatory action is needed in the form of stripping records set by steroid-abusing players or denoting such records with an asterisk, effectively jeopardizing the players' chances of admission to the Baseball Hall of Fame.

Finally, if your scandal takes place in the context of a *caring* relationship with a consumer, compensation should follow if the customers' needs were violated. Consider the case of Merck's blockbuster drug, Vioxx, a type of painkiller known as a COX-2 inhibitor that was launched in 1999. The company was forced to withdraw the drug from the market in September 2004 after conclusive evidence linking it to elevated cardiovascular (CV) risks became public. Particularly damaging to Merck's reputation was the fact that internal memos dating back to 1997 linked Vioxx to increased CV risks. Thus, although Vioxx was effective in performing the function for which it was designed, reducing pain, it also undermined the overall health and welfare needs of patients by placing them at increased risk of heart failure without their knowledge. The belief that compensation is warranted is supported by the more than 10,000 individual suits and 190 class action suits that were filed against Merck in the 18 months following the withdrawal of Vioxx from the market. Some of these lawsuits have subsequently been dismissed but others have resulted in multimillion dollar awards for the victims and their families.

*Intentional*   If the scandalous event or action was intentionally perpetrated, it is important to determine whether it was primarily due to a lack of competence or a lack of integrity. Scandals that occur because rules are broken or appropriate processes and protective measures are not followed are termed *competence-based,* whereas scandals that involve the violation of a moral social behavior and/or harm a vulnerable individual or group are termed *integrity-based* (Kim et al. 2004). When Martha Stewart used insider information to time the selling of her Imclone stock, she broke a rule, so the resulting scandal was competence-based. By contrast, when Michael Jackson was accused of child molestation, the charge involved far more than breaking the law; it implied a violation of fundamental moral principles regarding protecting the innocence of children, so the resulting scandal was integrity-based.

Whether a scandal is competence- or integrity-based influences the audience's mindset when considering any response that is issued. If the scandal is competence-based, positive information is likely to be given due consideration because there is a tendency to give normally competent people and brands the benefit of the doubt when a lapse in judgment occurs; a previous good track record goes a long way. However, if a scandal is integrity-based, negative information receives disproportionate emphasis because a single slippage on an integrity issue implies low *overall* integrity and, thus, generally dishonest behavior (Kim et al. 2004). The phrase "once a thief, always a thief" captures such reasoning.

The differential weighting of positives and negatives leads to the following recommendations:

- Emphasize *apologies* for competence-based scandals, but not integrity-based scandals. Apologies contain both positive (remorse) and negative (responsibility) components. The positives are more likely to receive substantial attention when the error is competence-based, whereas the negative side may be dwelled upon when integrity has been breached. Thus, an apology from Martha Stewart versus Michael Jackson most likely would have been received quite differently, had one been issued. Because her transgression was competence-based, Martha Stewart might have gotten significant mileage out of an apology—ironically, a path she seemed determined not to take during her ordeal. By contrast, the issue at the heart of the Michael Jackson scandal was integrity-based, and thus, may have been beyond the capabilities of an apology to repair.

- Emphasize *punishment* for integrity-based scandals to show that you actually do understand and believe in the moral and ethical code that has been infringed and thus deserve to be given a second chance after serving your sentence. This is likely to be especially effective if the violated standard is important and one about which there is strong consensus. Thus, if Michael Jackson had been found guilty of child molestation, severe punishment would been expected, given the strong agreement that child molestation is an atrocious crime and that it is important to preserve basic human rights such as personal sanctity and safety. By contrast, Mel Gibson's antics, while tactless and insensitive, did not pose a real threat to anyone's life or well-being. Thus, an apology was expected (and offered), and there was no groundswell of support for incarceration or other such punishment.

Having decided on an overall approach—and whether denial, apology, compensation, and/or punishment will be featured—decisions about specific response tactics can now be made.

## Step 4: Design a Specific Response

Implementing the strategic response requires making a number of tactical decisions, including: What issues should be addressed and in what detail? What tone should be taken? Who should deliver the response?

To answer these questions, it is helpful to first determine your audience's goal orientation or expectations for the brand. If the audience views your brand as a means of achievement or advancement (i.e., women may purchase Martha Stewart products in an effort to achieve a lifestyle that she represents), the brand is seen as facilitating the achievement of *promotion* goals and a scandal constitutes a failure to reach these desired goals (i.e., Martha Stewart's insider trading scandal undermined the brand's ability to help customers achieve the goal of a genteel, domestic lifestyle). By contrast, if the audience expects your brand to provide protection (i.e., companies purchase Trend Micro anti-virus software to protect their computer systems from harm), the brand serves *prevention goals* and a scandal signals the loss of such protection (i.e., Trend Micro's flawed pattern file update not only failed to protect customers, it harmed their computers. See Idson, Liberman, and Higgins 2000 for more on the distinction between promotion and prevention goals).

Some scandals, such as the ones involving Martha Stewart and Trend Micro, fit relatively neatly into either the promotion or prevention category. Likewise, the Michael Jackson saga seems to fit into the prevention mold because it involved a lack of security and protection for the children who were involved. Conversely, the Mel Gibson mishap aligns more naturally with promotion because it relates to a failure to maintain an ideal of tolerance and respect for other people.

Other scandals are open to framing in either promotion or prevention terms. Consider, for instance, the Vioxx scandal. On the one hand, the problems with Vioxx could be cast in promotion terms because the medication failed to help its users achieve an ideal state of good health. On the other hand, the scandal could also be framed in prevention terms because Vioxx failed to prevent harm to patients' health. If there is an opportunity to help the audience frame the scandal, we recommend choosing a promotion rather than a prevention frame because losses have a greater impact on evaluations than gains (or lack of gains; Kahneman and Tversky 1979). Thus, framing a scandal in promotion terms may dampen its negative impact relative to framing it in prevention terms.

Goal orientation has been found to influence many aspects of how people respond to information. Thus, knowledge of the audience's goal orientation is very helpful when crafting a denial or an apology. Next we detail the implications of goal orientation for choosing the message content, emotional tone, and spokesperson for a scandal response. We illustrate several of our points by drawing on Mel Gibson's responses to his drunken driving/anti-Semitic tirade scandal. Mr. Gibson's words are quoted in the Appendix for reference.

### Message Content

*Counterfactuals*  On hearing about a scandal event, audience members often spontaneously construct "counterfactuals." This entails taking the bad (scandalous) outcome and mentally altering the elements in the scenario that would have changed the outcome to be positive ("this is what could have happened instead"). Therefore, when responding to a scandal, it is important to anticipate and address prominent thoughts about what should have happened (or not happened) to avoid the scandal in the first place.

Events that are framed in promotion versus prevention terms have been found to generate different types of counterfactuals (Roese, Hur, and Pennington 1999). *Promotion* failures prompt "additive counterfactuals" in which an element that could produce a positive outcome is mentally inserted into the original scenario. For instance, Mel Gibson's scandal presumably involved a promotion frame, because people look to Gibson for entertainment and/or aspire to be like him. Thus, after learning of Gibson's drunken tirade, audience members most likely constructed an additive counterfactual scenario in which they imagined the additional acts of Gibson calling a friend for a ride home or drinking cola all night rather than tequila—both of which would have dramatically changed the way events unfolded.

By contrast, when considering *prevention*-framed events, audiences rely on "subtractive counterfactuals," where an element that produced the negative outcome is deleted from the scenario. For example, in the Michael Jackson scandal, the audience might have reasoned that threats to a child's safety could have been avoided by parents simply refusing to allow private visits between the singer and their children.

Understanding the promotion versus prevention framing of a scandal can provide useful guidance on content for messages that are issued in response to scandal outbreak. Specifically, whereas promotion-framed scandals call for responses that address what should have been done to produce a more positive outcome (what action to add), prevention-framed scandals demand responses that speak to what should not have been done (what action to subtract).

Applying these guidelines to the Gibson case perhaps helps to explain why his management team felt it necessary to issue two formal responses rather than just one. Examining his first statement, it is noteworthy that there is virtually no reference to additive actions, which would have been appropriate to the scandal's promotion framing. Instead, the focus is primarily on things Gibson should *not* have done that night, such as driving a car, acting like a person out of control, and saying despicable things. The mismatch between this message focus and the promotion view of the scandal may explain a lukewarm reception to the statement, which presumably led to the issue of the second one. In the follow-up, we see a slightly better alignment between scandal framing and message focus. Although there is still a heavy emphasis on things that should not have been done (anti-Semitic remarks, harmful words to law enforcement), there is also an acknowledgment of what should have happened instead. Gibson highlights a desire to meet with Jewish leaders for help in cultivating greater regard for the Jewish people—feelings that, if added to the initial scenario, could have prevented his anti-Semitic rant.

*Level of Specificity*    A second consideration in deciding what to say is whether the response should be couched in relatively abstract or concrete terms. Here again, research on how goal orientation affects processing is informative. There is evidence that when in promotion mode, people tend to process information at a macrolevel (Forster and Higgins 2005). As a result, fairly abstract language is appropriate when addressing a promotion-oriented scandal

(Semin, Higgins, and de Montes 2005). Conversely, a prevention orientation focuses thinking on concrete details of the situation and, consequently, a more specific response is optimal.

The language level of Mel Gibson's response—and particularly his second statement—appears to be well calibrated for a promotion-framed scandal. The concepts he references prominently, such as "charity and tolerance as a way of life" and "existing harmony in a world that seems to have gone mad," are fittingly broad and sweeping in nature. By contrast, had his scandal taken on a prevention framing, he would have wanted to couch his response in more concrete terms, perhaps providing specific details as to his rehabilitation plans, rather than vaguely issuing a request to meet with Jewish leaders with an intention to define an "appropriate path for healing."

***Tone***   It is also important to consider the general tone that should be struck in delivering the response. Events related to promotion versus prevention goals tend to evoke very different emotions (Brockner and Higgins 2001; Idson et al. 2000; Leone, Perugini, and Bagozzi 2005; Roese et al. 1999). Specifically, promotion-based events prompt dejected emotions, such as sadness, disappointment, and dissatisfaction, whereas prevention-based events elicit more agitated emotions such as anxiety and nervousness. Ideally, the "look and feel" of the response to a scandal will match the audience's emotional reaction to it.

Imagine yourself in Mel Gibson's shoes following his DUI arrest. Realizing that your scandal is likely to be construed in promotion terms, you might anticipate that the public will react with disappointment and disillusionment. Thus, what tone should you strike in order to achieve the greatest positive impact? Certainly, a subdued and remorseful voice, which can tacitly acknowledge the audience's mood, would be in order. Interestingly, this was precisely the approach that Gibson took, sprinkling his message with downcast yet unexciting terms such as "disgraced" and "unbecoming."

How might the ideal tone of his response have changed if had he been embroiled in a prevention-framed scandal? In that case, the audience's emotions would likely have been characterized more by anxiousness than disappointment. It follows that a suitable tone might have been one of calmness and serenity, with perhaps more usage of terms like "path for healing," to help pacify the fretful nervousness that might have been evoked by the scandal.

***Spokesperson***   Finally, a spokesperson must be chosen to deliver the denial or apology, as well as any news about punishment and/or compensation. Knowing whether the scandal is promotion- or prevention-focused is again helpful, because different types of role models are effective in each situation.

Research suggests that when the issue is promotion-oriented, people tend to be influenced by positive role models who can highlight strategies to achieve success. By contrast, when the issue is prevention-oriented, people prefer to hear from role models who emphasize strategies for avoiding failure (Lockwood, Jordan, and Kunda . 2002). In the Mel Gibson example, it is significant that both his earlier and later statements are written from a first person vantage point, positioning Mr. Gibson himself as his sole spokesperson. Was this the best choice? The wisdom of serving as his own spokesperson depends on whether Gibson is likely to be viewed as a role model in domains relevant to his scandal. Having freely spouted ethnic epithets (albeit under the influence of alcohol), Gibson seems to be a dubious model for religious tolerance and peaceful coexistence. This leads to a general rule of thumb: Third parties may be best to deliver response messages for promotion-framed scandals because it is difficult for someone who has been personally involved in a scandal to quickly reappear as a positive role model.

However, if the scandal is prevention-based, those involved in the event may be quite effective spokespeople. When in a prevention frame, individuals prefer to receive information from someone who can convincingly highlight ways to avoid failure. The person who has been directly involved in the scandal itself—and who can speak from the experience of having learned a sharp and painful lesson—may be very credible in addressing a prevention-based scandal. Thus, it was appropriate that the CEO and president of Trend Micro served as spokespeople when the software failed to protect their customers.

## CONCLUSION

The challenge of managing a brand scandal is complicated by the variation in the types of scandals and, hence, the need to adapt the response to the particulars of the situation. No one formula will work in all situations. Accordingly, this chapter presents a four-stage framework and related questions to guide the manager in assessing the likely damage to the brand and crafting the most appropriate strategic and tactical response. The stages, and related questions, are summarized next:

*Step 1: Assess the Likelihood That Your Brand Will Be Affected by Asking the Following Questions:*
- Will the potentially scandalous incident gain significant attention?
- Is the audience committed to my brand?
- Is the scandal likely to spillover to brands beyond the perpetrating brand?

- If my brand is not the perpetrating brand, is it similar to the perpetrating brand on the scandal attribute?

**Step 2: If Your Brand Is Likely to Be Affected, Issue an Immediate Acknowledgment That Includes the Following:**

- An expression of concern for any parties harmed by the scandal event,
- An outline of the steps that are being taken to investigate and/or remedy the problem,
- Identification of a person in charge of the investigation and an outline of the timetable for providing progress reports,
- And, if appropriate, a summary of any immediate actions taken or underway to insure no further harm occurs.

**Step 3: Formulate a Strategic Approach Based on Answers to the Following Questions:**

- Are the allegations true or false?
- How intentional is the scandalous action perceived to be?
- Is the offense competence-based or integrity-based?

**Step 4: Design a Specific Response Based on the Specific Issues Involved in the Scandal and the Audience's Likely Goal Orientation:**

- Does the audience view the brand in a means of achievement or advancement (i.e., promotion goal) or as a means of protection (i.e., prevention goal)?
- What are the implications of the goal orientation for the message content and tone and the spokesperson?

# APPENDIX

### Mel Gibson's First Statement

"After drinking alcohol on Thursday night, I did a number of things that were very wrong and for which I am ashamed. I drove a car when I should not have, and was stopped by the L.A. County sheriffs. The arresting officer was just doing his job and I feel fortunate that I was apprehended before I caused injury to any other person. I acted like a person completely out of control when I was arrested and said things that I do not believe to be true and which are despicable. I am deeply ashamed of everything I said and I apologize to anyone who I may have offended. Also, I take this opportunity to apologize to the deputies for my belligerent behavior. They have always been there for me in my community and indeed probably saved me from myself. I disgraced myself and my family with my behavior and for that I am truly sorry. I have battled the disease of alcoholism for all of my adult life and profoundly regret my horrific relapse. I apologize for any behavior unbecoming of me in my inebriated state and have taken necessary steps to ensure my return to health."

### Mel Gibson's Second Statement (Excerpts)

"There's no excuse, nor should there be any tolerance, for anyone who thinks or expresses any kind of anti-Semitic remark. I want to apologize specifically to everyone in the Jewish community for the vitriolic and harmful words that I said to a law enforcement officer the night I was arrested on a DUI charge . . .

"But please know from my heart that I am not an anti-Semite. I am not a bigot. Hatred of any kind goes against my faith . . .

"I'm not just asking for forgiveness. I would like to take it one step further, and meet with leaders in the Jewish community, with whom I can have a one-on-one discussion to discern the appropriate path for healing . . .

"Again, I am reaching out to the Jewish community for its help. I know there will be many in that community who want nothing to do with me and that would be understandable. But I pray that the door is not forever closed."

## REFERENCES

Ahluwalia, Rohini, Robert E. Burnkrant, and H. Rao Unnava. 2000. Consumer response to negative publicity: The moderating role of commitment. *Journal of Marketing Research* 37 (May): 203–214.

Alicke, Mark D. 2000. Culpable control and the psychology of blame. *Psychological Bulletin* 126 (4): 556–574.

Brockner, Joel, and E. Tory Higgins. 2001. Regulatory focus theory: Implications for the study of emotions at work. *Organizational Behavior and Human Decision Processes* 86 (1): 35–66.

Darley, John M., and Thane S. Pittman. 2003. The psychology of compensatory and retributive justice. *Personality and Social Psychology Review* 7 (4): 324–336.

Deutsch, Morton. 1976. Theorizing in social psychology. *Personality and Social Psychology Bulletin* 2 (2): 134–141.

Forster, Jens, and E. Tory Higgins. 2005. How global versus local perception fits regulatory focus. *Psychological Science* 16 (8): 631–636.

Idson, Lorraine Chen, Nira Liberman, and E. Tory Higgins. 2000. Distinguishing gains from nonlosses and losses from nongains: A regulatory focus perspective on hedonic intensity. *Journal of Experimental Social Psychology* 36 (3): 252–274.

Jones, Edward E., and Victor A. Harris. 1967. The attribution of attitudes. *Journal of Experimental Social Psychology* 3 (January): 1–24.

Kahneman, Daniel, and Amos Tversky. 1979. Prospect theory: An analysis of decision under risk. *Econometrica* 47: 262–291.

Kim, Peter H., Donald L. Ferrin, Cecily D. Cooper, and Kurt T. Dirks. 2004. Removing the shadow of suspicion: The effects of apology versus denial for repairing competence versus integrity-based trust violations. *Journal of Applied Psychology* 89 (1): 104–118.

Leone, Luigi, Marco Perugini, and Richard P. Bagozzi. 2005. Emotions and decision making: Regulatory focus moderates the influence of anticipated emotions on action evaluations. *Cognition and Emotion* 19 (8): 1175–1198.

Lockwood, Penelope, Christian H. Jordan, and Ziva Kunda. 2002. Motivation by positive or negative role models: Regulatory focus determines who will best inspire us. *Journal of Personality and Social Psychology* 83 (4): 854–864.

Roehm, Michelle L., and Alice M. Tybout. 2006. When will a brand scandal spill over, and how should competitors respond? *Journal of Marketing Research* 43 (3): 366–373.

Roese, Neal J., Taekyun Hur, and Ginger L. Pennington. 1999. Counterfactual thinking and regulatory focus: Implications for action versus inaction and sufficiency versus necessity. *Journal of Personality and Social Psychology* 77 (6): 1109–1120.

Semin, Gun R., E. Tory Higgins, and Lorena Gil de Montes. 2005. Linguistic signatures of regulatory focus: How abstraction fits promotion more than prevention. *Journal of Personality and Social Psychology* 89 (1): 36–45.

Treviño, Linda Klebe. 1992. The social effects of punishment in organizations: A justice perspective. *Academy of Management Review* 17 (4): 647–676.

# CHAPTER 8

# MANAGING PUBLIC REPUTATION

## DANIEL DIERMEIER

**R**eputation has moved to the top of the agenda for many CEOs and senior executives. What used to be a "nice to have" is now increasingly considered a core asset that needs to be protected and managed. Reputational damage can hurt a company in many ways. Take the example of Wal-Mart. Over the past two years, Wal-Mart has been the subject of negative news coverage on topics ranging from environmental and labor concerns to allegations that Wal-Mart has a negative net economic effect on local communities.[1] These accusations (whether true or false) have already had an impact on Wal-Mart's business performance. According to a leaked internal study, about 2 percent to 8 percent of shoppers have taken their business elsewhere because they were no longer comfortable shopping at Wal-Mart stores. Perhaps more importantly, Wal-Mart has encountered increased resistance to opening new stores, especially on the West Coast and in the northeastern region of the United States.[2] As a consequence, Wal-Mart's stock price has been depressed over the past two years. To address the concerns Wal-Mart has engaged in an extensive reputation management initiative,[3] and the *Wall Street Journal* has called Wal-Mart's CEO Lee Scott the de facto "Chief Reputation Officer."

New (user-generated) media have only accelerated this trend. When rats were found in a Taco Bell restaurant, the corresponding YouTube video made sure that any customer anywhere in the world could take a look for himself.[4] Similarly, the ability to repeatedly watch and listen to the racially offensive marks by controversial talk show host Don Imus even days after their initial broadcast led to a ground-swell of outrage that eventually led to Imus' being fired.[5]

Yet, while awareness of these issues is undoubtedly increasing in C-suites and boardrooms, companies are not much closer to effectively navigating these treacherous waters. Reputation management is still largely the domain of the communications department, and while CEOs increasingly recognize the importance of effectively communicating to the public, in many cases, communication departments still lack sufficient funding and credibility within a company. In part, this lack of influence may reflect senior management's suspicion of the business value of effective communication. However, it also reflects the inability of communication experts to integrate their craft effectively into what really matters to a business: value creation and cost reduction.

Consider the example of Starbucks. Starbucks' success is based on creating an enjoyable experience for customers. This experience is not only based on coffee of consistently high quality, but a welcoming atmosphere and ambiance, friendly, knowledgeable staff, the ability to have one's coffee prepared exactly as one likes it, and so forth. For many customers an important aspect of this experience is a belief that Starbucks is a decent company that treats its employees well (e.g., health-care benefits even for part-time employees) and cares about the environment (e.g., policies on shade-grown coffee). Now suppose (hypothetically) that a Starbucks customer, while waiting in line for her latte, picks up a copy of the *New York Times* and reads a front page article that accuses Starbucks' purchasing department of using its purchasing power to put the squeeze on poor coffee farmers in Guatemala. Reading this story may thoroughly destroy the pleasurable experience for this and similar customers. Suddenly, the customer may experience a strange aftertaste after sipping from her coffee, vaguely reminiscent of "guilt."

The financial consequences of reputational crises can be substantial. Consider the crisis recently experienced by Bausch & Lomb, a producer of soft contact lenses and lens care products. On April 10, 2006, the U.S. Center for Disease Control and Prevention linked a surge in potentially blinding fungal infections with Bausch & Lomb's ReNu with MoistureLoc contact lens solution. As a result, Bausch & Lomb's stock price dropped by about 20 percent within a few days, a loss that was sustained for roughly a year and amounted to the destruction of roughly $630 million in shareholder value. Bausch & Lomb subsequently experienced accounting restatements and was acquired by private equity firm Warburg Pincus.[6] Other examples come from the mutual funds industry. Putnam Investments, at the time a division of Marsh & McLennan, not only paid $110 million in penalties and restitution with Federal regulators, but lost roughly $100 billion in assets under management as a consequence of the scandal.[7] Current examples include concerns over safety of products manufactured in China. This led to numerous recalls, including three recalls by Mattel in the span of four weeks in the summer of 2007.[8]

These effects are particularly important as companies adjust their value propositions from a product-focused to a customer-focused perspective. As companies strive to provide an "experience" or provide "solutions" for customer problems, more of the value for customers becomes psychological; the value increasingly resides in the mind of the customer. Of course, achieving a close customer connection can be of tremendous value for companies' product commoditization, provides additional value to customers, and other advantages, but it also bears additional risks. In many cases, developing a closer relationship with customers requires mutual trust. But the dark side of trust is betrayal, and the fall-out from customers who feel betrayed can be massive.

An important lesson not only from the fictitious Starbucks scenario, but also from Wal-Mart, Bausch & Lomb, and Putnam is that a company's reputation among customers is only partially shaped by direct experiences with the company. There are whole population segments with very firm opinions about Wal-Mart that have never set a foot into Wal-Mart stores. Similarly, both existing and potential customers of Taco Bell may choose to never set foot into a Taco Bell restaurant once they are exposed to the rat video. In other words, perfect execution at the typical customer "touch points" is not sufficient for building and maintaining an excellent reputation. Rather, third parties, especially the media, play an important role in shaping customer perceptions (Figures 8.1 and 8.2).

In the case of the recent concerns over manufacturing quality in China, the reputational impact of Mattel and other toy companies (including retailers) stems from the practices of their suppliers, not the company itself. In other words, a company's reputation can be damaged not only by its own actions but by actions of business partners in its value chain. The charge against the company is not that it itself engaged in the offensive practice, but it failed in its oversight over its suppliers. These effects will be most pronounced for companies that either have a strong brand or are engaged in an industry where trust is crucial (food, children's products, financial services, health care, etc.). By outsourcing key parts of their value chain, companies may lower costs and mitigate both operational and (to some extent) legal risks, but the same is *not* true about reputational risks, especially for well-known consumer brands: If you live by the brand, you die by the brand.

While our focus so far has been on customers, the business impact of reputational damage does not stop there but may lead to regulatory and legal consequences all the way to significant freedom-to-operate concerns. Wal-Mart's inability to open stores in time, as well as the lawsuits and regulatory action in the Bausch & Lomb and Putnam cases are just a few examples. It is important to recognize that prosecutors and regulators themselves are subject to public opinion. Consider a typical accounting scandal. First, management is under

**Figure 8.1**
**Shaping Customer Perceptions**

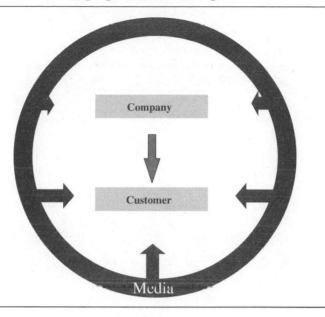

**Figure 8.2**
**Impact Beyond Boundaries**

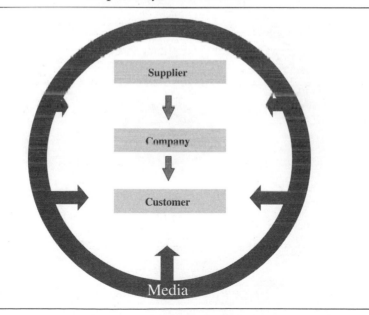

attack by shareholders, regulators, perhaps even prosecutors. Then, attention will turn to the auditors. In many cases, potential inquiries can be settled behind closed doors, but in cases where an issue receives substantial media interest, such approaches are likely to fail. The problem is that, in those cases, public officials have to manage their own reputation and demonstrate that they were not "asleep at the wheel" or, an even more serious charge, "in the pocket of the industry." A true and tested approach to dispel these public concerns is to come down hard on the affected company or industry (Figure 8.3).

This effect is particularly prominent in the case of regulators that are subject to oversight by other members of the executive branch (e.g., a minister) or legislators (e.g., an oversight committee). That is, if regulators do not proactively act tough they may be subject to hostile hearings or reprimands. This further increases the incentive to take a hard line against the company. In many cases, public officials may shift their stance on an issue in response to mounting pressure. In an evolving scandal such shifts may be sudden and

**Figure 8.3**
**Reputation of Regulators**

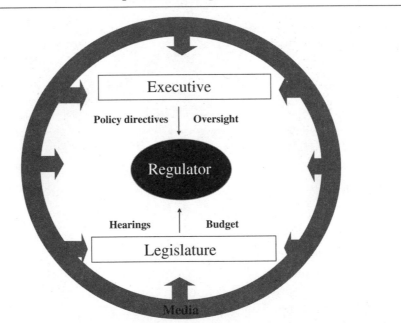

unexpected. Companies are sometimes stunned by the fact that the same regulators who were highly cooperative only a few weeks ago now refuse to meet
or return phone calls. Public opinion is dynamic, and skillful public officials
will adjust either directly or indirectly through the oversight process.

Clearly, reputational concerns have moved to the core of managerial responsibilities. Long the domain of public relations and legal experts, they are
now increasingly a core concern of areas such as marketing and risk management. But the question remains how to best manage those challenges. This is
where new concepts and frameworks are needed.

## CONCEPTS, FRAMEWORK, AND PROCESSES

There are three core difficulties in managing corporate reputations:

1. Lack of *control*.
2. Limited *credibility*.
3. Overwhelming *complexity*.

### Control

As demonstrated in the previous examples, companies cannot directly control
third-party messages. Consider the example of a credit card company. If a customer is unhappy with a late charge, a customer services representative can
directly engage with the customer on a one-on-one basis and rectify the situation, for example, by waiving the fee or at least convincingly explaining its
rationale. In contrast, if the *New York Times* runs an article detailing the alleged
abuse of late fees among credit card companies, the company cannot reach all
the readers of this article, certainly not among *potential* customers. Direct-to-
consumer advertising in many cases is not a successful remedy for this dilemma
because companies frequently lack credibility with customers or the public as
a whole.

### Credibility

When third parties (e.g., journalists or scientific experts) play a role in shaping
a company's reputation, companies need to realize that in many cases their
own credibility is much lower than that of the experts. In the competition
over a company's reputation, companies are at a disadvantage compared to
scientists, doctors, even nongovernmental organizations and governmental

actors. Importantly, which third parties have high credibility varies from country to country. In Northern Europe, nongovernmental organizations have some of the highest credibility scores. This is not true in Japan or the United States where some government agencies (e.g., the FDA) have more credibility with customers. Companies need to understand that what works in one market may not work in another. During the introduction of genetically modified food, Monsanto successfully used the FDA to overcome customer concerns about the safety of its products in the U.S. market.[9] A similar strategy in the European market, however, dramatically backfired, in part because the corresponding Health Ministry's reputation had previously been damaged after it mismanaged the occurrence of Mad Cow Disease in the United Kingdom.

## Complexity

Customers usually do not understand the complexity underlying certain business decisions. As a consequence, they will form their own beliefs on whether the company's behavior was appropriate. In many cases, they will rely on heuristics and rules of thumb when forming an opinion about a company. Social and cognitive psychologists have demonstrated that risk perception is subject to various biases and so-called "framing effects."[10] For example, customers will overestimate the risk to themselves if they empathize with the reported victim of allegedly improper business practices, especially if the victim comes from a particularly vulnerable group such as children or the elderly. Food safety concerns are a prime example of such processes, especially when they involve items consumed by children, such as milk or cereal.

These few examples point out that reputation management not only can be extremely challenging, but can affect the core assets of a company, especially if maintaining high levels of trust among customers, regulators, investors, or other stakeholders is necessary for sustained business success. It follows that reputation management should not be relegated to functional specialists such as the legal or public relations department. In many cases, reputational challenges have their origin in ordinary business decisions such as market entry (Monsanto and genetically modified food), marketing (charges of predatory marketing practices by credit cards), or product design (prepayment penalties for subprime loans). Once reputational challenges have reached the desk of the corporate counsel or the head of public relations, they frequently have reached crisis proportions. It is therefore much better to integrate reputational considerations into the day-to-day business decisions of the managers that run the business.

To successfully manage reputational challenges, companies need to develop three core capabilities:

1. A functioning early warning system.
2. Ongoing measurement of the reputation of the company, its markets, and its products.
3. Rapid situational assessment by issue, product, and market.

We discuss each capability in turn.

***Early Warning Systems***    Often, reputational challenges have their origin in areas not frequently monitored by companies. For example, a data privacy issue may first be voiced in an obscure computer science conference and not raised again until it has reached mainstream media. Companies can completely avoid or at least mitigate reputational crises by changing business practices, stakeholder outreach, or through detailed communication plans. But developing such responses takes time, the one thing companies do not have once an issue has reached crisis proportions. In retrospect, the warning signs could have been identified but they never reached the key decision makers. Moreover, in many cases, issues that turned out to be enterprise-critical were not even identified as potential risks; they never made it onto the radar screen. As "unknown unknowns," they never could be integrated into a proper risk management framework.

This is the value proposition for investing in early warning systems. This may range from informal monitoring of various media sources over proactive stakeholder outreach to the development of an internal issue anticipation group. In many cases, the critical information already resides with an organization (e.g., in call center or sales representatives) but is not aggregated.

Of particular promise is the use of information technology in this area. Companies are increasingly benefiting from using sophisticated tools from computational linguistics and artificial intelligence to identify and monitor emerging issues. Conceptually, the idea is closely related to the concept of "open source intelligence" in the area of national security. The idea is that in the context of emerging issues, the shortcoming does not rest in the *lack* of information but in *too much* information. Unfortunately, much of the available information is never aggregated to actionable intelligence. The "dots" were present, but not connected.

The Bausch & Lomb example discussed earlier presents an illuminating example. The U.S. Center for Disease Control and Prevention announced its findings on April 10, 2006. Yet, the link between the infections and ReNu had been uncovered almost *two months* earlier, on February 22, in a public announcement by Singapore's Ministry of Health. (Bausch & Lomb subsequently withdrew the ReNu solution from its markets in Singapore and Hong Kong.) The government announcement had been reported in the region's major newspapers, but had not been covered in the United States. Notice also Bausch & Lomb's stock lost a mere 3 percent from $71.51 at the close on February 21 to $69.40 at the close on February 23 with very low trading volume (Figure 8.4).

Effective early warning systems have essentially three components: identification, evaluation, and monitoring. The purpose of issue identification is to list all issues that may affect a company's reputation or other nonmarket risks. This is where tools from computational linguistics and text analytics can be most fruitfully applied. The general problem is that information about reputational risk is usually not available in a structured or numerical format (in contrast to, say, financial information). Rather, it is buried in documents, news articles, web sites, blogs, and other media. This makes information extraction and evaluation a challenging task. Fortunately, recent technical breakthroughs in the automatic processing of unstructured data permit organizations to identify emerging issues more easily.

**Figure 8.4**
**Bausch & Lomb Stock Reaction to Infection Disclosure**

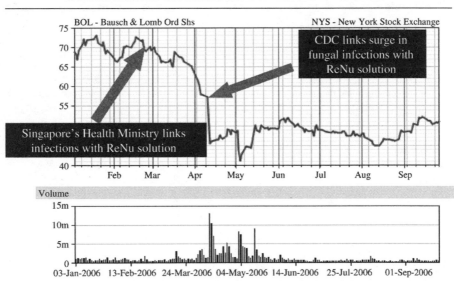

Next, companies need to evaluate which issues are *enterprise-critical*. This requires defining and assessing risk-profiles that are specific to an issue, a product, or a company. Figure 8.5 outlines a methodology for creating such risk profiles.

Here risk segments are characterized by two dimensions. The dimension of *Business Centrality* measures how closely an issue is connected to a company's core value proposition. In the examples given, the issues of data privacy are of a much higher concern to a financial services company than to a food company; the reverse will be true of food quality. In both cases (food quality for Nestle, data privacy for American Express), the issues directly touch on a core competency that the respective company needs to consistently demonstrate in order to maintain the trust of its customers.

*Media Centrality* refers to a different risk dimension. Here the point is that certain issues are likely to create more and more hostile media attention. In some cases, this will depend on the nature of the issue. *On average,* issues related to food safety are considered better stories than issues of IT security. A mass audience will more easily connect with issues that are easy to understand and are of direct relevance to their daily lives. Of course, there are exceptions to this observation. As an example, consider the enormous attention focused on Y2-K or, more recently, issues of identify theft related to Internet

**Figure 8.5**
**Risk Segmentation**

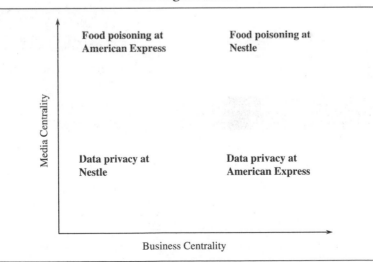

commerce. The point is that increased media centrality will make it more likely that customers and stakeholders (including regulators) will pay attention to an issue. This will usually lead to a more serious management challenge.

Identifying the Business Centrality of an issue is usually not a difficult task for companies once they recognize the importance. Anything that affects a company's value proposition, its core competencies, competitive advantage, or core values should trigger an alert. Media Centrality, on the other hand, is much more difficult to anticipate. In other words, it is easy to see that an issue has reached a high level of Media Centrality if it is featured on *60 Minutes* or the front page of *USA Today*. A much more difficult task is to predict which issues are more likely to create strong media interest and why.

A useful tool for this purpose is Baron's theory of the media.[11] According to Baron's approach, news coverage is largely driven by two forces: audience interest and societal significance (Figure 8.6). Audience interest drives the amount and likelihood of coverage, while the societal significance dimension determines how an issue is covered, for example whether an issue is merely reported or whether its segmentation of media coverage.

Depending on an issue's location in the interest-significance space, news coverage will change significantly. The most dangerous location for management is the high-audience-demand/high-societal-significance quadrant ("northeast"). This is the area where *60 Minutes* or *48 Hours* are located—

**Figure 8.6**
**Perceptive Drivers**

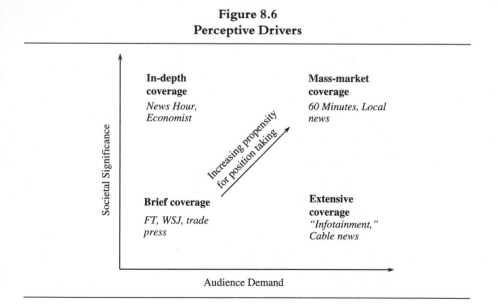

hard-hitting TV news programs that address controversial social issues, but need to present them in a format that is attractive to a mass audience. This format focuses on drama, individual cases ("victims"), easy to understand moral conflicts ("good" versus "evil"), and testimony instead of data. In this media environment, complicated arguments (e.g., the technical and regulatory limits for effective data protection) are very difficult. An approach that focuses solely on technical or legal aspects will almost always fail. Rather, the company must tell a compelling, credible story that can stand up to images with direct emotional impact (Figure 8.7).

As each issue segment is associated with a certain type of coverage, companies need to adopt strategies that are appropriate to the "reputational terrain" where an issue is located. For example, in the low-audience-demand/low-societal-significance quadrant ("southwest") much of the coverage is purely based on facts. Wire services or the back pages of the business press are good examples. In this segment, clarifying facts or pointing out inaccuracies constitute appropriate strategies. For example, an erroneous story about a planned bond offering can simply be clarified by a press release and so on. In the low-audience-demand/high-societal-significance quadrant ("northwest") we are dealing with sophisticated, in-depth coverage that is intended to convey the complexity of an issue and perhaps explore its various dimensions. The trade press or certain high quality publications (e.g., *The Economist*) fall into this

**Figure 8.7**
**Theory of the Media: Reputational Terrain**

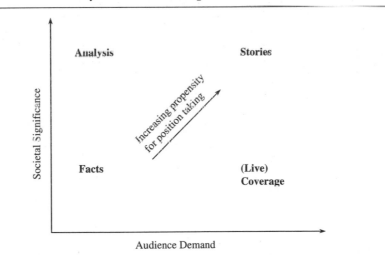

category. This segment is all about analysis and interpretation, and companies can shape the discussion by providing data, reports and so on. In contrast the high-audience-demand/high-societal-significance quadrant ("northeast") is all about *telling a story*. The focus will be on individual cases and how they are affected by an issue. A good story is built on dramatic tension around a few key characters: a victim, a villain, and a hero. Even though companies may perceive themselves as the victims of hostile media coverage, this perception is not shared by the general public. Companies are typically not the object of empathy: We do not feel sorry for powerful organizations, especially when they are perceived as wealthy and/or profit motivated. Of course, the public may empathize with individual workers losing their jobs, but the emotional reaction does not carry over to the company as a whole. The same is true of shareholders. Losing an investment does not elicit the same amount of sympathy as being the victim of fraud. This implies that, for companies, only two roles are available: hero or villain. The key difference between these two roles is their relationship to the victim. Heroes act on behalf of and in the interest of the victim. Villains do not. A company that responds to an injured child by referring to its exemplary safety statistics is perceived as uncaring, even monstrous. Appropriate strategies express direct and personal empathy for the victim and then commit themselves to "getting to the bottom of the problem."

On one hand, these communication strategies can be very effective once an issue has caught on, even if it has reached crisis proportions. On the other hand, companies have considerably more room to maneuver and prepare for potential crises if critical issues are identified early in their life cycle and assessed for media centrality. *Media Centrality* then corresponds to the *likelihood that an issue will end up in the high-audience-demand/high-societal-significance quadrant*. Anything that increases the likelihood of an issue leading to a "good story" is relevant. Examples include the presence of an identifiable, sympathetic victim or victim group (e.g., poor minorities as the subject of predatory marketing practices by unscrupulous lenders), the availability of visuals (consider both Abu Ghraib and rats at Taco Bell), involvement of a celebrity (e.g., Al Roker and weight-loss surgery), a well-known brand (e.g., recall of Thomas the Tank Engine), or a connection to a particularly controversial issue (e.g., abortion and the morning-after pill).

It is critically important to think about these dimensions from the perspective of the general public rather than from experts. Let us reconsider accounting scandals in this context. First, even major accounting scandals (e.g., WorldCom) usually do not involve sympathetic, identifiable victims. The injured parties are shareholders who do not elicit a lot of sympathy from the general public. Second, accounting matters are usually complicated and require extensive prior knowledge. That means that the overwhelming number of accounting crises will be characterized by low audience interest. With respect to regulators or prosecutors, this means that in most cases a settlement can be reached behind closed doors. There are some cases, however, where we move toward high-audience-demand/high-societal-significance. The prime example is Enron. First, we had identifiable victims (Enron's employees that not only lost their jobs but their pensions), a set of perceived villains (Enron's senior management) and many other factors that increase audience interest (the friendship between Enron Chairman Kenneth Lay and President Bush, the California energy crisis, the company's arrogant attitude, and the lavish lifestyle of its executive, the tearful TV interview with Mrs. Lay). All this added up to a great story with victims, villains, and heroes (the whistle-blowers and journalists).

In this context, the general public then learned about document shredding at Arthur Andersen, Enron's auditor. Andersen was immediately perceived as the accomplice and enabler of Enron's deeds. Here, public beliefs does not constitute a judgment about Enron's or Andersen's legal culpability, rather it is a statement about the court of public opinion. And here the judgment is clear: Guilty. This now leaves prosecutors and regulators no other option than to come down hard on Arthur Andersen and Enron, leading to the demise of both companies.

What does the Arthur Andersen tragedy teach us about early warning systems? First, the risk to professional service firms is largely driven by *client characteristics*. It was not the accounting issue per se that destroyed Arthur Andersen, but the verdict by the public and its representatives. But the public and the media paid so much attention to the issue because of its high level of media centrality. To see this compare the Enron case to the WorldCom case, the latter being a bigger bankruptcy with clear evidence of fraud by senior management but lacking the sensationalist elements that made Enron such an irresistible story.

Second, accounting firms should be monitoring the risk potential of their clients. For example, a moderate-sized hedge fund usually does not present a high-risk profile, unless the hedge fund counts Hollywood actor Sylvester Stallone as one of its investors, as in the case of Lipper Holdings. Then it becomes front-page news.

Third, client issues cannot be monitored by hand. The number of potential clients and issues is just too large. However, the text analytical methods discussed earlier can form the basis for such a system. The approach is to apply automated issue identification algorithms to a client portfolio, score the identified issues according to their risk profile, and then monitor their dynamics, while being prepared to take quick and decisive action if necessary. Note that the same approach can be applied to the monitoring of supply chains. Again the number of suppliers is usually too big to be monitored by people, especially for retailers. Automated (or semi-automated), open source intelligence systems provide a promising remedy.

***Measurement***   What gets measured gets managed. While financial and operational risk can now be (largely) quantified, this is not the case for reputational risk. If companies engage in any measurement at all, it is largely based on surveys or focus groups that make it difficult to obtain enough reliable data for a proper quantitative analysis. What are lacking are both operational measures (similar to customer satisfaction scores in marketing or quality measures in manufacturing) and financial measures that connect reputational with financial performance. Again, the sophisticated use of information technology provides a potential remedy. As discussed previously, media coverage heavily influences the perception of customers and other stakeholders. While measuring their beliefs directly may be prohibitively costly and impractical, we can measure the opinions expressed in the media and third-party sources. This can be accomplished by using computer algorithms that are trained to identify positive or negative opinions, using technologies not too dissimilar from a sophisticated spam filter. The effect of this approach is to generate quantitative data about a company's reputation that can then be further analyzed. For example, companies can compare the reputations of a given product in two different markets, measure reputational challenges over time, and assess whether a particular communication strategy has "moved the needle." Once such measures have been developed, they can be connected to a company's financial performance using standard event study methodologies. This allows an integration of reputational risk with other risk types.

***Situational Assessment***   Once critical issues have been identified and their impact measured, managing such issues requires rapid and reliable situational assessment. For example, many issues are "owned" by only a few journalists. Also, journalists frequently rely on the same group of experts that are then repeatedly quoted. Companies need to understand who is an "ally" or an "opponent." Of course, the list of opinion leaders, gate-keepers, and others is both issue- and market-specific and therefore requires ongoing monitoring.

Of particular importance is a good understanding of interest groups and opinion leaders that may move an issue to the forefront. Motivated activists may shrewdly utilize the media to advance their agenda. One of the most famous examples of this strategy is the confrontation between Royal

Dutch/Shell and the environmental activist group Greenpeace over the issue of deep-water disposal of the Brent Spar oil buoy in 1995. After an acrimonious battle between activists and the company—where sales in Germany and other European countries dropped by as much as 50 percent—Shell U.K. who had operating responsibility for the Brent Spar decided to abandon deep-water disposal and seek a license for on-shore disposal.[12] Only one year later, Royal Dutch/Shell was targeted again, this time over human rights issues related to Shell Nigeria. Royal Dutch/Shell subsequently engaged in an extensive reorganization and value-based change process to avoid similar issues in the future.

The key to Greenpeace's success was to create an irresistible story for the media. To generate sufficient attention to their issue, activists need to obtain media coverage in the northeastern corner. This is difficult. Competition for air and print space is fierce and many environmental issues, such as the Brent Spar disposal, involve complicated, technical issues. *Before* Greenpeace took action, the Brent Spar issue was located in the southwestern corner with little to no coverage in the media. Thus Greenpeace needed to stage its protests in a way that increased *both* audience interest and social significance. The Brent Spar occupation was an ideal means to increase audience interest. It provided drama, high stakes, and great visuals. Moreover, by taking a confrontational approach, for example turning on the water canons, Shell directly played into the hands of the activists by providing dramatic images of a high-stakes confrontation.

But increasing audience interest was not enough for Greenpeace. The activists also needed to provide the German public with a simple, straightforward reason to act. Ingeniously, Greenpeace framed the whole issue as a recycling issue, something German citizens care passionately about. The activists' line "Here I am dutifully recycling my garbage, and there comes big business and simply dumps its trash in the ocean," made the choice for German citizens an easy one. Since every upstanding German citizen recycles, Shell, by dumping the Brent Spar into the deep ocean, cannot be a good *corporate* citizen. It is important to recognize that by framing the issue as one concerning the moral duties of corporate citizens, the scientific, technical arguments brought to the discussion by Shell were powerless. They looked like feeble attempts by the company to avoid its onerous duty as good corporate citizen.

Companies need to understand that they are increasingly being scrutinized for their social impact. In other words, as companies are becoming the main engine of social and cultural change on a global scale, they are being held accountable for the consequences of such change. Food companies are being asked to promote healthy eating habits. Retailers and manufacturers are pressured to adopt sustainable business practices and require the same policies for their suppliers. Financial service companies are being targeted for "predatory" lending practices. Overall, these trends have substantially increased the risk for reputational damage at a global scale. Understanding these changing issue landscapes and stakeholder environments proactively is more and more becoming a critical capability for globally operating companies.

## CONCLUSION

Given that the importance of managing reputational risk is no longer much in doubt, companies need to develop appropriate processes and capabilities. Figure 8.8 summarizes the key components of an effective reputational risk management system.

First, companies need to develop appropriate internal decision systems. Delegation to reputation management "experts"—whether corporate communications, legal, or even a "Chief Reputation Officer"—is usually not the solution. Frequently, reputational challenges emerge from specific business practices, products, or markets. For example, a marketing campaign may target children or the elderly. Once these issues reach the legal or public relations department it is often too late. A much preferable approach is to integrate reputational concerns into core business responsibilities such as marketing or risk management.

Organizationally, this may mean forming cross-functional decision units with the main business function represented. Leading companies have started to set up such decision units under names such as "corporate relations council" or "consumer acceptance committee." In all cases, functional specialists

**Figure 8.8**
**Reputation Management System**

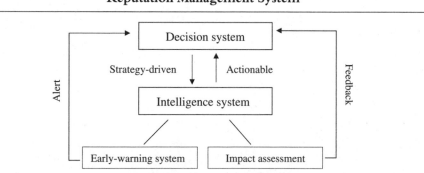

are closely connected to the business leads. Ideally, such senior decision councils are supported by tactical units that engage in the day-to-day operations.

However, even if companies develop appropriate decision systems—and many do not—there is much less appreciation of the need to create intelligence systems that allow a systematic anticipation and management of reputational risk. In the absence of core functionalities (early warning, measurement, situational assessment), decision units essentially decide in the dark, unsupported by data and largely based on the intuition of some key decision makers. Unfortunately, the many reputational crises suffered by corporations today make the need for such a system only too apparent.

## NOTES

1. C. Fishman, *The Wal-Mart Effect: How the World's Most Powerful Company Really Works–and How It's Transforming the American Economy* (New York: Penguin Press, 2006).

2. "Seeking Expansion in Urban Areas, Wal-Mart Stores Get Cold Shoulder," *Wall Street Journal,* September 25, 2006.

3. See note 2.

4. "Take a Rat to Dinner," *New York Times,* March 16, 2007, www.nytimes.com/2007/03/16/opinion/16shaw.html?ex=1331697600&en=fafe448c82627ccd&ei=5090&partner=rssuserland&emc=rss, Youtube.com Video: www.youtube.com/watch?v=su0U37w2tws (accessed September 11, 2007).

5. "Imus Suspended Over Race Slurs" *Wall Street Journal,* April 10, 2007, online.wsj.com/article/SB117612028739263955.html (accessed September 11, 2007).

6. "Warburg Pincus to Buy Bausch & Lomb," *Reuters,* May 16, 2007, www.reuters.com/article/businessNews/idUSWNAS167220070516 (accessed September 11, 2007).

7. "Putnam to Pay $110M in Penalties," *USA Today,* April, 28, 2004, www.usatoday.com/money/perfi/funds/2004-04-08-putnam_x.htm (accessed September 11, 2007).

8. "Mattel Recalls Third Batch of Chinese-Made Toys with Lead Paint," *Fox News.com,* September 4, 2007, www.foxnews.com/story/0,2933,295739,00.html (accessed September 11, 2007).

9. Daniel Charles, *Lords of the Harvest* (New York: Perseus Books Group, 2002).

10. P. Slovic, "Information Processing, Situation Specificity, and the Generality of Risk-Taking Behavior, *Journal of Personality and Social Psychology* 22 (1972): 128–134. See also D. Kahneman, P. Slovic, and A. Tversky, eds. *Judgment under Uncertainty: Heuristics and Biases* (Cambridge: Cambridge University Press, 1982).

11. David P. Baron, *Business and Its Environment,* 5th ed. (New York: Prentice Hall, 2006).

12. See D. Diermeier, *Shell and Greenpeace,* Harvard Business School Case P19, September 1, 1996.

# CHAPTER 9

# THE CONTRIBUTION OF PUBLIC RELATIONS IN THE FUTURE

## CLARKE CAYWOOD

**W**hile public relations (PR) has been a highly successful business tool for over a century, it has not played a leading role in marketing strategy despite its rich potential and its relatively low cost. When the American consumer goods leader Procter and Gamble (P&G) changed their strategy in the first decade of the new century to include heavy duty PR, both traditional marketers and business recognized that something "new and improved" had taken place. In a recent internal study, P&G concluded that the return is often better from a PR campaign than from traditional forms of advertising. In this chapter, I make the case that the relative importance of PR will continue to grow in the coming years. Some predict that PR spending will grow by almost 9 percent a year.

According to *The Handbook of Strategic Public Relations and Integrated Communications* (Caywood 1997), "Public Relations is the profitable integration of an organization's new and continuing relationships with stakeholders including customers by managing all communications contracts that create and protect the brand and reputation of the organization." Beyond this definition of the field, PR offers at least three important advantages over other marketing communications strategies. These relate to:

1. Credibility and reputation.
2. A broader and more dynamic view of the market as composed of stakeholders (and not just consumers).
3. Measurement and therefore accountability.

I explore these three key contributions of PR in turn. First I discuss the concept of credibility as it relates to the organization's reputation and brands

196

and the company's ability to protect itself during a crisis. Then I define and illustrate the unique and powerful concept of stakeholders that is part of the wider market and societal view that informs PR. Finally, I consider the measurable best practices of the field to which it should be held accountable. It is these three contributions that will distinguish public relations in the future from other marketing communications functions.

## CREDIBILITY

Many unfamiliar with public relations view it as only "free advertising." Public relations is thought of as unpaid media coverage of a product. It is advertising that has been slipped into the media and is justified mainly by its low cost. The term "free advertising" suggests that the company has somehow secured commercial space or time on the sly. Today, however, practitioners in the field of PR prefer to call it "earned press" or "product news," or even "brand journalism." The difference lies in recognizing that PR produces stories, or media content, that inherently have more credibility than an ad. This difference compared to the other strategies of marketing communications is significant.

People come to the media largely for content. Therefore product information in the form of content necessarily is more believable and trustworthy than advertising information. Advertising necessarily is a different kind of information. Public relations presents information in the form that is more valuable in that it is the kind of information people are coming to the medium for. A PR strategy should be based on the notion that information in PR form is more credible than a paid advertisement ordinarily can be.

This credibility is not just a matter of perception. It has substance. The substantive credibility of the PR message lies in the fact that it has been evaluated, edited, and filtered by standards of what is newsworthy. The appearance of the product in the media signals to the reader, listener, or viewer that a trusted third party, the newspaper, magazine, TV program, or other media, (and not just the promoter of the product) has judged mention of the product to be worthwhile. Because the information provided could be positive or negative, there is an underlying regard for truthfulness that is apparent.

Some marketers and academics have grasped the value of PR as a form of marketing information. Philip Kotler, marketing guru and leading textbook author from Northwestern University, notes "Some experts say that consumers are five times more likely to be influenced by editorial copy than by advertising. PR tends to catch people off guard who might otherwise avoid sponsored messages" (Kotler and Scheff 1983, p. 377). And the advertising pioneer and author, David Ogilvy (1983) states that six times as many people may read the average PR article as the average advertisement. An ad may only be read by one person in 20. And, although the press may be unwilling to document how much of their writing comes from or is influenced by PR, the total amount is probably high. I do not believe that this reflects any great laxity on the part of news organizations. I think it reflects the fact that they recognize that consumers do value this kind of information. One can think of PR from a media point of view as just another way of generating content. In a world of user-generated content, PR content does not seem at all exceptional.

I would argue, in fact, that PR practitioners are giving greater and greater vitality to marketing and to the diffusion of information about products. Consumers engage more with media content than ad content. Public relations is a way of infusing this engagement into the marketing communications process. The increase in the number of messages, number of senders, number of receivers of marketing communications combines with the decrease in the amount of time and the value and credibility of messages to make this engagement increasingly important. Public relations, deliberately and strategically, heavily relies on the idea of "third-party credibility." The premise, again, is that others outside the marketing organization inherently have more credibility for stakeholders. The term *newsworthy* captures the nature of this credibility. It is not that the information is considered infallible. It is that the information seems worthy of attention for the same reason that all of the information in a given media vehicle seems worthy of attention to the reader or viewer. Newsworthy suggests that a story or even a quote is highly relevant, that the information has some value within the realm of influence of the media vehicle. The information must have some value to the larger story being told by the media.

Obviously, value lies in the credibility of the media source as an independent and thoughtful filter of information. The reporting of the story and the mention of the company by a "third party" gives the story more value than a message that has been purchased. Other parties, including experts, often lend additional credibility. Experts' comments, credentials, and willingness to participate can provide an "endorsement" without the assumption of economic conflict. The same holds for other organizations that can be associated with a product. Museums, hospitals, schools, not-for-profit groups, foundations and even other companies can be seen as giving a story about a product more credibility. A science museum may have an exhibit that demonstrates a particular manufacturing process. Even with some financial support from a company, the visitors may be willing to give credit to the company for their work because the credibility of the museum and its scientists is seen as an untainted endorsement. The demonstration of a new product on a morning news and entertainment program is not merely about the product but the product in the context of everything else that the program is associated with. Similarly, during a crisis, stories including comments by experts that the company is taking the right action can give the answers by the firm more standing.

Still another way to look at credibility is in terms of reputation. Public relations has been given the responsibility of building the company reputation or the corporate brand for many decades. Each story, event, relationship, donation, or action that strengthens the perception of stakeholders about the positive qualities of the company builds this reputation. Corporate contributions to the community such as adopting an area school and supporting it with money and volunteers help build what accountants call "goodwill," which has value when a company is sold. Such actions, while often selfless, are also logically designed to improve the company reputation and give it more overall credibility. Each addition to the company's "trust bank," which is what the well-known PR executive Al Golin (2004) calls reputation for his client McDonald's, helps build a positive feeling and perception for the company that gives it more trust. These "deposits" of goodwill or trust can be very helpful when the company is under attack for recalls or mistakes. Johnson & Johnson, for example, survived a strong attack on its Tylenol product by virtue of the trust it had established with its customers.

In PR, the word *reputation* is often used to describe the earned position in the hearts and minds of various stakeholders. Once a company becomes credible, it is not just that its credibility is improved by information about it in the media, it is also that companies with strong reputations can speak credibly through the media.

## PUBLIC RELATIONS AS A BROADER VIEW OF THE MARKET

Not surprisingly, senior management in most companies focuses on broad financial issues. At the corporate and policy level of a firm, the focus is often on delivering shareholder value as interpreted by management. Public relations shares this broader focus. It does not, as other marketing communication functions do, focus only on the consumer. It also focuses on communicating with the shareholder. In fact, PR focuses on anyone that affects or is affected by the company. Public relations collectively refers to these different types of constituencies as stakeholders.

Going beyond a single-minded customer focus on consumers is perhaps the most important distinguishing difference between PR and other marketing communication functions. While PR is most often considered a marketing communications function, and it is, the field is also similar to general management given its broader orientation to a wide range of stakeholders, from employees to shareholders, to suppliers, to governments, to local communities, to nongovernmental organizations (NGOs), to the media, and finally to the customer. This broader definition means that PR is able to see the company as a whole and to see how different problems and opportunities are connected.

To understand the importance of the stakeholder approach to PR and to get a greater sense of this approach, a tool called the *stakeholder map* can be helpful. The stakeholder map permits us to agree on the identity of specific key stakeholders, their influence at various times, their potential influence, and who in the company is charged with tracking the actions and reactions of the stakeholders.

Many corporate leaders, and even political leaders, may not be able to articulate the wide range of stakeholders that have a stake in the success or failure of an organization at some specific point in its history. Experience driven by work with larger corporations with high visibility (such as AT&T and IBM) suggests that the ability to assign a professional manager to each stakeholder or a cluster of stakeholders gives the company an advantage in tracking factors and trends relevant to the stakeholders. And this is particularly useful in thinking about the future of the firm. For instance, my recent work with Chinese business leaders has demonstrated the value of the stakeholder map in helping them consider the rapidly growing number of stakeholders outside of traditional government and how these stakeholders are affecting their companies more and more.

Looking at a very simple example of a stakeholder map in Figure 9.1 may be useful before discussing a more complex one. A stakeholder map will

**Figure 9.1**
**Stakeholder Map**

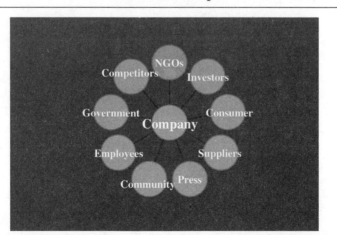

usually include a minimum of nine stakeholders related to the company: employees, consumers, suppliers, government, press, community, NGOs, competitors, and investors.

With some imagination and a high degree of knowledge of a specific company and its environment, a more comprehensive and detailed map usually is more useful. The map in Figure 9.2 uses generic labels for stakeholders, but it is based on work with hundreds of executives from all over the world brought together for a "stakeholder exercise." You can see that the stakeholder list can become quite specific. A more comprehensive map still might include alumni or former employees; types of suppliers and other vendors; types of shareholders such as individual or institutional activists; and types of NGOs including specific ones such as People for the Ethical Treatment of Animals (PETA), the Oxford Committee for Famine Relief (OXFAM), and international NGOs (INGO).

Other stakeholders could include journalists in popular newspaper, magazine, and broadcasting media; trade print and broadcast journalists; bloggers using a range of newer media including Second Life, You Tube, podcasts, and others; direct and indirect competitors as well as future competitors; federal regulators including the Federal Trade Commission (FTC), Food and Drug Administration (FDA), Centers for Disease Control (CDC); the International Organization of Standardization (IOS); universities that supply employees,

**Figure 9.2**
**Stakeholder Map**

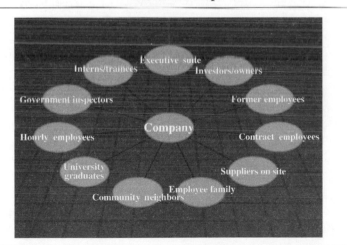

consulting and research help to companies; and research labs that are privately or government funded that provide continuing support for the company. It could even include advertising, PR, or other marcom agencies that advise the company or advisors such as the outside law firm or managerial consulting firm on an on-going basis.

To illustrate this idea of mapping stakeholders to obtain a broader perspective on problems and opportunities, consider how a map can be exploded to cover not only dozens of specific stakeholders but to include several dynamics, providing an even richer perspective. For example, a wide range of metrics can be added to the simple model to show the following variables: estimated degree of impact on the firm (size of circle), changes over time (dates), alliances between stakeholders (lines connecting stakeholders to each other), conflicts between stakeholders (jagged lines between stakeholders), boundaries of organization that are more porous or closed (thickness of circle line), frequency of contact (proximity to core circle), number of contacts (thickness of lines to circles), public and media perceptions of negative or positive relationships among stakeholders (+ or − symbols), and more. Data on sales volumes, numbers of employees, and other information can be included for more detail. As additional dimensions are added over time, the map becomes a model for thinking broadly and deeply about the organization.

The stakeholder map in Figure 9.2 and the list of specific stakeholder examples is intended to indicate the breadth of perspective that PR has come to assume. This broader perspective brings insights into problems and opportunities that would not occur with a typical marketing communication perspective. Focusing narrowly on the consumer means that we might miss things like, for example, the connection of a shareholder activist group to information showing up in online blogs that is the real cause of an emerging consumer product concern that is being picked up in newspaper stories. In the complex, flat world of the future, we need to be able to make connections like this. Public relations offers the perspective to do so.

The broader perspective that focuses on big picture connections is also well suited to scanning the future and assessing risk. A stakeholder map helps PR decision makers know that some firms, organizations, and even personalities are more likely to need more intensive levels of communication due to the inherently high risk they face. For example, McDonald's has worked with the PR firm GolinHarris since the founding of the restaurant chain in 1956. By definition, the nature of their product, which is ingested, potentially creates a health risk. That the company heavily serves children creates a high visibility risk, too. Both of these risks need to be monitored and possibly addressed with special communications. The distribution of toys to children represents yet another kind of risk. Similar packaging (foam clam shells at one point) can create an environmental risk and food selection creates a public health policy risk. McDonald's recognizes the value of PR as an important part of their risk management effort. The contribution of PR in risk management is applicable to a wide variety of other types of company risk. Risk levels will increase for all firms in the future and PR will play an increasingly important role in dealing with this. The person most likely to have a heightened awareness of risk and an understanding of it is the PR professional. This is not to say that others are not be able to address such issues, but the language, processes, and history of PR give it an advantage in this area.

## ACCOUNTABILITY AND MEASURED PERFORMANCE

Public relations sees its role differently from other marketing communication functions. It is more concerned with the company's business than with the business of communication. Let us examine how the industry sees its role.

"Chasing the prize" is not as important to PR as it often is to other marketing communication functions. For instance, I was once asked to judge classified advertisements published in newspapers for their marketing value. Another contest asked for judgments of the creative impact of a series of sales presentation product pages. There seems to be no end to the sorts of prizes that are of so much concern to marketing communication professionals. The big advertising awards are only the tip of the prize iceberg. All these prizes reflect that marketing communications is most often more concerned about doing outstanding communications work than about selling product. When I have been asked to judge communications for prizes, often there is often no information on the research, planning, execution (except for the ad itself), or the outcome of the ads. The prize is all about the ad or the communication piece itself. More rigorous standards than this are needed for judging best practices. Moreover, the real prize should be business success.

Instead of these too common nonstandards of performance in marketing communications, the discipline of PR has attempted to set standards and chronicle best practices. While all efforts can be improved, my involvement with the Public Relations Society of America (PRSA) over two decades indicates that this effort has been successful and bodes well for the future of the field.

The annual Silver Anvil awards (named to reflect the forging of public opinion) is especially indicative. Yes, it is a prize, but a prize with a difference. A team of professionals on the awards committee of the PRSA has defined the standards to reflect a far more strategic approach to the practice of PR and a concern for business outcomes. The annual awards process, which examines as many as 800 entries packaged in two- to three-inch-thick ring binders, applies rigorous standards by trained judges. An abstract from a winning example is shown next. Notice the focus on business results:

- *Summary:* Think of California and many images come to mind, movies, wine, and technology, to name a few. The Real California Cheese campaign, developed by the California Milk Advisory Board (CMAB), has made consumers care about where their cheese comes from, not a small accomplishment in a category largely built around commodity products. In just a few years, California has developed a reputation as being one of the national premier cheese-producing regions, boasting a growing cheese industry that is becoming the equal of its wine industry.

The lessons from the Silver Anvils are several. One, the criteria for judging demand that the entrants cover the *research* that led to the *plans* that gave support and budget to the *execution* of the *outcomes* that are finally reported. While these four categories are certainly strategic by any perspective, it is even more important to note that each of the four steps is counted equally (10 points each). This equal emphasis on such advanced strategic elements—research, planning and execution, and outcomes—is remarkable in a field in which the only thing that matters is often the ad (or direct mail, press release, web site, etc.).

My point is further underlined by the fact that the team of judges uses the questions that follow to evaluate the PR work. Each of the four categories includes 19 related questions. Each question becomes an item for a checklist and this list shows how PR thinks about its work:

### Research

- How thorough and relevant was the research to overall planning and audience ID?
- Did the research reflect a clear need or opportunity?
- Was the original or secondary research undertaken to achieve the desired results?
- How clearly was a baseline . . . defined . . . to gauge the program's success?

### Planning

- Did the plan clearly define objectives?
- How well did the objectives support the organization's overall goals?
- Did the strategy reflect research findings and supported objectives?
- How original was the strategy (big idea)?
- How thorough was the plan?

### Execution

- How appropriate were the tactics?
- How creative were the tactics?
- How well were the tactics implemented?
- How integrated were the various tools with one another?
- How efficient was the execution of tactics?

### Evaluation

- How successful was the organization in achieving its objectives?
- How thorough and relevant were analysis and quantification of results?
- Did the results clearly reflect the original strategy and planning?
- How well did the team work together?
- Were there continuous opportunities for learning and program refinement?

Of special interest to marketers may be the rapid growth of measurement of PR. There is now strong interest in such measurable variables as sales, stock price, employee retention, and other behavioral and nonbehavioral metrics. Sophistication in measurement is growing in PR and the field is increasingly using artificial intelligence and databases. The field has moved well beyond the traditional "clippings" that dominated PR metrics for decades. Clippings are simple counts of the number of articles in the media that are clipped. Sometimes they may include the measurement of column inches as a throwback to the belief that the number of column inches in the newspaper was evidence of results. Where the clipping appeared, on the front page or buried in a back section, or whether the article was critical or positive, did not matter traditionally. Now it matters and much, much more is considered in evaluating the outcomes of a PR effort and its success.

## CONCLUSION

Public relations is founded on an understanding of the value of third-party credibility. In a period in which the openness of a firm's actions and reporting transparency can save, build, or destroy a company, PR should have a more significant role than ever before. Consumers want more than information about a product, they want to know the story behind the product, and the larger story of the company itself. Brand journalism, of the sort recently begun by Ford and others, which literally takes people (online) behind the scenes of a company, is not a gimmick. It is the kind of thing that will allow PR to contribute even more to corporate reputation and brand credibility in the future.

The field also should be valued more in the future for the breadth of its focus on a range of stakeholders. As senior vice president of Grainger Corporation, Nancy Hobor, recently said: "CEOs are looking for leaders who can understand and integrate all corporate stakeholders, not just customers and not just business functions" (personal interview, September 16, 2007). A few years ago, I attempted to capture the breadth and depth of the field with a handbook of 37 chapters authored by practitioners and academics in the field (Caywood 1997). The book, like this discussion, was built on the assumption that the most significant contribution of PR to modern management is the extraordinary peripheral vision of the professionals in the field. Like other experts, journalists, scholars, and leaders, the strong PR professional is able to identify, track, communicate with, and evaluate dozens if not hundreds of specific stakeholders who may have a strong and continuing impact on the success or failure of the organization's decisions and actions.

Public relations may have a lingering reputation for being a "soft field" with writing as its major contribution to business. Certainly writing and editing will always be needed. but the PR field is now becoming more quantitative, looking for new ways to measure and track the vast volume of words, ideas, events, and activities that surround companies. As business environments get more and more complex, this new sophistication will allow PR to contribute more.

Public relations is uniquely poised to assume a larger role in the future. Its contributions to credibility, stakeholder vision, and measurement will be needed.

# REFERENCES

Caywood, Clarke. 1997. *The handbook of strategic public relations and integrated communications*. New York: McGraw-Hill.

Golin, Al. 2004. *Trust or consequences: Build trust today or lose your market tomorrow.* New York: AMACOM.

Kotler, Phillip, and Joanne Scheff. 1997. *Standing room only: Strategies for marketing the performing arts.* Cambridge, MA: Harvard Business School Press.

Ogilvy, David. 1983. *Ogilvy on advertising.* New York: Crown.

## CHAPTER 10

# USING *THREE I* MEDIA IN BUSINESS-TO-BUSINESS MARKETING

JAMES NEWCOMB

The conventional business-to-business (B-to-B) marketing organization, particularly within large industrial companies (such as heavy manufacturers) and the consultancies that serve them, has typically focused on supporting the personalized selling efforts of business development and sales teams. Business development and sales teams work with marketers to analyze highly detailed industry and customer-specific data gathered through surveys, trade shows, office visits, and other means. They use this analysis to shape materials including brochures, presentations, trade ads, and product cards. These materials are basic or introductory in nature and serve the purpose of attracting customers. Once the customer is connected to sales or business development, marketing moves into a useful, but subordinate, support role of backing up the selling efforts of the sales and business development teams.

This conventional set-up has always made a great deal of sense. And so has the execution because marketing materials, including traditional promotions as well as newer exhibit displays and video shows, are intended to generate interest in the broadest customer sets, which is how they have been used. Moreover, the high cost of developing materials has forced creators to develop materials

Special thanks to professionals at Boeing and Caterpillar who shared their time and insight for this chapter. They are: Susan Bradley and Diana Klug in Boeing Commercial Aircraft Division; John Williamson and Daniel Beck of Boeing's Integrated Defense Systems; Mary Kane of Boeing Image Licensing; and John Dern and Fritz Johnston of Boeing Corporate Communications; Martin Gierke of Caterpillar's brand management group; and David Cooper of Caterpillar's Visual Research Center.

that are typically more general and less personalized in nature than the rest of the B-to-B selling process. So, while innovative and eye-popping examples of innovative multimedia abound in B-to-B, these videos and efforts have tended simply to showcase a company or product's capabilities. Such highly polished productions are thought to become less helpful and less cost efficient as the personal selling process progresses. The most important part of B-to-B selling comes in the relationship-building activity that begins later in the process. And that activity has historically been the province of sales, not marketing.

As media, however, becomes "smarter" and more customizable, and the costs of rich high-quality production and presentation go down, marketers are finding new opportunities to create dynamic selling environments that allow them to engage more deeply and relevantly in the selling process than ever before. In fact, B-to-B marketing leaders are now developing innovative multimedia-based strategies that play an integral and powerful role in the success of the personal selling approach that is the core of the B-to-B model. What I call *THREE I* media—smart multimedia that is immersive, immediately configurable, and identity-linked—is moving marketing deeper into the personal selling process.

The following sections examine the role of personal selling in more detail; explore how the introduction of smarter, more information-rich multimedia environments can influence the marketing and personal selling mix; and describe how the conventional model is evolving at some of the world's leading B-to-B companies. For the purposes of this work, I will focus on the efforts of large-scale B-to-B corporations, but I believe the discussion also is applicable to smaller-scale operations that wish to employ multimedia in their sales and marketing efforts.

## PERSONAL SELLING CYCLE IN B-TO-B ORGANIZATIONS

We begin with a more detailed look at the personal selling cycle. Unlike the more mass-media model characteristic of business-to-consumer (B-to-C) organizations, B-to-B emphasizes relationships, two-way communication, and customization. The closest analogy to B-to-B in the B-to-C environment may be the market for custom housing because the configuration and customization of the product through the selling process is the defining element of the transaction. Further, given parity products, the more knowledgeable, skilled, and easy to work with a salesperson is, the better the results for the home seller or real estate company. The relationship between the seller and the buyer becomes still more important and more individualized as the price of the house increases. The closer a house is to the high-end of the scale, the more salespeople must be masters of their trade, and their ability to maintain two-way, ongoing, responsive, and tailored communication becomes more essential. This is very much like the environment in B-to-B marketing.

Considering this analogy, we can see why the selling process in a B-to-B firm is very logically structured. It begins with identifying existing and emerging customers. In larger industrial B-to-Bs, this is a fairly straightforward process that eliminates all but a relatively few companies based on qualification criteria and the relevance of the seller's offerings. Obviously, a company engaged in mining or road-building needs massive, powerful tractors but not commercial jets to conduct its business. Because of the infrastructure, financial resources and extraordinary engineering know-how required to enter major industrial businesses, the number of competitive offerings is relatively small (compared to, say, cellular phones). Firms getting into a business will most often contact manufacturers, retailers, or industry consultants early in the process, and those that have already entered the business are on the seller company's radar screen. Compared to B-to-C, the need for demand stimulation and prospecting is much more limited.

In B-to-B, customer awareness of a company's products or services, while not unimportant, plays a smaller part in the total B-to-B selling process than in B-to-C companies. Customer awareness is necessary in any purchase decision, but the distance between awareness and final decision for a custom purchase is considerably greater than it is for off-the-shelf purchases. As such, stimulation of awareness receives considerably less attention and considerably fewer financial resources in the conventional B-to-B organization than in the conventional B-to-C organization. So while a B-to-B company may spend $500,000 developing a video or multimedia production for trade show and direct-to-customer distribution, it will usually spend much more than that developing market data, traveling to visit customers, and preparing individualized materials to help a salesperson actively manage a sale *after* a customer has indicated interest.

Returning to the analogy of a custom home, it is easy to see how a salesperson's role is of pivotal importance where customization is essential and the ability to offer different configurations will dramatically affect product performance. In this environment, effective salespeople are experts in industry trends and extremely knowledgeable about materials and product specifications. They understand the importance of individual product decisions on the overall purchase process. They must help buyers explore options. This is just like a salesperson suggesting ways to configure the design of a home to fit the buyer's goals, helping the buyer to make trade-offs and to avoid unnecessary expenses. A salesperson will recommend that a buyer consider whether a more expensive grade of appliances is the best choice for a family who cooks only rarely, or will suggest that a fitness enthusiast consider building a fitness or spa room within a given footprint. By explaining the trade-offs in a complicated transaction and providing information ("People want high-end kitchens less this year than in years past, but fitness rooms are emerging as a hot item."), salespeople become partners, helping guide buyers toward their ultimate goals and increasing the relative value of their investments. Ideally, they are not simply convincing buyers to make a purchase or registering a sale. Indeed, *consultative selling* has become part of the day-to-day language of traditional B-to-B marketing.

As in our home-buying example, the better customer information can be matched to product information, the better will be the fit to the customer and the more likely the sale will be completed. In fact, most major industrial projects are launched with signed commitments in hand because companies often rely on their customers to help design a product or service to meet their specific needs. While this may be obvious for bottom-line-shaping purchases like airplanes, factories, or specialized industrial machinery, it is also true in service and consulting businesses that may assign top consultants to work with a major customer before developing a new "practice" within the firm.

The development of a B-to-B offering can take can take months or even years to reach its conclusion. The process is extremely dynamic in response to changes in the industry, the competitive set or the underlying product and financial data. Each major element in an offering is typically arrived at through ongoing, detailed back-and-forth negotiations between the salesperson and customer. This makes each proposal as different as the underlying configurations and changing market conditions demand. It is not unusual for the specific economic promises of a salesperson to be reflected throughout a final contract and for enforceable sanctions and financial penalties for failure to perform to be an essential part of the offering.

The development, maintenance and constant updating of decision-making data is an essential B-to-B core competency. Because this data is used in the creation of business proposals and for guiding the complex purchase decision process, it benefits both sides of the transaction. Logically, this is where much of the money is spent, with departments focused on ensuring that the best data is available to the company and its customers. Not surprisingly, the processes that drive the acquisition of a major piece of machinery, a fleet of vehicles, or a major consulting assignment are complex, rigorous, and designed to drive out emotion, check assumptions, and force the reanalysis of baseline scenarios. Further, because the industrial arena often involves big-ticket, bottom-line-shaping decisions, the offerings are analyzed and scrutinized by multiple layers of management and multiple functions to ensure that the quality of the data and the analysis is as good as it can be.

Once a sale is made, the selling process turns to maintaining the sale and extending the relationship with the customer. It continues with reevaluating the customer's needs until another purchase is in the offing. In many B-to-Bs, this activity is unending and is marked by regular customer briefings about the state of the industry. Sales and business development teams continue to reshape and share broader data and combine customer and product-specific data in personalized presentations and analyses. They are engaged partners who pay close attention to changes in market dynamics and the impact of new products on a particular business. The teams are active, trustworthy sources of expert analysis even when a new sales opportunity might not occur for years. The quality of information and its interpretation are the basic currency of the relationship. The development of the relationship, or more simply the establishing of mutual trust and a sense that salespeople and the company they represent actually want to help the customer, is everything. Thus, it is critical to recognize that the greatest part of the time and energy in B-to-B marketing is, and will continue to be, spent within the frame of the salesperson-to-customer relationship. Top B-to-B salespeople manage every element of customer relationships, ensuring that every contact strengthens the relationship and assures customers that they can trust the quality of the offering.

For B-to-B, personal selling is the medium for creating the customer relationship. Salespeople are the face of their company; they serve as the voice of the company to the customer. Therefore, for marketing to play a larger role in B-to-B, it is necessary for it to contribute to improve this medium by making personal selling more engaging.

## EXPANDING THE ROLE OF MARKETING IN B-TO-B WITH MULTIMEDIA

Given this structure, it is not surprising that sales directors sometime question the need for a greater role for marketing in B-to-B. In fact, the pressure to keep costs down in the hypercompetitive B-to-B environment can become stifling. An individual advertisement or trade show item, particularly those with high initial cost and a hard-to-track return on investment (ROI), is an easy place to cut costs. And all this is especially true for high-quality multimedia. Historically the cost of producing high-quality multimedia has been quite expensive, requiring producers, video production teams and photographers, writing and editing teams, and expensive equipment. Add the cost of voiceover talent or actors and buying music rights, the total cost can grow very high relative to other marketing items.

Because companies seek to reduce and repurpose assets to save money, and see marketing materials as limited to the introductory stage of building customer relationships, the resulting customer experience is often less emotionally powerful and relevant. Repeat showings to the same audience of a general video presentation has limited impact. A trade-show media presentation that is overused can undermine the interest-generating effect that it was intended to have in the first place. These problems can be overcome but until very recently making changes was as expensive as the initial production and, worse, usually took too long. For all these reasons, marketing materials have been more general and less customized than the more up-to-date, rigorously maintained information that is at the heart of the personal selling process.

Because of this history, business development and sales managers often score the development of smart or rich multimedia low in terms of marketing efficiency in any stage beyond the introductory stage of the personal selling process. They feel that videos and multimedia introduced later in the personalized selling effort can even negatively affect a sales effort by introducing a new element or new voice into the process. This risks creating greater distance between salespeople and their customers, which can occur simply by introducing something that is not perfectly tuned to the conversations that have already occurred between the salesperson and the customer. This opinion has limited the use of multimedia almost exclusively to the front end of the selling process where broad, overarching messages about quality and performance seem to make more sense. There they do not require the rigorous attention to personalized detail that eventually characterizes the selling process.

There is a growing realization, however, that rich multimedia can be used in a way that is consistent with the personal selling process. The dramatic evolution of a variety of technologies has created opportunities for marketers to use multimedia in this way. This in turns opens the door to expanding the role of marketing in B-to-B.

## NEW ENABLING ROLE OF SMART AND RICH MULTIMEDIA—*THREE I*

The evolution of multimedia allows marketers to play a more powerful role throughout the sales process by allowing them to create highly customized, realistic, and data-rich experiences—even whole environments. New immersive, immediately configurable, and identity-linked media can maintain the tenor of a particular sales effort by staying in sync as data changes and customer preferences emerge. These *THREE Is*—immersive, immediately configurable, and identity-linked—are key to creating media experiences with deeper relevance to the B-to-B selling relationship. We now examine how particular new technologies have made each "I" available to marketers and how they are changing marketing's role in B-to-B.

The first kind of technology—flat screens, touch-screen interfaces, and 3-D projections—have been available for some time, but only recently have matured to the point of being a platform for meaningful, real-time interaction. Life-sized images and rich, crisp visuals make multimedia seem more real. This is important if marketing is to facilitate the conversation with customers. Such marketing requires producing compelling and realistic experiences that increase levels of customer engagement. Just as a 50-inch plasma screen makes movie viewing at home more immersive and enjoyable, so does an array of screens or 3-D projection equipment that allows customers to become immersed in the experience of purchasing and analyzing a piece of equipment or a vehicle. This is the first key to *THREE I* B-to-B marketing— it must produce an *immersive experience*.

The second kind of technology—computer-generated imagery (CGI)— has been driven by dramatic increases in computing speed and power that bring critical improvements in computer image rendering software. One need only look at Pixar Animation Studios or any of the popular computer games that produce and quickly modify surprisingly realistic 3-D images to see how good digital rendering has become. For B-to-Bs, this increase in quality has been "table stakes:" It is the ability to personalize the scenario on the fly with real data that makes this software most useful. By creating realistic, customer-specific business scenarios that are displayed as a part of high-quality productions, the technology becomes relevant at every step in the selling process.

To appreciate the relevance of CGI, return to our custom-home selling example. Imagine how powerful the interaction between a salesperson and a buyer could be when a rendering of the house under discussion can change as a customer examines options. Imagine in this interaction that the customer can try out different options by touching a screen and then use his or her finger to drag and drop rooms and materials as the house is discussed with the salesperson. The salesperson's role is not diminished in anyway. The salesperson is able to make suggestions based on his or her knowledge of housing and the customer and to show the impact of the changes. This is, conceptually, how CGI is coming to be used in B-to-B, particularly in industries that sell vehicles or equipment before it is actually produced. Realistic images can be instantly modified to help customers visualize the product as part of their business operations. This is both a powerful selling tool for companies and a powerful purchasing tool for customers. This is our second key to *THREE I* B-to-B marketing—images must be *immediately configurable*.

The third kind of technology—which includes radio frequency identification (RFID) and other tracking technologies—allows computers to recognize which customer is standing in front of a screen, passing through a door or moving to a new area within a room. Computers can automatically personalize data for multiple customers in a short span of time whether they are in a virtual showroom, a tradeshow, or even a common meeting room. The same is true of web sites that customers may enter via passwords or through "cookies" left on their computer. These technologies have made seamless identification, configuration, and connections across platforms, such as web site pages or trade show floors, possible. By managing layers of individually specific customer data, multimedia becomes a consistent and individualized experience that exists as a part of the customer-company relationship. This is the third key to *THREE I* B-to-B marketing—it must be *identity-linked*.

Dramatic drops in the price of computing power and equally dramatic improvements in the sophisticated technology behind products and software programs have allowed the technologies discussed to migrate from the worlds of manufacturing and training where they were originally developed. The same basic CGI 3-D technologies that were used to allow rapid prototyping of machine parts are now inexpensive enough to be used as marketing tools to sell the products that the parts go into. The same is true of RFID chips, which were used to track products and parts within factories and shipping facilities and can now be used to connect customers to customized experiences. Improvements in microchips that speed computer processing have also allowed flat-screen TVs to become commonplace in almost every setting, from living rooms to corporate offices and exhibits. These price-drops have been enough to allow marketers to begin to combine these technologies to create *THREE I* experiences and in doing so, reimagine the role of marketers and multimedia in B-to-B selling.

Marketers are developing smart and rich multimedia experiences that facilitate the personal selling process and enable multimedia to be integrated into the selling process from beginning to end. As illustrated in Figure 10.1, the use of media used to peak in the early stages of the sales process. Now *THREE I* media is becoming ubiquitous at every stage, the backdrop of the sales process. Marketers are able to create uniquely powerful experiences that take purchase decisions into new environments and allow salespeople to use new tools to extend their ability to assist a customer in the visualization and configuration

Figure 10.1
*THREE-I* at Each Stage in the Sales Process versus Conventional
B-to-B Marketing

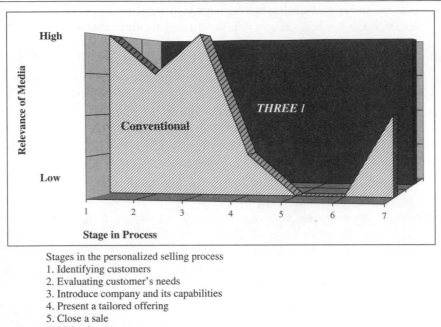

Stages in the personalized selling process
1. Identifying customers
2. Evaluating customer's needs
3. Introduce company and its capabilities
4. Present a tailored offering
5. Close a sale
6. Maintain customer
7. Continue to build relationship and reevaluate customer needs

of their purchase. Using *THREE I* media with sales and business development, marketers can dramatically extend their role and the value of their efforts much more deeply into the personal selling process than ever before, becoming true partners in the effort.

To make sure the connection to the selling process is clear, consider again the example of a buyer who wants to purchase a custom home. Now, instead of looking at a picture or walking through a model home, the buyer and seller enter a space outfitted with a large touch-screen monitor. Together they enter basic data that begins personalizing the content to reflect whatever features the customer has in mind. As the options appear, the customer is able to use the technology with a salesperson not just to learn about what is available in general but to virtually configure and react to options. Because the salesperson guides the customer's configuration and visualization of the product using *THREE I* multimedia, a deeper understanding of a customer's priorities becomes possible and facilitates the essential sharing of information that continues to be at the heart of the process. By engaging customers through interfaces that use dynamic multimedia, marketing creates a seamless process that extends the power of the sales team as consultative sellers.

Note that the development of tailored proposals can be done as an ongoing part of the configuration process, dramatically improving the experience. *THREE I* media can help by shortening the time between the configuration of the product and the submission of the proposal by allowing customers to configure the products virtually. This creates an environment that makes the transition to ownership more natural and similar to purchases that customers routinely make in their lives. In guiding the personal selling process in this way, marketers can in effect guide the decision-making process. By creating materials that are as dynamic as the selling process, marketing can aid sales and business development teams in a more meaningful way at deeper levels of the process. In this new role, marketing effectively mediates the customer's experience with the company, making ever more vivid, dynamic, and personalized media an integral part of the personal selling cycle.

## *THREE I* Case Examples

*THREE I* media are already in use at some of the world's most progressive and innovative B-to-Bs. Marketers are working with sales and business development teams to continue to develop and extend the value of the technology as it gets easier to use and less costly to acquire. A classic example of how a company has evolved naturally toward *THREE I* is Boeing, which I will discuss next. I then briefly note two other examples that show how *THREE-I* is evolving in very different industries.

---

### *THREE I* at Boeing

The Boeing Company has a long history of using dazzling live events to showcase its products. These include the appearance of its products at air shows (trade shows that include flight demonstrations) and crowd-thrilling public events where their aircraft are the stars of the show. Even the company's plant tours draw hundreds of thousands of visitors each year to experience the awesome scale associated with manufacturing the largest commercial airplanes. (Boeing's 470 million cubic foot assembly

*(Continued)*

---

building in Everett, Washington, is the world's largest building by volume.) These spectacles have always engaged an audience of aerospace enthusiasts and customers alike, with crowds ranging from 15,000 at a product launch "rollout" to millions at a public air show. At any of these events, the sales and business development teams attend to customers who are participating in the event, ensuring that their customers enjoy the whole of the experience. These events are truly immersive, with everything in the air and on the ground working to create a sense of excitement and awe.

*THREE I* multimedia at Boeing developed naturally from these air show environments as well as from Boeing's seminal role in the development of immersive simulations for pilot training and from the use of complex, 3-D rendering as part of advanced manufacturing and systems integration. The use of *THREE I* came first in trade show exhibits—mini-customer demonstrations that require constant innovations in order to keep them ahead of the competition. Since including flight-simulators and demonstrations of engineering technology, the company has grown increasingly sophisticated in the use of immersive environments at events. Today, the company has developed permanent exhibit-like structures (facilities) that have become key elements in its marketing and business development efforts. These include Boeing Integration Centers (BICs) for the defense group's customers and the Customer Experience Center (CEC) and Dreamliner Gallery for its commercial airline customers.

Boeing's first major investment in an exhibit-style, immersive experience using *THREE I* on a grand scale came with the opening of the first Boeing Integration Center in Anaheim, California, in 2000, and a second in Crystal City, Virginia, in 2004. The idea was to create a space to demonstrate the promise of network-enabled operations with the ability to manage and analyze live data from multiple sources, of multiple types, and sometimes in incomplete streams as if it were all part of one integrated system. This system-of-systems approach is the foundation of much of the U.S. military's next-generation battle planning and management philosophy—connecting individual soldiers, military assets, and satellites to share a more complete view of the battlefield, thus allowing commanders to respond to possible threats and changing scenarios faster and in a more coordinated way.

Network-enabled operations can be hard to envision for those who have not experienced how they can work, making Boeing's need to create an understandable technology demonstration very clear. This also set the stage for *THREE I*. The company decided to employ an immersive media experience because, ultimately, that is what they believed a successful network-enabled operations center would be. Only by experiencing what such a center could make possible would the diverse array of decision makers (customers) be able to appreciate it. To accomplish its mission, the center had to behave credibly with complex data that changed quickly and in unpredictable ways. BICs had to be more than simple mockups.

The center is built around four modeling labs, each with very large screens and theater-style seating (see Figure 10.2). On a screen is projected a comprehensive view of the battlefield simulation, with moving icons representing the assets of both friendly and enemy forces, ranging in scale from battlefield installations, to weaponry and machinery, down to individual soldiers. The data is received from simulated sources on the ground, vehicles in the air, and satellites in space. As the simulated data pours in, analysts, strategists, and commanders can access data from flat-screen computer terminals that line the front of the center or from hand-held computers. The system models information as it would in actuality come in, and allows leaders to experience seeing the battlefield in this way.

This smart, rich media demonstrates how the technology can be used in a real battlefield situation. Business development and salespeople have put the centers to very good use with more than 20,000 visitors to date. The centers make the dizzyingly complex computer analysis and combinations of data understandable by people who are experts in military strategy but not necessarily expert in networked-enabled operations. Moreover, military leadership and their suppliers can use the center to virtually integrate and deploy new technologies for realistic testing even before they make it into production, and more significantly, into operation.

Boeing's commercial airplanes division has also invested in the development of increasingly powerful and immersive customer experiences that align with the *THREE I* concept. The crown jewel of its marketing efforts is the Customer Experience Center (CEC), a 30,000-square-foot

*(Continued)*

**Figure 10.2**
**Boeing Integration Center (BIC)**

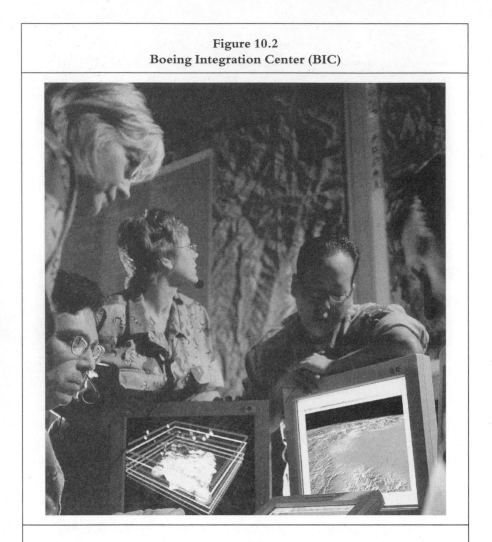

sales center that showcases its family of commercial airplanes and service offerings (see Figure 10.3). The center was specifically designed to facilitate dialogue between customers and the sales and marketing team. Most impressive is the high-tech and high-ceilinged Solutions Studio within the CEC, which is very different from the conference rooms and airplane interior mockups that are adjacent to it. The Solutions Studio is built around a series of assets that portray Boeing's overall programs, products, and services. Unlike traditional video or multimedia content,

**Figure 10.3**
**Boeing Customer Experience Center (CIC)**

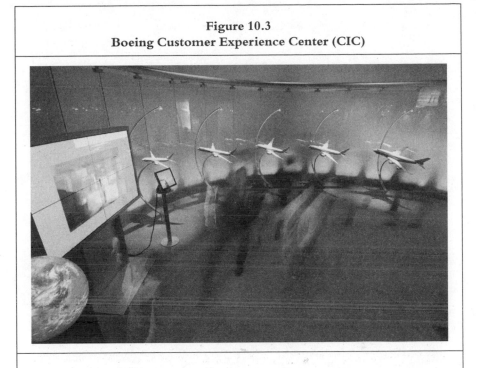

much of the content in the Solutions Studio, including 3-D projections and various kinds of flat screen media, is programmed to show how Boeing's products and services can help build the individual customer's business. This is done by carefully linking the visualizations to important details of the customer's business.

As a marketing or sales representative leads customers through the space, the content configures itself to fit the customer, individualizing the data as the group moves through the studio. Computer programs pull data to generate greeting text. Renderings of airline liveries appear on lifelike 3-D video models along with customized fleet data. The goal is to make sure the details of the experience are specific to the customer's own operations. The farther into the Solutions Studio a visitor goes, the more detailed and immersive the experience becomes. As they pass a line of large 8- to 10-foot-long Boeing liveried airplane models, flat screens behind the individual models display the number of each model type in that customer's fleet. At the end of the row, a map of the world

*(Continued)*

displays all of the customer's daily flights in action. The data can be modified to show where all of their aircraft are currently scheduled to be, where specific Boeing models are, or even where an individual model (or airplane) is.

The Solutions Studio is the most impressively customized element in the center. Boeing uses RFID technology, its detailed knowledge of its customer's business and a giant touch-screen interface to allow customers and Boeing sales representatives to explore the impact of different levels of service support. Customer data is used to create crisp, customized, and visually compelling scenarios that bring abstract ideas and hard-to-visualize data to life. Importantly, the system is not static. The more a customer wants to know, the more detailed the information the system provides. The interaction, however, is guided by the salesperson. At no time does the technology supplant the salesperson's relationship with the customer. It simply mediates the relationship.

In 2006, Boeing opened another facility, the Dreamliner Gallery, which for the first time allows customers to completely configure the interiors of their airplanes, including seating, galleys, in-seat media, and customer-service capabilities, in one location. Largely filled with mock-ups and actual equipment, the center also offers a complement of visualization tools, both physical and computer-based, to help customers configure their 787 Dreamliner airplanes. The center helps further extend *THREE I* into the personal selling process by using it to engage the customer in configuring the airplane interiors to match their needs. It helps customers to more completely evaluate the trade-offs they need to make. There is one particularly insightful example of the use of *THREE I*. Boeing created a kitchen-configuration area where flight attendants can test out a number of virtual designs and share their reactions with customer and Boeing executives.

By looking at what Boeing has created in its business units, we can see that differing examples of *THREE I* can be developed and successfully deployed. The BICs, the CEC and Dreamliner Gallery all use smart and rich multimedia in different ways to create immersive, configurable environments that change their content to fit the needs of each individual customer. In all cases, the sales and business development teams still manage discussions with the customer, but they are able to do so in environments that offer a much more engaging customer experience.

### *THREE I* at Caterpillar

Caterpillar has a long and successful history of building B-to-B relationships. It too has a history of introducing products through high-profile product launch events and trade shows. Caterpillar first started using 3-D imaging and multimedia technology in the production and training simulation areas and has now expanded their use further into the company's selling and relationship building efforts. But Caterpillar has a somewhat more complicated challenge, as its partner dealers manage much of the personal selling effort. Caterpillar meets this challenge by using immersive and immediately configurable technology at a few key steps in the sales process to support a dealer.

The first stage where a customer may encounter Caterpillar's approach to *THREE I* is in the company's Caterpillar Immersive Technology Environment (CITE). This immersive and interactive experience facility allows customers to enter and operate new vehicles. With 3-D goggles, Caterpillar creates a virtual cab environment. Customers have the opportunity to tell Caterpillar and their dealer or sales representative what they think about the cab's configuration, how they believe it should be laid out, and how well they think the sightlines work. This interaction is extremely important to Caterpillar because it gains valuable intelligence about how the customer sees the product and the language they use to describe what they want—all this without Caterpillar having to build a physical prototype.

The Edwards Demonstration and Visitor Center is a stop for some customers on a visit to Caterpillar in Peoria. This center, expanded in 2006, now features a 150,000-square-foot facility with two indoor demonstration arenas and an outdoor demonstration area with grandstand seating for 225 people. Visitors can see product demonstrations of digging, grading, leveling, or a variety of other tasks. Caterpillar even puts on an occasional fireworks display as the highlight of its choreographed, synchronized parade of products that can include mining equipment, backhoes, and highway graders in action. If it sounds a bit like a Las Vegas show, this is no accident. Caterpillar employees even describe it as "a bit like infotainment."

Whether customers and dealers come to the center to hold meetings, see a demonstration, or to be trained on a new piece of machinery,

*(Continued)*

Caterpillar encourages them to use its virtual training simulators. These simulators have large screens, cockpits, and controls that replicate the feel of driving a real vehicle. Developed to allow safer, more cost effective, and more educationally effective training, Caterpillar discovered that operators and purchasing agents alike found them to be fun. In fact, while a CEO or CFO of a company that uses grading equipment would never take on the risk associated with driving a real machine, the virtual simulator gives them the opportunity to experience what it is like to do so. The sales representative or dealer who accompanies the customers as they enjoy the demonstration show and the simulators gets a great opportunity to build their relationship and to learn more about what customers really want and need.

Whether in the CITE or at Edwards, Caterpillar is able to bring customers and salespeople closer together to facilitate better sharing of information and to reinforce the brand values of Caterpillar. These efforts allow Caterpillar to mediate interactions with dealer-partners, Caterpillar salespeople, and customers in a way that builds and improves the overall relationship.

### *THREE I* at Accenture

Accenture, a spin-off from Arthur Andersen, but no longer able to use the name Andersen Consulting, was forced to reinvent itself in 2002. It is not surprising given the circumstances that Accenture launched a new brand-driven campaign to announce themselves and to reassert themselves in the crowded consulting marketplace. What is interesting is that it has leveraged this by creating public multimedia experiences that have put it at center stage for some of its most important target customers.

The Accenture Interactive Network at O'Hare Airport opened in May 2006 with a 10 foot × 15 foot high-definition touch-screen kiosk in Terminal 3. The kiosk offers travelers a variety of information on news and entertainment topics with all of this set against Accenture's familiar Tiger Woods-themed advertising campaign. The facility uses a touch-screen that users must get close to use. Once a person is up close, the experience becomes immersive rather than just visually interesting. Multiple parties can use the touch screen at the same time and the kiosk continues to react quickly. This gives a sense of customization and allows users to escape from the crowded atmosphere that is too much a part of the airport experience. Above all, the kiosk reinforces the company's "High Performance Delivered" brand positioning simply by delivering a high-performance experience.

Accenture clearly is promoting the *THREE I* potential of this product to business customers, showing them how it can create immersive experiences. What is intriguing about this is that it suggests what more companies could do. Imagine the power of video walls that can recognize and communicate with potential customers as they make their way to their next destination, whether it is in Asia or just a short flight away. Imagine a wall in an airport where a customer can see himself or herself behind the wheel of a new BMW or on a Hawaiian beach as he or she returns from a weeklong business trip. Imagine an interactive wall that could provide flyers with all manner of destination information. Accenture is letting potential customers experience *THREE I* and is thereby showcasing its capabilities in this area.

## CONCLUSION

Boeing, Caterpillar, and Accenture are excellent working examples of marketers who have employed *THREE I* or elements of *THREE I* to usefully extend their presence and their relevance into the personal selling cycle. Boeing has developed completely immersive, identity-linked experiences that allow customers to explore their products and services in customized ways. Caterpillar has facilitated the selling efforts of both their dealer partners and salespeople Accenture is the first to bring a sense of what is possible with *THREE I* to a larger universe of companies who are potential clients. All three of these or ganizations point the way forward for using smart multimedia in B-to-B sell ing efforts. As packaged solutions become available in the future, the sales process should be transformed in many other companies as well. The promise that *THREE I* holds in the B-to-B environment is that it gives marketers the ability to deepen and enrich customer relationships by creating mediated environments where customers and salespeople can work together. By creating these environments, marketers can become truer partners with sales and business development. Marketing and sales organizations that once found themselves pitted against one another can instead work together.

# CHAPTER 11

# COMMUNICATING *WITH* CUSTOMERS

CHARLES SPINOSA, DAVID LE BROCQUY and
BOBBY J. CALDER

Advertising through paid media has been the dominant form of marketing for most large companies for over a century. The logic has been simple: Communicate the benefits of the product to customers and count on the resulting increase in awareness, knowledge, and evaluation to lead to higher sales. This formula has been the key to the creation of countless successful brands. Today, however, in a world of hypercompetition, parity products, and consumer overexposure to advertising messages, it is widely recognized that marketers need to go beyond the conventional formula. Alternative marketing services such as direct mail, online advertising, and branded entertainment already account for a greater share of marketing budgets than traditional advertising.

There is more at issue though than the need to spend more on other forms of marketing communications. There is certainly a need to invest in alternative media, interactive advertising, and the like. But there is a bigger challenge. Advertising alone, no matter how sophisticated, may not be sufficient to ensure that consumers are highly engaged with a brand. We believe that companies need to expand their view of communications beyond advertising *to* customers. A company needs to give equal weight to communicating *with* customers. By communicating with customers, we mean listening to customers about their concerns and talking to them about these concerns. In short, we mean having the kind of conversations with customers that they want to have. This applies not only to companies like retailers who by their nature already have extensive contact with customers but also to companies that may now have contact limited to call centers and the like. Consumers may want to have conversations even more in the latter case.

It will always be important to get the product's message out to customers. The effectiveness of even the best advertising will be limited, however, if customers feel cut off from the company, talked to but not listened to, unable to interact with the company. Consumers may be receptive to what the advertising message *promises* but they increasingly will also want specific *commitments* as to what they can expect in dealing with the company and, surprisingly, what the company expects from them. Even the clearest of advertising promises (such as "always the lowest price") needs to be coupled with two-way communication in which the company commits to listening to customer issues and responding to them.

The challenge is not just to deploy the tools of customer relationship management (CRM). Call center technology and the like may be useful, even necessary, but they are not sufficient. The challenge is not merely one of handling customer questions and complaints. Nor is it just a matter of the organizational alignment of company functions (Kaplan and Norton 2006). It is about truly connecting the organization as a whole to the customer. Companies need to project their advertising into the activities of the internal organization. Companies like Starbucks, Apple, Whole Foods, and Nike are already showing that customers find the experience of truly interacting with a company highly engaging. Having a company communicate *with* you is becoming an essential part of a positive customer experience. In our view, both traditional and alternative approaches to advertising need to be paired with a parallel strategy directed at the interaction of employees and consumers.

## COMPANIES NEED BOTH AN ADVERTISING STRATEGY AND A COMMITMENT STRATEGY

A commitment strategy must be inside out. The aim should not be one of simply communicating internally with employees. The goal is to engage the employee, so that the organization itself becomes a *medium* of communication with consumers. The goal is to surround the product or service with a communications experience that engages the customer. A commitment strategy comes most naturally to companies such as retail, service, and business-to-business (B-to-B) companies that sell products through intensive sales and service interaction with customers. Yet, we emphasize again that a commitment strategy may be needed even more where consumers may not feel that the company has any natural or existing avenue of communication with them.

Developing a commitment strategy to parallel your company's advertising strategy requires thinking more broadly about communications. CRM and internal (company to employee) communications can play important roles but the challenge is to make customers feel that the company is truly communicating with them. A commitment strategy must engage both employees and customers.

In this chapter, we provide a design framework for thinking about communications in this way. The framework treats a company's operations as a *network of commitments*. It focuses management attention on employee-to-customer conversations and employee-to-employee conversations about customers. It leads to employees making commitments to customers and then to employees making commitments to each other to fulfill those commitments to customers. Advertising tells consumers about how the company's product offers better benefits than its competitors. A commitment strategy applies to what employees say and do in interacting with customers about this. L. L. Bean thus goes beyond *promising* customer satisfaction to a *commitment* that any item can be returned for full value or replacement at any time with "no questions asked" in the communication experience. "No questions asked" is a good example of what we mean by a commitment. Good commitment strategies go well beyond simple examples such as this, however.

First we will describe some companies on the cutting edge of using commitments to manage communication with customers. We do this in some detail in order to convey better the meaning of commitments and their power in communications. Then we present our framework for designing a commitment strategy. Last, we relate this specifically to conventional internal communications programs and more generally to integrated marketing. As we will see, having a commitment strategy as well as an advertising strategy can become an important part of implementing an integrated marketing strategy for a brand. As described by Malthouse and Calder ( 2005), such a strategy can turn CRM tactics into strategically driven marketing contact points.

## MANAGING COMMUNICATION THROUGH COMMITMENTS

A commitment, first of all, transforms communication between the company and the customer into a conversation. The brand message no longer lives just in the mind of the customer but becomes part of the conversation between customers and front-line employees. If the commitment is, as most successful ones will be, a conditional one, where the customer has certain responsibilities as well, this conversation will create a relationship between the customer and the employee. The explicit commitment to the customer will have a personal flavor. Both the customer and the employee will feel obliged to fulfill it, not just for its own sake, but also for the sake of the relationship. We honor most commitments we make because we care about and respect the people to whom we make them.

Second, when there is an explicit commitment, a virtuous circle begins. Employees not only take pride in fulfilling the commitment but also tell the customer when they have done so. Customers explicitly acknowledge the fulfillment with gratitude. That gratitude in turn makes for more enthusiastic employees who take more initiative to earn more thanks.

Third, and most important, fulfilling the commitment to the external customer sets up a communications discipline that runs through the entire organization. Instead of having front-office and back-office people focused on their own processes in order to achieve company objectives, commitment-based companies have front-line employees *asking* back-office employees for *commitments* to complete work at a certain level of quality and by a certain time. The work does not satisfy a general competitive standard, but satisfies the external customer. Most of today's internal corporate conversations, even those in high performance companies, are filled with justification, defensiveness, and silo-focused reports. These conversations should be more about commitments to the customer.

A handful of companies are leading the way in these three regards. Some examples worth looking at closely are Lloyds TSB Scotland, Pacific Trust in San Diego, and John Lewis in the United Kingdom.

### Commitments at Lloyds TSB

Lloyds TSB Scotland is exemplary in deploying the concept of commitment and developing a customer communication experience around a series of commitments made by customers and employees. In 2001, Lloyds TSB Scotland offered its direct mortgage banking to brokers in the Scottish market. The bank confidently expected the Direct Mortgage Unit to have sales of £70 million for its first year, but eight months after its launch, it looked as though it would be lucky to hit £50 million. Worse, with less than 1 percent of the mortgage market, the sales team was reduced to "begging" for business. Brokers viewed the mortgage unit as the lender of last resort for their subprime clients. Lloyds TSB Scotland had an average of 95 percent loan to value.

To find out what he could do to change this, Norrie Henderson, head of mortgages, studied mortgage brokers in the Edinburgh area. The Scottish mortgage market is unusual in that Scottish homebuyers make no-contingency bids on homes before having mortgage approval or any prior financing. So most buyers use a mortgage broker to secure a mortgage loan quickly. Consequently, brokers are harassed into making lots of follow-up calls to lenders to whom they have submitted applications in order to satisfy anxious buyers. Henderson found that the brokers were in a classic bind. They wanted to go out and make more sales, but they were constantly servicing their current nervous clients. Worse, with most of the lenders, there were frequently additional calls for information long after it appeared that the application was complete. This confusion around the completion of applications produced much anguish among buyers and brokers alike. Lloyds TSB Scotland was considered among the worst in requiring additional information and lots of follow-up.

To turn his business around, Henderson decided to make a distinctive *commitment* to the brokers in Edinburgh, one that could be linked to an advertising message, but which would also be an explicit part of the unit's conversation with brokers. The commitment had to be one that would speak to the anxiety the industry created for both brokers and borrowers. Although back-office staff chafed, Henderson instituted the commitment that brokers would receive a "good as gold" decision on a short, preliminary mortgage application within three hours of submission. The "three-hour" commitment meant that Lloyds TSB Scotland would be bound by the decision unless it later discovered a misrepresentation of facts in the full application.

Henderson advertised this commitment to a target group of brokers in the form of membership in a club for brokers sponsored by the bank, which he named the Spearhead Mortgage Club. The result was an immediate upsurge in applications. But then applications dropped off. Henderson engaged in a second round of interviews with the brokers. He asked if they were satisfied. Many said that they were not because their loan applications had been rejected. But when he asked them if they had received an answer in three hours without making follow-up calls, the brokers agreed that they had.[1] The rejection rate was high because the brokers were still using Lloyds TSB for their high-risk applications. At this point, Henderson saw that his commitment was one-sided and easily taken for granted. The commitment needed to be expanded to include a reciprocal commitment by brokers to submit applications that represented the broker's actual mix of business. The bank would commit to a speedy decision on the application but it would ask that Lloyds TSB get a "fair share" of the broker's total business and a "fair mix" of the business, not just small, risky, high loan-to-value mortgages. "Fair share" and "fair mix" constituted commitments on the part of brokers.

At this point, the commitment worked as a two-way communication experience. The conditional "three-hour" commitment drove Spearhead Mortgage Club growth exponentially. Thirteen months from the start of the Spearhead program, mortgage loans were £350 million, well exceeding market growth. The loan to value ratio went from 95 percent to better than 75 percent and average loan size increased by 40 percent. The growth continued.

In 2004, mortgage lending was up 42 percent, and it was attracting other lending (up 27 percent) and growth in account balances (up 19 percent). Market share went from under 1 percent to 13 percent in the first 13 months. Lloyds TSB Scotland Direct Mortgage Unit enjoyed better than 150 percent compound annual growth rate (CAGR) in mortgage lending from 2001 through 2005.

### Commitments at Pacific Trust Bank

The Lloyds TSB results are no fluke. In San Diego, California, the community bank Pacific Trust grew from $43 million in assets in 2001 to $318 million in assets in 2006 (a 49.2 percent CAGR), increased its number of branches by 33 percent, and is getting much more public attention than its size would warrant. Hans Ganz, the flamboyant CEO, is emphatic that he differentiates his bank on its customer communication experience. Like Lloyds TSB, he set out to relieve an anxiety felt by most banking customers. Surveys and focus groups show that banks are often seen as a necessary evil. Consumers think that banks gouge customers with hidden fees and service charges. Many bank customers feel their bank treats them with indifference, or as wrong until proven otherwise. No matter how many years a customer has kept money with the bank, the minute the customer is in need of credit, the bank may well abandon them. Banks keep the customer's business by making it hard for them to switch. Conventional bank advertising does little to overcome these anxieties.

Hans Ganz instituted commitments designed to break the hold of the typical perceptions of banks on both his staff and customers. The first commitment met with little internal resistance but caused quite a stir in the market. Ganz promised to pay customers $50 to leave if they were not satisfied after six months. He wanted to upset all notions of consumer bondage. He composed the basic commitment himself: "Give us six months. We guarantee you'll be completely satisfied with our service or we'll give you $50 to leave."[2] Notice that, as with Lloyds TSB, the bank had to request the behavior it wanted. It had to elicit a commitment from the customer. If a customer decided to collect the $50 and leave, Ganz had one requirement: "All you need to do to receive the $50 guarantee is provide us with a brief explanation on how we failed to provide the service quality that you deserve."[3] The commitment was paralleled in advertising as shown in Figure 11.1.

Building on the "$50 to leave" commitment, Ganz also changed the tone of the conversations bank employees and customers had. Bank employees committed to conversing in a hardworking, friendly, neighborly way. For instance, they called out "Hello" the minute a customer walked in the door. Though advertising is modest, it parallels the commitments. The bank boldly displays signage (in-store) that says:

**Figure 11.1**
**Pacific Trust Advertising**

You have the right to expect good service. We're all human, so you shouldn't expect perfection. But, when mistakes happen, you should expect timely correction of problems, to be made whole, and to be treated well in the process.[4]

When was the last time you heard bankers openly admit to making mistakes?

These commitments caught the attention of customers and the press, but they were insufficient to create a completely new communication experience. Ganz knew he had to make a commitment that would emphasize to everyone throughout the bank that each was responsible for communicating with the customer. One Monday, he announced to his senior management team and his branch managers that he wanted them to publish their private cell phone numbers and invite customers to call if they were ever dissatisfied with the bank. The response was immediate and negative. The vice presidents and branch managers felt as though he was asking them to give up their private lives, their spouses, and their families. They said, "Why don't *you* do it?" and he said he would and that he and they would go even further; they would all list their cell phone numbers on the bank's web site at: www.pacifictrustbank .com/info/ServiceTeam.html. With the commitment that customers could call the bank's president, vice presidents, and managers on their private cell phones, Ganz fundamentally changed the customer's communication experience. The bank's advertising messages built on the "call the president" commitment with copy such as: "Do you know of any other bank where customers with a problem are encouraged to pick up the phone and call the bank's president? Can customers with problems at other banks get past the branch manager?" More than the promise of personal service, there is the commitment to it. During the first couple of weeks, Ganz received a number of calls, mostly from people who just did not believe the promise. Now, a few years into the promise, he says he receives about three calls per month.

The commitment has changed everyone in the bank. As SVP Branch Operations, Rachel Carrillo says, "No one on the front line wants to receive a call from the president or branch manager saying that a customer has called with a problem." With the telephone number commitment and a little coaching, the front-line staff learned quickly that a friendly, caring attitude was the best way to communicate with customers and stave off calls to their bosses.

What about the back-office functions though? In the past, front-office employees blamed back-office folks for mistakes. The back-office folks replied that the front-office people did not know what they were doing. Ganz and his senior team decided to look at this problem just as if it were one between staff and external customers: How could he turn issues and complaints into commitments that would facilitate communication?

Ganz made all employees responsible for turning their complaints into requests or offers. If the back-office staff did not think that the front-office employees knew the details necessary to provide a service, then the back-office staff was responsible for designing and delivering a training program to the front-office people. Likewise, if the front-office staff felt that the back-office staff had created overly burdensome procedures, they were to request that a back-office person spend time in the front to figure out a solution. The "training program" and "spend time" commitments were the start of a virtuous circle. Both front- and back-office employees became more flexible by virtue of their commitments. Commitments affect the entire corporate culture in this way.

## Commitments at John Lewis

John Lewis, the U.K. retailer, has a marketing approach similar to the upmarket service promise of Nordstrom's in the United States. John Lewis, however, also commits to its customers that it is "never knowingly undersold." This commitment appeals to customers because it relieves them of the responsibility to shop around and check prices before making a purchase. Beyond this commitment and the promise of the brand comes a behind-the-scenes commitment that all employees, "partners" at John Lewis, check the prices of local competitors to discover "undersells." Bonuses are awarded to partners who find products sold at lower prices at local retailers. And if a customer spots a lower price at a local retailer, the store manager immediately lowers the price for all customers. These interlocked commitments may seem straightforward, but they are not because John Lewis must apply this commitment to a wide range of up-market products that might well be discounted at other stores. Thus, buyers have to focus not only on the usual criteria for product selection but also on acquiring merchandise that discounters will tend not to carry and other stores will be less likely to discount. Additionally, the "never knowingly undersold" commitment ultimately not only touches buying strategies but also departmental budgeting, displays, training, compensation, and virtually every other aspect of the business. The commitment shapes the entire John Lewis corporate culture.

As with Lloyds TSB Scotland and Pacific Trust bank, John Lewis's chairman, Stuart Hampshire, tells his customers what he wants from them. He wants customers who care about workers' conditions, using environmentally sensitive materials, treating others with respect, and dealing with retail employees who are treated with respect by their employer.[5] Although John Lewis will never knowingly be undersold, it does not cater to customers who care only about "getting a bargain." John Lewis promises superior service and commits to keeping the customer from having to shop around to compare prices. It asks the customer for a commitment for something in return and makes this commitment clear. The "never knowingly undersold" commitment itself is linked to the condition that customers must care about others.

John Lewis customers take both sides of the commitment seriously. We have repeatedly observed participants in focus groups say that they like the service promise but enjoy shopping at John Lewis because they feel a strong sense of dignity there. Notice in the consumer quotes that follow how the reciprocal commitments color the entire shopping experience:

> I shop at John Lewis for carpets, not Carpets Plus. I don't have to worry about comparing prices. I know that John Lewis has only quality goods. And John Lewis gives me a price guarantee.

> At John Lewis, the sales associate always takes me to the product if I ask a question. I get treated with dignity. At other places, the sales associate will just point.

> John Lewis is my favorite store because the sales associates really care about getting me just the right product, even if it is one that is not as

expensive as the one I wanted when I came in. And I can be sure the price is right.

I know that John Lewis wants me to care about how it treats the world. I do.

## DESIGNING A COMMITMENT STRATEGY

There are four key steps in designing a commitment strategy to complement your advertising. Since the communications process is cumulative and on-going, think of the following steps as iterative:

1. *Identify specific commitments that follow from the overall brand promise advertised to customers.* The brand promise may be more or less well developed but it will ordinarily always imply some commitment. A good way of thinking about this is to consider what anxieties a customer could have about the promise or perhaps even about the general product category if the promise is a very general one. What might customers worry or wonder about? What might they need to know? What might they want to inquire about? Commitments address such anxieties.
2. *Map out the commitment conversation that customers would ideally have with front-line employees.* It is critical to view the commitment in terms of a conversation with the customer and to map it out as a two-way communications loop. The goal is to *design* the commitment conversations that you want to happen.
3. *Map out the network of commitments that will connect front-line employees with other staff.* Work backward to identify the chain of conversations that will need to happen if the basic commitment to the customer is to be honored.
4. *Monitor customer satisfaction with commitment conversations and the overall communications experience.* Remember the initial problem with Lloyds TBS Scotland where the original "three-hour" commitment needed to be modified to include the reciprocal "fair mix" commitment. It is crucial to obtain feedback on whether the commitment is working as it should be or is breaking down.

Let's examine this logic in more detail.

### Identifying Commitments

All nontrivial brand promises generate some consumer anxiety. With Lloyds TSB, the idea of shorter turnaround was very appealing but brokers and their clients feared that they would be less likely to secure the loan. Hans Ganz knew that most bank customers feared that banks make offers to get their business and then gouge them six months later with hidden fees. John Lewis knew that retail customers worried they might be duped into paying super-high prices by the promise of superior service.

The most difficult part of constructing a commitment is to answer the anxiety inherent in the brand promise. Norrie Henderson and Hans Ganz excel at this. Three guidelines serve them well: (1) Design as though you trust your customers; (2) Make a bold commitment that clearly faces *one* dimension of the anxiety; and (3) Make the commitment measurable: "We'll provide a decision in principle within three hours." "We will pay you $50 if you leave us after six months." Make the initial promise bold and clear. Later, you may need to make other commitments if you need to take up another anxiety as with the example of publishing private cell phone numbers.

Do not forget the need for reciprocal commitment. Many marketers find it difficult to state the behavior they want from their customers beyond purchasing behavior. Norrie Henderson asked for what he needed to compete successfully: a fair share of the brokers' best customers. Hans Ganz asked for an explanation on which he could act. Stuart Hampshire of John Lewis asked for customers who will genuinely appreciate his corporate values. Such reciprocal commitments rebound to the benefit of customers as well. John Lewis customers take pride in shopping at John Lewis.

Often changing the brand or designing a subbrand is key to bringing out a commitment. It is important that the commitment be made manifest and tangible in order to create an actual communications experience. To embody the "three-hour" commitment as something concrete, Henderson named the club of brokers he created "Spearhead" and sent invitations to join on specially made arrows featuring the broker's corporate colors (see Figure 11.2). These were mailed in specially designed Lloyds TSB's tubes. Henderson also staged events around these invitations such as archery contests. A typical launch mailer invited targeted brokers to an introductory archery event where Henderson explained the mutual commitments. It is important that commitments take concrete form.

### Commitment Conversations

Conversations around commitments solve two of the biggest problems companies have:

1. Sales teams promising whatever it takes to make the sale and
2. Service representatives who act like compliance police as in, "You did not enter your customer number correctly."

**Figure 11.2**
**Spearhead Invitation Pack**

With well-coordinated commitment conversations, customers and front-line employees spend time talking about how they could make things better and not lodging complaints, arguing over what was promised, or playing GOTCHA.

But since commitments need to be made by the whole workforce, they need to evolve. Most of the time, it is best to test new commitment conversation designs with small customer segments. Conversations generally need to be refined based on actual front- and back-office practice. For instance, Lloyds TSB back-office staff collected historical information about where homes were selling, the types of customers, sizes of mortgages, trends in down payments, and so forth. As front-line employees started talking to the brokers about their mix of business, they found that they could usefully draw on this information. Hence, the back-to-front office conversation about trends became standard.

Thus, one of the most important things in the entire process is the ongoing redesign of commitment conversations. Once a company makes and starts living up to a commitment, a revolution occurs. Both customers and employees will expand the original commitment into a larger one. Norrie Henderson discovered that the true heart of his revolution was not the "three-hour" commitment itself. Rather it was the change in the role of the underwriter. Most banks keep their underwriters from ever speaking to a client or a client's representative. Underwriters protect the bank from risk. Henderson had his underwriters explain their decisions and offer alternatives by speaking directly to the brokers. It is critical to evolve commitments emerging from conversations into a "core" commitment by the company. Hans Ganz discovered that customers wanted trustworthy, responsive, neighborly conversations with bank employees. The core commitment became treating every customer as a close neighbor. John Lewis' core commitment is fast becoming employees who get carried away getting inside the customer's head and finding just the right product and explaining why it is the right product.

The design of commitment conversations is a way of implementing the commitments that have been identified.

## Commitment Loop: The Basic Design Tool

We turn now to mapping out commitment conversations and networks of commitments. Mapping is a powerful design tool for creating and understanding interconnected conversations where people make offers and commitments and then fulfill them. Carefully aligned commitment conversations enable employees to make responsible commitments to customers and to ask for certain behaviors in return. Commitment conversations should be designed to follow the phases of a commitment loop, which is the basic atom of any network of commitment conversations. The loop shows how to make commitment conversations operational.[6] Loops are connected together to map the network of commitment conversations necessary to take complex action.

A commitment conversation starts with an external (or internal) customer and a performer, who is the key employee in the conversation. These roles are defined within the conversation, and the performer in one conversation can be the customer in another. A unit manager might ask the CFO for a report on her purchasing spend. Although she is less senior in the organization than the CFO, she functions as the internal customer to the CFO who will be the performer. On another occasion, the CFO could ask the manager to submit her annual budget, in which case the manager is the performer and the CFO the customer.

The commitment conversation goes through four phases in the loop between the external or internal customer and the performer: preparation, negotiation, making it happen, and acknowledgment. Three of the four phases end with an action-oriented speech act—a request, promise, or declaration. We will exemplify the four phases and the typical speech acts with an example of how the conversation loop generally works at Starbucks.

*Preparation*     Normally, Starbucks customers prepare to make a request by thinking about which beverage they want to design and what the Starbucks people call it. They check to see if they have the money and the time to drink it and then walk into the closest Starbucks. When the Starbucks employee beams a huge smile at you and says, "Do you want your regular today?" you know that you have someone tuned in to your interests. "I'd like a vente black coffee, not my normal grande." With that request, the preparation phase is complete.

***Negotiation***    The negotiation phase begins with a simple, strictly win–win negotiation. "Would you like something to eat? The scones are great today. Also, we have a free sample of our new holiday drink." The scone might appeal or trigger another idea for a snack or remind you that you have a scone-loving friend back in the office. In general, negotiation brings in considerations of the larger context on both the customer's and the performer's side. "Just the coffee, please." "It's coming right up." Thus negotiation phase ends with the promise from the performer.

"It's coming right up" could be a disinterested prediction, and at many businesses it is. "Your package is in the mail. I can give you a tracking number if you'd like." But at Starbucks baristas and counterpeople promise fulfillment. They typically take responsibility for making sure that you get your drink in a reasonable amount of time at reasonable quality and compensate you if you do not.

***Making It Happen***    "Did you say you wanted foam?" "No thanks." Conversations in the making-it-happen phase involve new insights that arise in the process, new offers the performer can make, new desires that the customer has. "Here is your skinny grande cappuccino with two shots and cinnamon," the counterperson or barrista says after making it happen. That declaration or report completes phase three. And in many organizations, that's the end of the conversation.

***Acknowledgment***    At Starbucks, there is almost always a follow-up. "I'll see you later." Or "Have a great day." These valedictory acknowledgments are not just niceties. They are ways of finding out if the customer is satisfied. If the customer looks or sounds dissatisfied, the employee will ask, "Can I get you something else?" In most cases, the customer simply says: "Thanks very much." The declaration of gratitude, an acknowledgment, leaves the barrista feeling better about her work and the customer feeling better about life.

Conversations designed to follow this loop draw customers and performers into relationship with each other, even in such a simple transaction as

**Figure 11.3**
**The Commitment Loop**

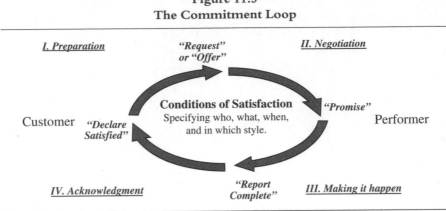

*I. Preparation*     *"Request"*
*or "Offer"*     *II. Negotiation*

**Conditions of Satisfaction**
Specifying who, what, when,
and in which style.

Customer   *"Declare*
*Satisfied"*     *"Promise"*   Performer

*IV. Acknowledgment*     *"Report*
*Complete"*   *III. Making it happen*

purchasing coffee. Obligations are expressed and felt. When that happens, communication takes on a personal character that companies often value but find hard to achieve. The loop as a design tool gets at this by including among the conditions of satisfaction a statement of the style with which the conversation takes place. At Starbucks, baristas and cashiers make commitments in an uplifting manner.

With this understanding of the basic commitment conversation loop, let us turn to implementing commitments through linked loops. (See Figure 11.3 for a schematic representation of the commitment loop.)

## Designing the Network of Commitment Conversations

Let's examine how Lloyds TSB Scotland used networked commitment conversation loops to fulfill the commitments it identified, first with the "three-hour" response commitment and eventually with the core commitment of having underwriters help brokers solve problems. The steps Norrie Henderson went through are typical and illustrate the design process well.

After interviewing his broker customers, Henderson began his internal diagnosis by mapping the key commitments that his managers made to him. He began with managers in charge of marketing and advertising. Henderson's initial diagnostic map appears in Figure 11.4.

Starting with the marketing managers, Henderson noted that the company's advertising focused on the clearly established brand attributes, vigorous, powerful, and fast, attached to the Lloyds symbol, the Lloyds black horse. Ads

# Figure 11.4

## Diagnostic Commitment Map of Direct Mortgage Unit

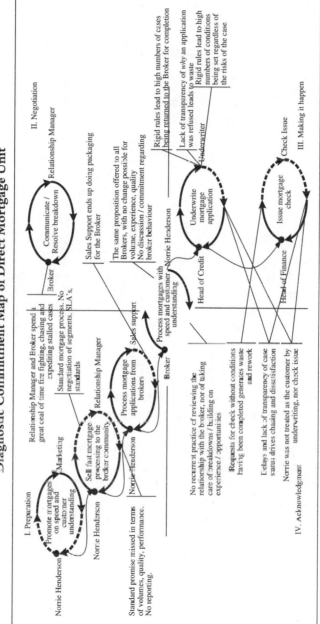

showed the horse with various voiceovers about particular products. The Direct Mortgage unit sought to match the overall brand's 4 percent share, but was struggling to hit 1 percent. The advertising promises of brand benefits simply were not having their carry-over effect to direct mortgages. Nevertheless, the commitment conversation with marketing still focused on broad brand themes. Henderson realized that he was not asking marketing or the ad agency to acknowledge the results or examine their assumptions. Henderson drew dashed lines in the acknowledgment and preparation phases while noting that the central commitment of the conversation was wrong.

Next came the commitment conversation of the relationship managers. Since they did not negotiate with Henderson or with other internal managers, he drew a dashed line for negotiation and performance to indicate that it was deficient. Since he did talk to the relationship managers about how they were doing in sales, he left the acknowledgment line solid. He concluded that the relationship managers were promising whatever would get the sale, which was usually impossibly fast processing times. Henderson characterized the conversations of the relationship managers as desperate.

Since the agreement of a broker to apply required another step, Henderson mapped the conversation of a third group dealing with the brokers. The sales support team helped the brokers complete the application. The sales support team issued the one-size-fits-all application to brokers and resentfully chased the broker and customer to complete the supporting documentation (the packaging). They saw their role as efficient processors. But since the brokers needed help evaluating whether certain documents and information satisfied the requirements, sales support took time out from their compliance work to help. Henderson indicated this deficiency in understanding of their role with a dashed line in their performance phase.

Note that in Figure 11.4 all of the commitment conversations occur in the upper left quadrant of the map. In the context of the entire network of conversations, all three are about Preparation. It is useful to capture this higher-order structure by labeling the quadrants of the graph as Preparation, Negotiation, Making It Happen, and Acknowledgment. The overall structure thus follows the phases of the individual conversations. This is often useful in organizing the network of conversations in a map. Thus, after considering the three Preparation commitment conversation loops, Henderson turned to the Negotiation quadrant.

He discovered that very little negotiation actually occurred. His underwriters and sales support teams had come up with a one-size-fits-all mortgage application form that, once complete, would enable—or so they thought—fast underwriting decisions. Lloyds TSB Scotland sought speed by cutting negotiation with the brokers. But since the brokers and their clients found the one-size-fits-all application burdensome and confusing, they made frequent complaints to their relationship manager. The relationship managers could do little more than harass the sales support team into helping the brokers out. The sales support team did not have a recurrent commitment conversation with the relationship managers. So the relationship managers were reduced to begging the brokers to be patient and begging the sales support team to help. That was the negotiation that took place. Henderson represented this with a detached, floating loop in the Negotiation quadrant.

In the Making-It-Happen quadrant, Henderson saw the most important commitment was for underwriters to review applications and make decisions quickly. The underwriters made their commitment, however, to do this to the head of credit, whose commitment to the bank was to maintain a safe risk profile. He did not promise speed, flexibility, or an interest in growing market share. Hence his underwriters were conservative and slow. They frequently demanded complete applications even when they would not use the missing data. They did not explain their decisions, not even to the extent of telling relationship managers what changes in the application, such as increasing the equity, would enable acceptance. Rather, when a loan was borderline acceptable, they would issue an acceptance with complex conditions. Henderson characterized the conversations around the underwriters' promise as aloof and risk-averse. The underwriting obscurity led to slowness both in issuing letters of acceptance and also in cutting the check. The team that issued the checks had to be sure of compliance with the conditions. Thus, the conditions turned the other performers into nervous compliance checkers.

Henderson had no recurrent follow-up with brokers to check their level of satisfaction or collect feedback on what could be improved. Thus, there was no conversation loop in the Acknowledgment quadrant.

Overall, Henderson's diagnostic map showed a classic manufacturing bureaucracy: almost all sales and production with little listening or care for the customer, no real negotiations, no real acknowledgment. Looking at all these commitment breakdowns, he made five critical observations.

1. The whole conversational process was trying to respond to the broker's desire for quick decisions. That promise was one brokers did appreciate.
2. But since sales support, relationship managers, and finance determined what would count as quickness by their own lights, they ended up creating huge inefficiencies from the brokers' perspective.
3. Henderson needed to have all critical commitments in the process made to him. Key elements of the process worked like autonomous nations.

4. Other than the relationship manager's initial conversation with the broker, all the other conversations were in one way or another about compliance. That had to end.

5. As a commitment process, Henderson's implicit central commitment to the brokers was to run a mortgage processing shop not a service organization.

No wonder the business was failing to meet its goals.

Two challenges screamed out from the diagnosis: (1) Relationship managers had to able to make a reliable commitment to brokers regarding speed; and (2) Henderson had to obliterate all the follow-up that kept brokers from going after more business and made the Lloyds TSB back-office into compliance checkers. Consequently, he changed his central commitment to the broker community. He committed to simplifying the brokers' businesses with fast, no-need-to-follow-up mortgage loans.

Working out from the new, provisional core commitment, Henderson saw that three key problems caused delays and follow-up calls: the all-purpose application, the complicated packaging, and the uncommunicative underwriters. To remedy the situation, he drew on one of the fundamental principles of commitment-based design: Structure commitments on the assumption that people tell the truth. He asked, "How much information did the underwriters really need to decide whether they could approve a loan?" Henderson's underwriters came up with about a half-dozen questions, which if answered fully and truthfully, could enable them to make a decision and then issued a slimmed-down application form.

On the basis of the new questions, Henderson refined his core commitment to the brokers. He committed to a mortgage loan decision within three hours of submission of the answers to the questions. No follow-up needed! Moreover, unless the supporting information showed misrepresentations in the original answers, Lloyds TSB would honor that three-hour decision. It was as "good as gold." See Henderson's first redesign in Figure 11.5.

The redesigned network of commitments solved the problems Henderson diagnosed. He accepted a commitment from marketing and its agency to promote a special subbrand, "Spearhead," on both quickness and accuracy. The new commitment conversation with marketing was one of continuous invention. Relationship managers agreed with Henderson to sell the three-hour mortgage commitment in exchange for a fair mix of business from the brokers. Where there had been no negotiation, Henderson inserted the most important conversation in the whole transformation. He told the underwriters to talk to the brokers directly and explain their decisions. The underwriters

**Figure 11.5**
**Initial New Commitment Map of Direct Mortgage Unit**

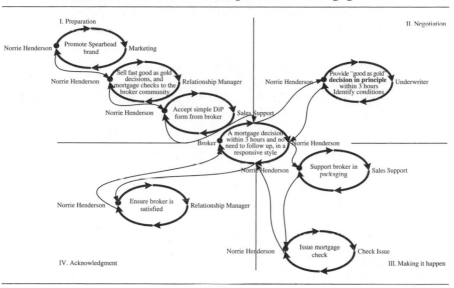

also agreed to support the business goals by finding ways to approve mortgages within the risk model and within the three-hour time period. This conversation was both tough-minded and inventive.

Once the broker, the broker's clients, and the underwriter agreed on the mortgage terms, the sales support team went back to work helping the broker complete the necessary packaging. The conversation was about help and not compliance.

Last, Henderson insisted that relationship managers frequently get back to the brokers to discuss the level of satisfaction on both sides and to find ways to help each other succeed in the business. To everyone's surprise, the brokers started to call up the relationship managers to check on the relationship manager's satisfaction with the business mix. The style of conversations became responsive in contrast to the earlier compliance-oriented style. In fact, as described earlier, an even stronger core commitment evolved out of this.

Several months after ramping up the program, underwriters found themselves engaging in conversations with brokers that no one ever expected them to have. If the decision was "no" for a £100,000 loan, the broker might negotiate and say, "What if my client put more money down?" The underwriter could come back immediately and say, "I could approve an £80,000 loan for this property" Similarly, the underwriter might suggest a longer term, a zero-interest product, or even another financial institution that would accept the higher risk. Even when the answer was "yes," brokers and underwriters engaged in conversations over where they were seeing lots of business.

When Henderson learned how highly the brokers valued this conversation, he developed a training program for the underwriters to increase their skill in conducting them. He also changed the core commitment that Lloyds TSB made to the brokers. The company committed to finding the best mortgage deal for brokers and providing them with valuable information to improve their businesses. The final map of the Direct Mortgage Unit's network of commitment conversations appears in Figure 11.6. You can see that all conversations are aligned around promoting and supporting the underwriter's conversation with the brokers.

How well did this commitment strategy work? We need only look at the competitive situation. Other banks have made competing advertising claims, one has even promised a 20-minute decision. But Lloyds TSB has kept growing its market share based on its attention to actual commitment conversations.

**Figure 11.6**
**Final Redesign of the Commitment Map of Direct Mortgage Unit**

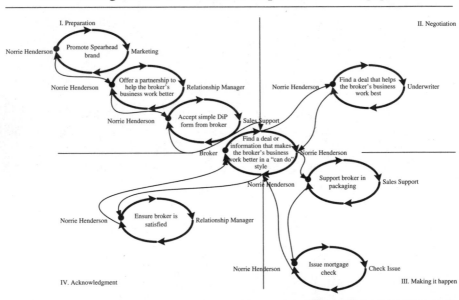

## Commitment Conversations over Time

You need to constantly adjust both the internal and customer-facing commitment conversations in response to feedback. When Hans Ganz published the cell phone numbers of his branch managers, he found an unexpected change taking place. As more customers called and got to know the branch managers, those managers started to take their branches more seriously. They started acting as owners and demanded that they be able to develop their own promotions to fit *their* market area. Ganz responded to this (internal customer) feedback by making this happen. No branch can be without a children's play area, a change machine (for fast deposits of all that change that mounts up at home), and a clear line of sight from the counter to the doors, enabling staff to greet everyone who walks in. But each manager can choose his or her monthly promotions in accord with the branch's neighborhood.

Commitment conversations inherently open a two-way chain of communication that extends into the corporate culture and its values. Employees do not need to be told what customers think because they are linked to customers. The company does not need to preach that customers matter because employees make personal commitments to them. At Lloyds TSB relationship managers learn about the brokers' businesses as the brokers learn about how to succeed with Lloyds TSB. The culture has changed so that underwriters have, improbably, adopted entrepreneurial, deal-making values. At Pacific Trust, Hans Ganz loves asking customers, "How are we doing for you?" You frequently hear customers answer, "You're the best bank in the world." You can be sure that if he repeatedly failed to hear these magic words, he would find a new commitment.

As we have tried to suggest, a good commitment strategy, like a good advertising strategy, can have a cumulative effect. At John Lewis, partners have become famous for their product knowledge. According to Simon Fraser and Andrew McMillan, who are in charge of the customer experience at John Lewis, their partners love to teach their customers. They are mavens. Who would have guessed that "never knowingly undersold" would lead to a kind of product maven culture? It is typical, however, that, as customers show gratitude, employees show more enthusiasm and change in response.

This discussion has illustrated the process of designing a commitment strategy and conveyed some of the richness of looking explicitly at commitment conversations. The Appendix at the end of this chapter presents a more systematic explanation of how to use the commitment mapping design tool.

## ROLE OF INTERNAL COMMUNICATIONS

Almost all companies of any size already have an internal employee communications program or perhaps even a large department devoted to this function. How does a commitment strategy fit into this? Presently internal communications in most companies focus on explaining to employees what is going to happen and why it is the right thing to happen. It might portray a current problem, but it will almost certainly describe a bright future.

Recently, there has been a trend toward opening up internal communications. John P. Kotter, a leading thinker in the area, emphasizes the following. Keep it simple; use metaphors, analogies, and examples; use many different forums (large group meetings, memos, newspapers, posters, informal one-on-one talks); repeat, repeat, repeat; walk the talk; address seeming inconsistencies, listen and be listened to.[7] And in the best cases, internal communication is more likely to involve listening carefully to employees. But on balance we think it is fair to say that the communication is still more top-down.

As our examples have shown, a commitment strategy, while not necessarily inconsistent with conventional internal communications, looks at communication in a different way. With a commitment strategy, internal communication is more the conversations employees have with customers. It focuses on commitment conversations. Thus, in a commitment-based company, leaders and managers do not spend time in every meeting justifying the corporate vision or strategy and then laying out how to fulfill it. They give enough background to what they are thinking to make requests of their employees. Leaders negotiate with employees, then, in order to get into action. Employees realize that in accepting a request, they will be shaping the idea into action. And as the employees and their leaders acknowledge what worked and what did not, they will be reshaping the idea for another go around. At the end of a commitment-based meeting, an employee does not say, "I get your vision and endorse it" (or more quietly, "I'll wait until this one blows over"). The employee commits to making something happen.

All this is not to say that some of the activities typical of conventional internal communications cannot be useful for a commitment strategy. Take celebrations. Celebrations already play an increasingly important role in corporate life. Celebrate wins. But in most places wins are defined in terms that the financial community would appreciate, lower costs, higher rates of customer satisfaction and retention, and sometimes such intangibles as increased morale.[8] In contrast, at John Lewis each store has to generate three legendary stories each year about an employee helping a customer with a product. These are celebrated with videotaped reenactments. John Lewis even has its annual film festival where the legendary stories are judged.

In a company that links its internal communications to a commitment strategy, the company and its leaders must constantly observe and report on how commitments are kept, and then help to celebrate them.

## COMMITMENTS AND INTEGRATED MARKETING

We began by arguing that advertising alone may not be sufficient for success in a changing marketing world. A commitment strategy turns an advertising promise into a commitment conversation that consumers can experience in their interactions with a company and employees can experience in their interactions with each other. One of the authors recently had a service interruption with his Internet connection. A call to the provider resulted in the usual telephone tree nightmare. On finally navigating this, a representative came on the line and began by reading a script explaining how much the company valued customers and wanted to provide good service. The customer was then told that he should wait a day or so to see if service resumed. After considerable protesting, a supervisor came on the line and, after more protesting, said that she would call back after checking with a technical representative. She probably tried, but was unable to reach this person or resolve the problem, but in any event, she did not call back. The customer had to call and start over with another representative. And so on. We find that such experiences have become symptomatic. Consumers are quite simply becoming sick of companies that are not able to communicate with them.

Advertising cannot remain above this. Internal communications cannot remain oblivious to this. The solution is not about more or technically better CRM. Advertising and internal communications need to be integrated with a commitment strategy for employee-customer and employee-employee communications. This strategy needs to be highly concrete and action oriented. It should ideally be designed around a specific set of commitment conversations that deliver on an overall core commitment that the company is making. That core commitment should be integrated with the advertising promise. From an integrated marketing point of view, commitment conversations with the customer represent contacts or touchpoints of a different kind than traditional ads and both should be integrated with advertising into a seamless marketing plan. Once advertising strategy is integrated with the commitment strategy, employee touchpoints become the way a company validates and makes concrete the brand promise conveyed by advertising.

Commitment conversations are also important from an integrated marketing perspective because they inherently lend themselves to and even often require customization. In the commitment conversation process, of preparation, negotiation, making it happen, and acknowledgment, customers invariably will be treated in a more individualized way. Malthouse and Calder ( 2005) describe why such customization is important for branding. It is through contacts in which consumers are treated in a more subsegmented way that marketers can build a relationship brand. To have customers experience a brand as similar to having a relationship with someone is a great goal of marketing. A commitment strategy thus not only makes the brand promise more concrete it also can help to create a relationship experience with the brand.

We emphasize one other closing note. As we have said, a commitment strategy lets the consumer experience the advertised brand promise. It also can change how consumers regard the advertising itself. Consumers who experience commitment conversation contacts may actually become more engaged with advertising. They realize the advertising is about something they are experiencing in their lives. Commitment can even create its own buzz that causes consumers who might not otherwise be affected by the advertising to engage with it. No doubt John Lewis customers engage more with its advertising because of their in-store commitment conversations with sales partners. And these customers make other noncustomers notice John Lewis' high-service advertising message by telling stories about their commitment conversations to other people.

## APPENDIX
### Guidelines for Mapping Commitments: Basic Map, Diagnostic Map, and Redesign Map

❖ Basic Map
  • Draw a main loop in the middle of the page. Draw cross hairs to divide the page in four parts with the loop in the center of the page. Write "Preparation" in the upper left hand corner quadrant, "Negotiation" in the upper right corner, "Making it Happen" in the lower right, and "Acknowledgment" in the lower left.
  • Identify the main customer for the business activity. This customer is usually an external, paying customer. Identify the customer by the segment name ("mass affluent") if applicable.
  • Identify the role of the individual who is the main Performer. That is the person, generally the business-line leader, in charge of all the key

activities for selling and delivering the product or service. Map from the perspective of this key performer.

- Write inside the central loop the tentative commitment the key performer makes to the customer. Ideally this commitment should reflect the advertised brand promise. Characterize the style of communication (e.g., in a neighborly style). The general form is: "Take care of a customer concern within a time frame in a certain style."

- From the perspective of the key performer, jot down on a scratch pad the top 10 to 12 commitment conversations necessary for a sale. Once inside the map, if a new commitment conversation comes to mind, eliminate another on the map. Note that some key conversations will remain implicit: tacit hand-offs or inexplicit expectations (sales notifies marketing of changes in customer behavior). Give these tacit commitments voice but do not clutter the map.

- *Preparation Quadrant:* Ask who or what incites the customer to contact your business. An ad created by the agency? A business developer? Sales? Draw conversation loops for each of the critical conversations, no more than three, and write the commitments inside. The loop representing the conversation farthest from the actual customer request should be farthest from the center. The one where the request is made goes closest to the center. Add the roles of the performers on the right side of those loops and the external customer or the internal customer on the left. Leave the customer space blank if the activity just happens automatically or by habit. Likewise, if the commitment is vague, write your best guess in red.

- *Negotiation Quadrant:* Ask who responds to the customer's request and determines how the business will commit to fulfill it. Salesperson? Sales manager? Specialist engineer? Project manager? The loop closest to the center shows the commitment made to the customer.

- *Making-It-Happen Quadrant:* In order to get the job done, what are the three main commitments made by various people and to whom are they made? Complete loops for the three key conversations.

- *Acknowledgment Quadrant:* Identify the performer who asks the customer to declare satisfaction or dissatisfaction. This conversation is often initially missing. Marketing surveys and customer service do not count. How is this conversation connected to other conversations internally?

❖ Diagnostic Map
- Some diagnostic judgments have already been represented in the basic map: red commitments indicating vagueness and missing customers. Examine each of the 12 loops outside the main loop and ask whether

there is a clear request, a clear commitment, a clear report that the work is done, and an acknowledgment by the customer of satisfaction or dissatisfaction. Draw red lines where the conversation phases are weak, black where they are clear. Look out for quadrants such as negotiation and acknowledgment where conversation may be missing. (Annual reviews typically do not count as acknowledgment of a particular request's fulfillment.)

- Next, diagnose the alignment of commitments. Write alignment diagnoses in call-out boxes. Consider the following:
  - *Preparation Quadrant:* Do the commitment conversations add up to exploring the customer's concerns behind the request? Change the style in the central loop to match the style of listening to the customer.
  - *Negotiation Quadrant:* Do various commitment conversations add up to the customer and performer brainstorming the best solution together? If not, then the commitment in the central loop is the delivery of a simple product or service, not a solution, valuable experience, or strong brand promise.
  - *Making It Happen Quadrant:* Do the commitment conversations add up to staying in touch with the customer, supplying updates, and finding out about changes? If not, revise the central commitment to say the product or service is standard.
  - *Acknowledgment Quadrant:* Do the commitment conversations add up to treating the customer as the boss and seeking closure on the activity while creating openness for others? If not, then the style of the central loop will have to be official, bureaucratic, or cold.

❖ Redesign Map
  - Generally, the redesign comes from looking at the core commitment and comparing it with the brand promise. Most leaders want their business to add higher value than it does in fact. Write the new central commitment consistent with the brand promise in the center.
  - Make appropriate changes in the 12 commitments around the core commitment so that they are in alignment with the core commitment and phase goals: make sure that Preparation yields a well-defined request, Negotiation is win-win, Making It Happen is responsive to change, Acknowledgment has the key performer, or a real representative, listen to the customer.
  - Change the performers as necessary.
  - Create more tightly linked commitment conversations by making the key performer the stand-in for the external customer where possible.

## NOTES

1. We thank Richard Flinn and David Singh for their personal reflections on the follow-up meetings with brokers, November 25, 2005. We also thank Don Sull for his analysis.

2. www.pacifictrustbank.com/products/guarantee.htm.

3. See note 2.

4. See note 2.

5. Article by Stuart Hampshire published in *Retail Week,*  May 2006, www.johnlewispartner ship.co.uk/Display.aspx?MasterId=4b9ceba8–9f69–4dc3-a86a-0cad0d41aa38&Navigatio nId=562/.

6. For more on commitment-based management, see Don Sull and Charles Spinosa, "Promise-based Management: The Essence of Execution," *Harvard Business Review* 85, April 2007, 79–86, and "Using Commitments to Manage across Units," *Sloan Management Review* 47.1, Fall 2005, 73–81. Fernando Flores and Chauncey Bell first developed the commitment loop. See Terry Winograd and Fernando Flores, *Understanding Computers and Cognition* (Norwood, NJ: Ablex, 1986), 65.

7. John P. Kotter, *Leading Change* (Boston: Harvard Business School Press, 1996), 89–100, particularly p. 93.

8. See note 7, p. 120.


## REFERENCES

Kaplan, Robert S., and David P. Norton. 2006. *Alignment*. Boston: Harvard Business School Press.

Kotter, John P. 1996. *Leading change*. Boston: Harvard Business School Press.

Malthouse, Edward C., and Bobby J. Calder. 2005. Relationship branding and CRM. In A. Tybout and T. Calkins, ed. *Kellogg on branding*, 150–168. Hoboken, NJ: John Wiley & Sons.

Sull, Don, and Charles Spinosa. 2005. Using commitments to manage across units. *Sloan Management Review* 47; 73–81.

Sull, Don, and Charles Spinosa. 2007. Promise-based management: The essence of execution. *Harvard Business Review* 85: 79–86.

Winograd, Terry, and Fernando Flores. 1986. *Understanding computers and cognition*. Norwood, NJ: Ablex. (Reprinted Addison-Wesley, 1997.)

# CHAPTER 12

# CHANGING THE COMPANY

JULIE ROEHM

**C**hange is a scary word for most people. Particularly if you are a chief marketing officer (CMO) faced with improving the business in a company that has experienced success in the past. The scary part is changing the approach to the business because as a CMO, if it doesn't work, you are criticized for making a change from what has always worked and if it does work, people react skeptically wondering whether it was just a fluke or wondering whether that approach can create consistent results.

As marketing and new technologies race forward, CMOs and marketing leadership are under more pressure than ever. With average CMO tenures measured in months—the average tenure for CMOs being 23.2 months in 2006, down from 23.5 months in 2005 according to SpencerStuart—it is more important than ever that they stay attuned to what is new. At the same time, CMOs will need to be able to determine what is right for their brands and more important, what can be proven to add value for them.

The first step in the process is realizing that a change needs to be made. There are many potential reasons why the CMO tenure is so short and why marketing communications is so slow to change. It is likely that the shortening in tenure is due to marketing going through a dramatic shift in which many CMOs are left behind and the accountability of the CMO on the executive team is misaligned with what their real role should be. The CMO should be a permanent student of the industry and the need for change.

## MARKETING AND OPERATING SYSTEMS

Today, it is difficult to pick up a book, read a newspaper, or have a conversation without someone referring to upgrades—the idea of a 1.0 or a 2.0 solution for something. Tiger Woods was on the cover of *Sports Illustrated* with a

254

headline of "Tiger 2.0." There is an entire magazine dedicated to the idea of evolution and innovation in business called *Business 2.0*. The Web is discussed in Web 1.0 and Web 2.0 terms. This language that is now part of the everyday dialogue mimics that of the operating system of computers.

These operating systems (i.e., Microsoft Vista or Mac Leopard) were developed by Bill Gates and Steve Jobs as a platform for human interaction with the computer. As the speed of computer chips and the capacity of hard drives increase, so does the capabilities they afford its users. These changes and increases in performance are realized through upgrades and are necessary if we are to keep up with the changing landscape.

The idea of upgrades has inadvertently transformed the way we think and speak about our world, not just our computers. It is a good metaphor for marketing because it is a shorthand that allows us to better understand complex systems.

## MARKETING 1.0/2.0/3.0

Marketing has transitioned through three significant eras that we will describe using the upgrade model as Marketing 1.0, Marketing 2.0, and Marketing 3.0. These eras were brought about by massive technological shifts in the media landscape that required wholesale adaptation in marketing.

Marketing 1.0 saw the development of modern advertising in a landscape of simple but powerful media. Marketing 1.0 can arguably be defined as the golden age of advertising when there were only a few media and few channels from which to build your media mix. In this world, your media mix was made up of TV (from three networks), radio, print, and perhaps billboards. It was possible to reach 85 percent of any audience through TV, print, and radio and advertising clutter did not exist. Measuring success was as much in terms of office chatter as it was in the actual increase in sales of whatever was being sold.

The advertising agency and the client were true partners. The agency worked with the client on the business problems or opportunities. These conversations included strategic brainstorming on the business as a whole, including packaging, product development, and all forms of advertising. The results created not only some of the most provocative advertising of our time, such as Apple's *1984* ad, but also created new products. The advertising agency Campbell Mithun is credited with helping to invent stick butter at Land O'Lakes. This type of collaboration and partnership helped to generate the notion of the full-service agency.

Marketing 1.0 was also the age in which brand management was born and that research into consumer's lives was spawned. It can largely be summarized as the analog era in which client and agency worked as a team to help define the audience in mass terms and to develop strategies and tactics through limited mediums in order to sell more products (Figure 12.1).

Marketing 2.0, the upgrade from analog to digital, is the world in which we live today. It includes interactive advertising, viral marketing, social communities, free content, and consumer-generated content. It is a world where digital interaction is king and YouTube can command $1.65 billion from Google without ever having generated a single dollar in revenue. It is complex, constantly in flux, and difficult to keep track of long enough to even get it into the marketing plan.

The Marketing 2.0 era was ushered in by the advent of the digital revolution. This world is exciting and fast-paced, where new mediums and modes of content pop up like spores in an uncontrolled environment. Consumers are exerting control over their worlds and because of technological advances are demanding brands and communication on their terms. Consumer-generated content is not just a fad, but a major part of the marketer's to-do list.

**Figure 12.1**
**Marketing 1.0**

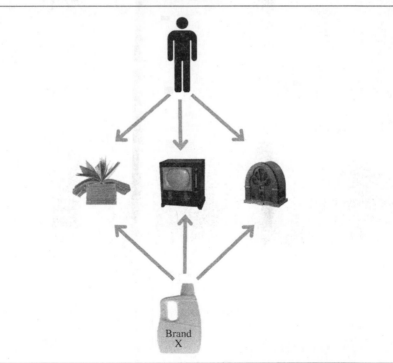

When a consumer can create a 30-second spot for the Superbowl and have it lauded as one of the best, it is time to realize that we as advertisers are no longer in control. This coupled with the fact that the ad itself cost just over $12 signals that there are no more barriers to entry in the media and content worlds.

This is a major factor in the spore-like explosion of mediums that are depicted by the gray boxes shown in Figure 12.2.

Brands, too, are experiencing change. They are seeing a far greater number of line extensions and product evolutions as they seek to keep up with the changing environment and complex consumer. In their drive to continuously reach and be relevant to their consumer, brands are spending more time segmenting their audience and defining it through not only demographic but also psychographic terms.

**Figure 12.2**
**Doritos Crash the Superbowl**

Agencies are also fragmenting. The 1990s saw the uncoupling of the media from the advertising agency. Today, there are as many types of agencies as one can imagine. These "adjective" agencies- interactive marketing, viral marketing, guerilla marketing, event marketing, permission marketing, duct-tape marketing, shopper marketing, and more all exist to help the client better reach the elusive customer.

Figure 12.3 helps to visualize the complexities that exist in the Marketing 2.0 world.

We suggest that Marketing 3.0 will be more about the network than the Internet. It will be activated by the semantic Web where information will go from silos to an intelligent knowledge network of applications and screen-based devices. No longer is the TV screen the place to watch content, or the computer screen the place to research a topic, or the mobile phone screen the place to look up a phone number and place a call. *All*

**Figure 12.3**
**Marketing 2.0**

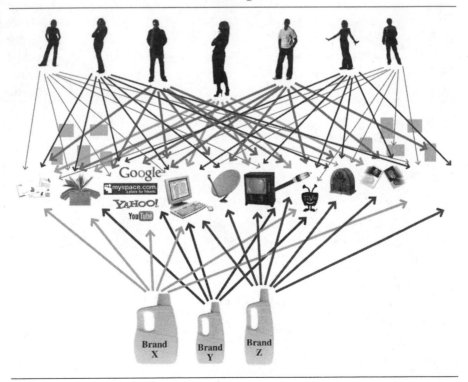

screens will offer *all* of these options. The choice of which screen to use will be up to the consumer.

In this world, there will be an artificial intelligence-driven network that will power the interactions between the screens and the data. This means that your devices could speak to one another so that you can e-mail someone about wanting to meet in the next two weeks and your computer or handheld will instantly offer up times where your calendar shows vacancies . . . without you ever asking or typing in a command. Imagine being able to plan an entire trip without having to go to multiple web sites and make multiple phone calls. The semantic Web would understand your preferences and suggest airlines (based on your Frequent Flyer preferences), hotels (based on your preferences), restaurants (based on your preferences), times for meetings and scheduling activities all on one screen at one time in a fraction of the time it takes today.

This will be a world where instead of typing in key words in a search box, you will simply be able to type in a phrase, question, or statement and the system will understand what it is you are seeking rather than simply seeking out the words that you typed.

In this world, the customer is at the center of all that we do. She is the creator and controller of her world and to be successful, we must be a part of her world by connecting to it instead of marketing at her (Figure 12.4). A recent study found that when Adidas placed content on the home page of MySpace.com, the greatest impact on customers was *not* from the individual who grabbed the content and placed it on their personal MySpace page. Instead, it was those who visited the MySpace page of the person who added the

**Figure 12.4**
**Brand, Entertainment, Fashion, Technology, Friends, and Family**

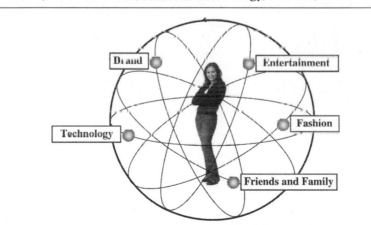

Adidas content that were the most impacted. It is the shift in thinking that will be required for marketers to succeed.

Marketing 3.0 is the space where we increasingly live today. It is somewhere between the digital revolution and the smart network. Upgrades can aid us in getting between the two points in time. To determine which upgrades are required, we must first agree on an operating system.

## MARKETING RESEARCH AND DEVELOPMENT

Research and development (R&D) departments are common in most industries and companies. What is less common is the notion of R&D in a marketing communications department. Without some commitment and structure to change and innovation within a marketing communications department, the ability to test and progress in this quickly changing landscape will be difficult. We can take some lessons from companies who have succeeded in implementing R&D as not only departments but philosophies for change and innovation into their culture. This system for R&D is the foundation for the operating system for marketing communications.

More than 100 years ago, 3M was established as a company. They established the Seven Pillars for Change that still exist as a pivotal part of their overall culture of innovation (see *BusinessWeek* online article, May 10, 2006). There are six that are particularly poignant to this discussion. The first pillar is a commitment to innovation. They believe that from the CEO on down, the company must embrace a culture of change. In fact, they dedicate 6 percent of their revenue to R&D with one-fifth of that going to "pursuits with no immediate practicality." This is a far cry from companies seeking change via the insertion of a change agent or by changing partners. A commitment to innovation exists in every facet of the company that can be recognized by its constant questioning of the status quo.

The second pillar is to tolerate mistakes. The third is innovation via a broad base of technology. In this instance, 3M is referring to their belief that companies who become unilateral in their thinking and do not apply their innovation from one realm to another typically run out of ideas quickly.

The fourth is to talk, talk, talk. By this, they mean networking in both a formal and informal manner with their researchers. The fifth is to quantify efforts. R&D is not a synonym for a slush fund. To be accepted, results must be captured and quantified.

The final pillar is to tie research to customers—a fairly straightforward mantra. There is one story that illustrates the majority of their principles as well as one of their greatest successes:

There was a researcher who participated in the church choir and recently had a failure at work. At work, he was asked to invent a super strong adhesive for paper and he was unable to perfect the adhesive, yet his "failure" was tolerated. While he was at choir rehearsal one day, he noticed that the members all marked songs in their hymnals with scrap pieces of paper that would fall to the ground periodically. This got him thinking about his recent "failure" at work. When he got back to the office, Arthur Fry applied that failed adhesive to paper and invented what we know today to be the Post-it note.®

Google, a company that is a fraction of the age of 3M also has a culture that embraces innovation and change. They, too, do this through words and through the commitment of resources. Twenty percent of their resources go to "whatever you think will most benefit Google"—this was stated in their founder's letter in the Google IPO filing. It was in this pursuit that AdSense was invented. This program has been one of their most successful inventions to date.

By approaching the marketing communications business with a disciplined structure and a resource allocation, the company will have permission to plan and strategize in a progressive fashion within the realm of the overall business. To that end, there is a perfect model for innovation that is designed for companies interested in adapting this philosophy yet requiring a slightly more measured approach to resource allocation.

We have dubbed our model, or operating system, the *70/20/10* model (Figure 12.5). The idea is best illustrated through the use of a single dollar as an investment into marketing communications. If you have $1.00 to spend on marketing, we suggest taking $0.10 and putting it toward the true R&D for marketing communications. Specifically, we suggest spending $0.01 on 10 different programs, ideas, and mediums that align with the overall strategy and goals for your organization. It is likely that one of those 10 pennies will hit on something worthy of greater analysis and review. We suggest taking $0.20, in this example, and placing it toward that one idea that showed merit and measuring its success across a broader array of products, categories, or services. This will allow the team to understand the opportunity and limitations the idea may have across the network. From there, we suggest taking that idea and placing it among the $0.70 of the planning spend which we liken to the core of the plan.

From an execution standpoint, the $0.70, or the core, is where the majority of the current marketing spend takes place and is typically managed by the advertising agency. The $0.20 and $0.10, if it is being considered at all, is typically being relegated to the interactive agency. While this may be bearing some fruit, it is our contention that the ability to stay abreast of the burgeoning

**Figure 12.5**
**Marketing 2.X**

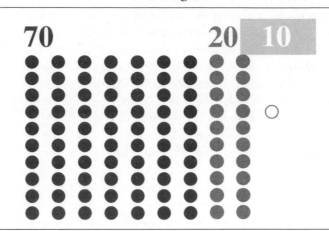

marketplace in the media and content realm is impossible for one single agency, tasked with specific interactive assignments, to successfully add to its scope.

So, you may ask, how do you find the places to spend your $0.10? We suggest an approach that is based on the Hollywood producer model.

In Hollywood, prior to the antitrust laws of the 1940s, the entire movie production system was handled within the studio. The theaters themselves, the script production, actors, producers, costume designers, set designers, and everyone else were all employed by the studio. After the antitrust laws, the studios chose to spin off the theaters and to keep the intellectual property of the movie-making business.

As the contracts for the talent began to expire, they began to unionize. From here the talent agencies were born. Producers became the people that were hired by the studios to understand the vision of the project and get the project done. They knew who to go to for the operational aspects of the production as well as the right talent to best realize the vision of the studio. In essence, they were business people who could speak the language of the studio operators as well as creative people who spoke the language of the cast and crew and they were well networked. As a result, they became the center of the entertainment world. Think Jerry Bruckheimer.

It is this combination of business and creative talent that can be applied to the 70/20/10 model. Hiring a "producer" allows the client to engage people who understand their needs and yet are networked and versed in growth areas. The producer will need to tap into that network to hire the right people for that specific task. Unlike an agency model that requires the utilization of the assets or talent already hired, this model allows for the use of free agents for a limited engagement appropriate for that need.

The hiring of these specialists can be likened to a SWAT team. SWAT teams can be defined as a small team of skilled and experienced practitioners who can pull a failing project out of the ditch. The team does not tolerate political interference as it makes decisions and takes actions to bring the project to fruition. This team will vary dependent on the need of the client and the project. The ability to hire the best team for the project will allow the client to experience new modes of execution, and results.

Another benefit of the model is that it allows the client to keep their agencies focused on the areas that they were hired for and eliminates the need to expand a scope or to hire yet another agency tasked with finding "what's new." Internally, the structured approach will likely be lauded and creating this change with people from the outside may be more readily accepted for the CMO and ultimately, less scary and threatening.

Some may argue that the advertising agency is capable of managing this R&D. This is a tall order. Agencies today realize that the world is changing but they are stuck in a Catch-22. If they reorganize or add overhead to expand their capabilities, they must either have a client willing to utilize this capability or be able to introduce it in a way that does not overtly increase the overhead and fees passed on to their existing clients. For this reason, many choose to wait for the client to push them to do this. When pushed, the agency reacts by purchasing companies that seem to fit the need (e.g., Publicis and Denuo, or WPP and 24/7 Real Media). This may solve the problem in the short term but eventually, it will be impossible to buy out all the talent and pass off the costs to clients. For this reason, we believe the producer model combined with the SWAT team is more productive and efficient.

A disciplined model such as the 70/20/10 model, allows you to tackle the marketing communications problems that face your business. It may be a far better approach that allows the organization to crawl, walk, and run without jeopardizing the culture or stability of the organization. It allows the team to approach problems in nontraditional ways, generate results, and insert some new thinking without creating a threatening environment for other departments or even the agency. At the same time, it provides access to the market at large without a commitment to a large fee structure that is not used on a daily basis.

## Compensation

Assuming you commit to a new model such as the 70/20/10 model, it will be important to ensure that the compensation plan is geared to deliver results.

Historically, agencies were paid on commission. This structure incentivized the agency to build in as much creative as they could to place it in as much media as possible. Unfortunately, in today's world, the "more everywhere" theory is neither possible nor efficient.

This model evolved to a model where the clients delivered an annual work plan by which the agency could estimate the types of people and the amount of time required to complete the task. While this system did a much better job of aligning work, it ended up commoditizing the agency personnel. Contracts became filled with full-time equivalents (FTEs) that did not differentiate talent levels by anything other than price. It placed contracts firmly in the realm of the procurement teams because it became much easier to negotiate FTEs in the same way widgets were negotiated. Agencies quickly began to play with overhead and costs in order to hide profits.

More recently, a pay-for-performance model has been implemented by companies. This system requires the client to be very specific on deliverables in a quantifiable fashion. The fees are negotiated at a fairly low rate with large upside returns based on performance reviews of the agency. Basically, the agency gets quarterly reviews with one final review based on the previously agreed-on metrics. The resulting "grade" is associated with a bonus that incentivizes the agency to be completely aligned to the client's goals and quantifiable metrics. One major concern of this model has been the client's gaming of the system. Some clients leave the metrics fuzzy so that at review time, it is easier to grant a lower grade, and therefore a lower bonus that can aid the client if they find themselves in the midst of a budget crunch.

The newest and least tested model is the intellectual property (IP) model. This model presumes that the client pays to license the IP of the agency. The agency then delivers for the client and reaps a share of the revenue derived from their implementation. This model is interesting in many ways, not the least of which is the incentive to deliver true bottom line results and to compensate the agency based on intellectual capital versus an FTE.

We believe that the R&D model can be delivered effectively through the IP model as well as the pay-for-performance model.

Once you have committed to the model, hired the producer and SWAT team, determined how to properly incentivize the team, it is time to deliver the problem or opportunity to that team. This may seem obvious but in today's complex marketing world, it seems we may have added so much fodder to our business that the real business problem is not always clear.

The normal way to engage an agency is through a marketing brief. The marketing team writes a one- to two-page brief that outlines the basics of the marketing problem or opportunity complete with the 4Ps. This is given to the agency who then translates it into a creative brief that will allow the creative team to deliver an idea that hits on the objectives.

While this system is thorough, it may be masking the real problem with additional information. Take for instance the automotive industry. It was customary to write a marketing brief for the agency several times a year asking for their "big idea" for this year's sales event. But this brief did not highlight the marketing problem and therefore did not tap into the agency's ability to actually deliver a program that could solve the problem. The brief, instead, asked for a creative solution to a tactic—the sales event. Had the agency been given a brief that said that there were 50,000 trucks, located in certain markets, that needed to be sold by a certain date, the resulting program might have been something other than a sales event. The point is best made by David Belasco, a famous playwright, director, and producer of the 1920s who said, "If you can't write your idea on the back of my calling card, you don't have a clear idea." Simplification of the problem will allow your partners to be more creative in their solutions.

The objective of this chapter has been to highlight the need for change and innovation in the world of marketing. Our contention is that the first step is recognition of that fact and the commitment to a model, specifically, the 70/20/10 model. Once this model, or operating system, has been accepted, the need to upgrade will become obvious. We have outlined five upgrades that will point you toward successfully navigating the Marketing 3.0 landscape (Figure 12.6).

By implementing these plans, the CMO can be actively participating in the media and marketing evolution instead of being left in the dust. Choosing not to participate, or to "wait and see" may well lead to consistent results but likely will not lead to improved results. Perhaps Albert Einstein said it best: "Insanity is doing the same thing over and over again and expecting different results."

**Figure 12.6**
**Marketing 2.X Upgrades**

1. What's in your 10?
2. Hire a Jerry Bruckheimer.
3. SWAT team it.
4. Work on the problem.
5. Show me the money!

# CHAPTER 13

# THE INTEGRATION OF ADVERTISING AND MEDIA CONTENT: ETHICAL AND PRACTICAL CONSIDERATIONS

RICHARD KOLSKY and BOBBY J. CALDER

**M**arketers are turning the media world upside down. Not only are they shifting billions of advertising dollars from traditional media to online and other marketing services, there is also growing interest in integrating advertising into media content. Product placements are everywhere. Advertisers are even becoming entertainment and information content providers themselves, in effect competing with traditional media companies. Anheuser-Busch has launched BudTV.com, its own online TV network; Busta Rhymes hip-hop hit boosted Courvoisier sales; Victoria's Secret produces its own TV show; and Kraftfoods.com is now the second most popular food site on the Web. These are all examples of *integration,* which is the term for the blurring of the line between media content and advertising.

Integration is more than a tactical shift in media buying. It is a different way of thinking about advertising and media. The opposite of integration might be called *separation*. For much of the past century, most companies thought about media as something you bought space or time in for an ad. The audience for a media vehicle came to it for its content. The audience was exposed to an ad simply because the ad appeared along with the content. The ad and the content were separated so that it was clear which was which. And this separation carried over into how this was all managed. Media companies produced content and marketers and agencies produced ads. The actual buying and selling of the advertising space or time was a relatively tactical matter of media planning. Separation was the dominant way people thought about advertising and media.

Integration is more than just another trend. It represents a paradigmatic shift in management thinking, a move away from separation to integration. It is also controversial. Many, particularly on the media side, still embrace separation and view integration with considerable unease. They worry that blurring the line between media content and advertising will damage the production of quality content. Beyond whether integration is practical, many worry as well about whether it is ethical. Doesn't it compromise the journalistic integrity of information providers or the artistry of entertainment providers?

There are those who strongly believe that a boundary must be drawn between content and advertising and that to blur the two is even immoral. Integration is not just wrong, it is WRONG. There is an ethical divide that should not be crossed. Many media organizations have even institutionalized this, referring to it as The Wall. In some cases The Wall has literally taken the form of walls, with content people sealed off from business people in order to avoid corruption and preserve journalistic or artistic freedom. We have often heard the story, repeated with considerable nostalgia for the good old days, that at "Colonel" McCormick's *Chicago Tribune* building there were actually separate sets of elevators for newsroom people and business people. Building Walls to keep away the business barbarians is both fact and cultural mythology in the media world.

Yet integration has its advocates and is proceeding at a breakneck pace, even if it seems driven as much by hype and circumstance as by discipline and rationality. Inevitably, the forces of creative destruction will ultimately settle the conflict between integration and separation. It would be a good thing, however, if we could avoid some of the chaos, or at least take some of the moral fervor from it. In this chapter, we try to suggest a third way, an alternative to both separation and integration. We call the alternative *collaboration*. Our contention is that it is both practically and ethically superior. We begin by putting the conflict between separation and integration into more of a historical context.

## HISTORICAL PERSPECTIVE ON ADVERTISING AND MEDIA

Tell a journalist or TV producer to incorporate advertisers' brands into the creation and delivery of their content and they will cringe before taking out the cross and the garlic. "I'll create world-class content to attract the audience, then you get the advertisers to pay for the eyeballs." The thought of a newspaper recommending books to its readers that it then tries to sell to them is anathema to the journalist. A leading newspaper in Germany, however, does just this. It is easy to jump right into an argument over cases like this. We think it helps first to look at this kind of thing in a larger historical context.

Integration has a long history. The original baseball cards were "published" by tobacco companies, soap operas were written by advertising executives, the Texaco Man was a mainstay on the Bob Hope show, and there were few bits more entertaining than watching Johnny, Ed, and Doc performing a live Smucker's commercial. Product marketers have long recognized the power of integrating advertising into the content itself. And content providers have thought that this was a good idea. Integrating advertising and media content goes way back.

Procter & Gamble (P&G) began advertising with small newspaper ads in 1838. It soon began using high-quality illustrations in emerging magazines like *Ladies' Home Journal*. In the 1920s, it turned to product-oriented radio programs such as one hosted by Emily Post on etiquette. The product was blended into the program content. But the company felt that consumers preferred dramatic content so they soon developed programs such as *Oxydol's Own Ma Perkins* and slice-of-life commercials that mimicked the dramatic content of these soap operas. "I've found a new soap called Oxydol, dear. No more backaches for me." P&G turned to TV in 1939 using the sportscaster Red Barber to advertise Ivory soap on a baseball game (Neff 2003). Soap operas like *The Guiding Light* migrated from radio to TV. The "Light" was "family" and the program famously followed life in the Bauer family. The "Light," of course, also harkens back to the company's original product, candles. Procter & Gamble Productions, Inc. still produces *The Guiding Light*. The involvement of P&G has not kept the program from being widely recognized both for the quality of its acting and writing as well as its impact on popular culture through its treatment of men's roles (Williams 2001). As of this writing, Rafe is hurt that Daisy had an abortion and didn't tell him.

Today network TV viewing is down. So P&G is turning to online with programs like *Crescent Heights*, a scripted, short video program about a young woman just starting out on a career and her circle of friends. Clothes are naturally part of the woman's life, and hence the connection to Tide. The company works closely with GoTV Networks to produce the program.

Integration is not a newcomer to journalistic content either. Consider the history of the newspaper. In the nineteenth century, newspapers were closely aligned with political parties. Political advertising was their main source of revenue. From this, newspapers evolved to be more commercial enterprises. This explains why historically newspapers turned more to targeting women and to softer features such as food, fashion, and entertainment (Baldasty 1992). In many ways, commercialization actually fostered separation. Perhaps along the way, the business side of newspapers did lessen the historical ties of a free press to the founders' concern for an educated citizenry (Starr 2004). But over the long-term, newspapers have become more independent, not less. It is the breadth of media coverage of consumer topics that invites integration. Advertorials for products like automobiles do blur the line, but this should be seen in the context of the involvement of newspapers and magazines in consumer culture themselves.

From a historical perspective, what seems to have happened is this: The past 50 years or so have been good times for both advertising and media. With baby boomers gobbling up hit TV shows like *MASH* and popular magazines like *Time,* major advertisers could afford to sit back and let the media deliver the audience. Media companies could afford to sit back and sell the eyeballs. Integration could take a bit of a holiday. All that has happened is that both the media and advertising worlds have recently gotten more complicated. With change comes a search for new ways of thinking, and quite naturally integration is back on the table. Interestingly, an early sign of this was in the late 1980s when less well-known advertisers began creating infomercials as a new way of using TV. Then in the 1990s, advertorials, advertising supplements, and product placements became popular. MTV began using music industry advertising (music videos) as content. And the integration "trend" was reborn. These days the webisode *It's a Mall World* runs on MTV as programming. It was developed by the retailer American Eagle Outfitters and is about young people who work in a mall with an American Eagle store. It is distributed not only online and on MTV but in American Eagle stores as well.

The determining factor in all this is that major advertisers increasingly recognize that information and entertainment offer more than access to eyeballs for promoting their brands. They have become an integral element of the consumer experience that defines their brands. For advertisers like Verizon and AT&T, entertainment and information content has become a major differentiator. Other brands, like Kraft, under the threat of low price competitors and margin-squeezing channels, are using homegrown publications and the Web to change the consumer's relationship with their brands, offering valuable advice and support, such as recipes and meal plans.

But many people in both advertising and media grew up with separation. To them, it seems the norm and integration is a violation of the status quo. Successes like HBO's original programming are celebrated as testament to the power of artists freed from the bounds of focus groups and advertiser demands. Journalists like Dan Neil are canonized. He is the maverick auto critic, transferred from the newsroom to the advertising department, and soon fired by the advertising manager for alienating local dealers. Cases like that of Mark Willes and the Staples chain are held up as new low points for the industry.

In historical context, however, separation is simply the main way the system worked for a number of years. In different circumstances, integration could have played a much greater role than it did. If it had, it would seem much more normal today.

None of this is to say that The Wall is not real. Many believe with high conviction that advertising should be separated from content. It should not be thought, however, that this belief is justified by the fact that separation has been the norm and that integration is an encroachment on this norm by a sinister new force. Build it (audience) and they (advertisers) will come. This was the way things mostly were for awhile, not the way they had to be.

## MOVING ON

The conflict between separation and integration should be an examined one. We need to examine the received conviction that separation is necessarily the way advertising and media ought to operate. If we maintain an open mind, there are obvious advantages and disadvantages to each. Separation has the potential advantage of allowing journalists and artists the full freedom of their craft. The disadvantage is that merely pairing advertising with this content may not optimize, or even be enough to justify, the advertising expenditure. Integration, on the other hand, has the potential advantage of leading to more powerful advertising. The disadvantage is that the integrity of the information or the quality of the artistic vision may be threatened.

The problem is this: We want high-quality content that wins Pulitzers, Emmys, and Oscars *and* advertising that maximally benefits from an atmosphere conducive to products. But does Ralph Lauren in the venerable *New York Times* "Spring Men's Fashion Supplement" help with the Pulitzer? Is there any doubt that Spike TV had beer companies in mind when it devised its current programming? Is any of it likely to win an Emmy? Both separation and integration resolve the conflict between content and advertising in the same way. Separation makes the overriding goal content. Integration makes the overriding goal advertising. Neither gives any hope of a win–win solution.

What are media companies and advertisers to do? Is there a way to preserve their integrity, delight the public, and serve their clients as well? Yes, but only by taking a fresh, consumer-driven approach to the problem, as outlined in the next section.

## A WAY FORWARD

Even if we leave behind some of the historical baggage, it still looks like we are left with something of a Hobbesian choice. If what you care about is content, there is really no choice but separation. If what you care about is advertising, there is no choice but integration. And there is no doubt in our minds that right now those disposed one way or the other, craft or business, would choose accordingly. No doubt as well that those choosing separation would feel that they have made the more ethical choice, the journalist upholding the public trust, the artist respecting their muse.

Let us suggest another way of thinking about this. Two points before we begin. One, we emphasize that we *are* concerned with the ethical considerations arising with advertising and media content. We are not trying to dodge them. We take a utilitarian approach not only because it speaks to practical considerations but also because it is one way of dealing with moral ones. One way of deciding if something is ethical is to ask if it contributes to the greater good. Something is morally justified if it contributes to the total utility of everyone involved. Second, we try to be as clear as we know how to be in spelling out our logic. The language of economics will be helpful for this reason.

Three simple principles guide our recommended approach to managing advertising and media content. We first state these, and then elaborate on them:

1. Content and advertising synergy can help consumers.
2. Content and advertising synergy can also increase the value of media content to advertisers.
3. Cooperatively tapping this synergy can increase not only consumer value, but also advertiser and media company profit potential.

### Content and Advertising Synergy Can Help Consumers

With all the talk about ad avoidance, we tend to forget that consumers actually need and value advertising as both entertainment and information. How else could we get our wives to watch the Super Bowl with us? The value to a consumer of a media and advertising experience ($V_{M+A}$) might be characterized as:

$$V_{M+A} = V_M + V_A$$

But this is a myopic view of the value of advertising to consumers, one rooted in the historical baggage that assumes that content and ads are valued independently. But who would buy *Vogue* if not for the ads? Ads make the content more valuable and the content makes the ads more valuable. We need to explicitly recognize that this synergy, or interaction, between content and advertising can be part of the value of the experience to the consumer:

$$V_E = V_M + V_A + V_{A/M}$$

Advertising, both in and of itself, $V_A$, and through synergy with content, $V_{A/M}$, contributes to the value of the consumer experience. And this total value, $V_E$, is what produces audience. Thus we have:

$$I = f(V_M + V_A + V_{A/M})$$

where I is the number of eyeballs attracted and again $V_{A/M}$ represents the synergistic effect of advertising and media content on the value of the consumer's overall experience. For example, a consumer motivated to lose weight could be better off if an ad promoting the launch of Kraft's new South Beach Diet line of products was part of an article about weight loss and diet fads. At the end of the day, the value to the consumer of their media and advertising experience depends on how well it has helped them achieve their desired outcome, be it a belly laugh or advice and support for shrinking their bellies. Of course, there is always the danger that thinly veiled attempts to tap synergies that benefit only advertisers (e.g., plugging a one-star movie on the *Tonight Show*) might create negative synergy, and our logic will allow for this.

## Content and Advertising Synergy Can Also Increase the Value of Media Content to Advertisers

Obviously, the consumer is not the only beneficiary of media experiences. The eyeballs attracted, I, are worth money to advertisers per eyeball ($W_A$). How much the advertising is worth depends not only on the stand-alone effectiveness of the ad being watched by the right eyeballs ($W_S$), but also on how well the media content experience strengthens the message being delivered ($W_{A/M}$):

$$W_A = W_S + W_{A/M}$$

where W is measured on a per-eyeball basis. The stand-alone effectiveness of the ad, $W_S$, is the analog of the ad's value to consumers, $V_A$, and likewise $W_{A/M}$ is analogous to $V_{A/M}$. Advertisers have long recognized this. Gatorade is likely to value consumers watching its commercials during the Tour d' France more than during the *Late Show* with David Letterman because consumers are more engaged by the Tour. This recognition lies at the heart of the *Good Housekeeping* model. Companies are willing to earn the seal of approval before their ads are allowed to brighten the magazine's pages because the seal is useful to *Good Housekeeping's* five million loyal monthly readers. Similarly, product placements in recipes on Rachael Ray's cooking show will likely be of greater value to advertisers (per eyeball) than those on the shelf of Rachel Green's kitchen in *Friends*. This is the engagement effect that is currently receiving considerable attention in media and advertising circles.

## Cooperatively Tapping This Synergy Can Increase Not Only Consumer Value, but Also Advertiser and Media Company Profit Potential

Using our model in its simplest sense, let's assume that the media company looks to maximize the profitability of its content ($p_M$):

$$\pi_M = P \times I - C_M$$

where P is the price per eyeball paid by advertisers, I is the number of eyeballs attracted, and $C_M$ is the cost of creating and delivering the media content (perhaps including costs supporting some higher-order social purpose). Simultaneously, the advertiser is also trying to maximize bang for their ad bucks:

$$\pi_A = (W_A - P) \times I - C_A$$

where $p_A$ is the profitability of the advertising, $W_A$ is again the worth (per eyeball) of the advertising, P is again the price paid to the media, I is again the number of eyeballs attracted, and $C_A$ is the cost of creating the advertising.

Is there a win-win solution here in which both advertisers and media companies reap maximum profits from a partnership and even consumers win, a win-win-win? Let's start with the partnership's bottom line and its joint profit, JP.

$$JP = \pi_M + \pi_A$$

or,

$$JP = P \times I - C_M + (W_A - P) \times I - C_A$$

This simplifies to:

$$JP = W_A \times I - (C_M + C_A)$$

and by substitution to

$$JP = [(W_S + W_{A/M}) \times f(V_M + V_A + V_{A/M})] - (C_M + C_A)$$

Note that the price of the advertising access drops out of the equation and simply becomes a means of dividing up the profit. You can see then that both the media company and the advertiser should be motivated to maximize the total value to the consumer, which is $(V_M + V_A + V_{A/M})$, and that this includes $V_{A/M}$ the synergistic effect of advertising and media content. The simple logic here is that more profit is created through maximizing total value to the customer. And, since the worth to the advertiser, $W_S$ and $W_{A/M}$ can only be captured when the advertising is also valuable to the consumer ($V_A$ and $V_{A/M}$), the partnership's profit ultimately depends on value to the consumer and costs. This formula indicates that there is more profit for both the advertiser and the media company to share when the value to the consumer is higher, and obviously the consumer is better off as well—a bigger pie for everyone.

There is a complication, however. We cannot assume that the synergistic effect, $V_{A/M}$, is always positive. There could be a negative synergy. This could happen for many reasons, but can be thought about this way. On any particular dimension of collaboration it is possible to go too far. If an advertiser gets too involved in the development of a movie script there may be diminishing returns, to the point that the impact of synergy on the consumer is lessened or even becomes negative. If an advertiser were to get involved in the coverage of the business section of a newspaper, the same adverse consequences might result. The advertiser might exceed its expertise in the content area or just overemphasize features that are more in their interest than in the consumers'. The notion of diminishing returns to collaboration is shown in Figure 13.1.[1]

Some degree of collaboration is in consumers' and advertisers' best interests, but eventually pushing collaboration too hard can undermine the quality of the experience and backfire. But, that does not mean that we have to ignore the existence of positive synergy. In fact, by ignoring synergies, we are hurting both the consumer and the media and advertising companies. In fact, neither

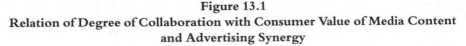

**Figure 13.1**
**Relation of Degree of Collaboration with Consumer Value of Media Content
and Advertising Synergy**

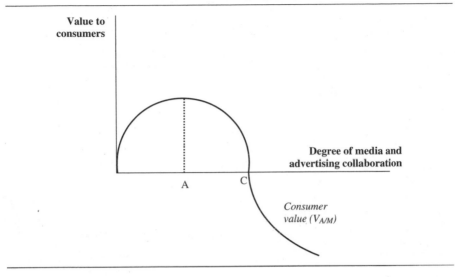

full separation nor integration best serves the interests of consumers. Collaboration makes better sense than either polar extreme.

Separation, that is, ignoring potential synergies, leaves us at point "0" in Figure 13.1, and is clearly *not* in the consumer's best interests. In fact, any synergistic collaboration up to C is more valuable to consumers than none. With a "build it and they will come" mindset, no attempt is made at creating synergy, and any synergistic value is coincidental. On the other hand, Integration ignores the legitimate point that there could be diminishing returns and even a point of negative return on the value of the consumers' experience of media content and advertising synergy.

It is also instructive to consider worth to the advertiser a little more; as noted above this may not be perfectly aligned with consumer value. In Figure 13.2, the consumer value of media content and advertising synergy is maximized at A, but combined advertiser and consumer value are maximized at point B.[2] What this means is that it is likely that advertisers would be willing to sacrifice a few eyeballs and some consumer value for more effective marketing impact. Furthermore, if advertisers focused solely on the advertising value, there is a chance that the synergy might extend beyond point B, and head into the "dissynergy zone." Therein, lies an additional problem with

**Figure 13.2**
**Relation of Degree of Collaboration with Consumer and Advertiser Value of
Media Content and Advertising Synergy**

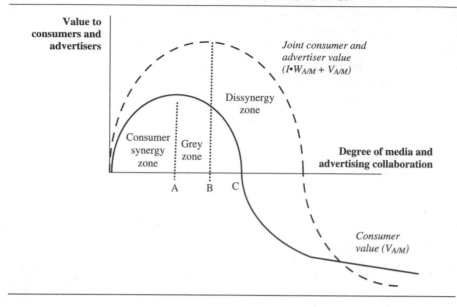

Integration—from a consumer perspective, the ideal degree of synergy is at A, whereas the joint interests of advertisers and media companies would push the synergies to B.[3] We have labeled the area between A and B the "grey zone," where, overall, media content and advertising synergy are still beneficial to consumers, but *incremental* collaboration effort detracts from consumer value while enhancing advertiser value. Collaboration points the way to both the win-win-win and the potential pitfall.

Is collaboration ethical? The answer is yes, because there is the potential for consumers, content providers, and advertisers to *all* be better off. Of course there are other ways of judging whether something is ethical or not. Perhaps the oldest is the Aristotelian way. Virtue is found in avoiding extremes. Collaboration passes this test as well. It seeks to navigate between the extremes of ignoring the value of media content and advertising synergy for consumers and going too far and risking negative impact. Another test is the Kantian "categorical imperative." Something is ethical if no one who is party to it would object to its being done. We do not see why consumers, media providers, or advertisers would object to collaboration.

We anticipate the criticism from some that our formulation rests on producing value for consumers and profit for the media company. Isn't profit what gets in the way of ethics? Should journalistic or artistic quality be subject to profit? The answer is that journalistic or artistic excellence in a company must be supported by profit. If a newspaper wants to pursue, say, public journalism (Rosen 1999), this either has to generate a profit or be absorbed as a cost covered by profit. The only alternative is to do journalism as a not-for-profit organization with other means of support. (At this writing, a group is trying to offer investigative reporting in exactly this way.) The conclusion is that by contributing to profit, collaboration is actually making more money potentially available for journalistic or artistic excellence within for-profit companies. Whether the organization expends the money for this purpose is a different question. Many (e.g., Klinenberg 2007) indict "big media" for not serving the public interest. To the extent this is true, collaboration should not be viewed as a cause of the problem. It is actually more of a solution.

## WHERE TO DRAW THE LINE

We have spelled out our argument for collaboration because we are sensitive to the views people now hold. One of us tells the story of talking to participants in a program for newspaper executives about advertising and media content. A man in the first row, immediately on grasping the subject being raised, folded his arms tightly around himself, and said with palpable conviction, "This is unacceptable to talk about!" Then there was the senior executive in a leading media planning firm that, when told that a project proposed for a major magazine company would be resisted by editors as an intrusion on The Wall, replied, "How does anybody have time to worry about that kind of thing?"

All we are really saying, of course, is that advertisers and media content providers need to have a conversation and that conversation should be about value to the consumer. Consumers experience value through content, through ads, and potentially through synergy between content and ad. If we can increase the value of the consumer experience, both the media company and advertiser are better off. As both a practical matter and an ethical matter, we should look at increasing value to the consumer through creating synergy between content and ad.

The only question is where to draw the line. We do not think that this is necessarily as difficult as it may sound. Consider Oprah's Book Club, which has done a masterful job of creating win-win-win outcomes, while preserving and perhaps even enhancing the integrity of the media enterprise. By choosing a specific book, encouraging her loyal audience to read it, and then organizing a discussion show and forum around the book, few would argue that she has not created a valuable consumer experience. Clearly, part of this is the synergistic experience between Oprah's (implicit) advertising of the book and the entertainment and information value of the show itself. The book's publishers are also big beneficiaries of this powerful endorsement (boosting sales up to 1 million copies). Interestingly, in this case the book publisher is the fortunate recipient of most of the profit, as they do not "pay" directly for the synergy, although the publishers have, at Oprah's urging, contributed more than 500,000 copies of the books to libraries and schools. So Oprah has in effect been paid and has chosen to use this profit in the public interest.

But where to draw the line? Suppose Oprah, for whatever reason, picked a really bad or inaccessible book. Consumers might well experience the synergy between her endorsement and the show in a negative way. "I expected to like this book but I don't get it and feel let down by her. I am feeling worse about myself, not better." It is easy to see in retrospect that this would cross the line. Our point is that it might be easier to see it in prospective if Oprah and the book publisher had a conversation about whether the particular book would make for a positive consumer experience. Discussion about the line becomes a key part of collaboration.

This is not to say there will not be close calls. Suppose Oprah writes a book and selects it for the club. Over the line? Maybe, maybe not. The synergy between her endorsement and the show could still be positive, contributing to a more valuable overall consumer experience. But the synergy could be negative if the endorsement made the discussion show awkward. A closer call, but still one where discussion with the book publisher would be useful. Note that, in any case, there is nothing, per se, ethically wrong with Oprah doing her own book. Everyone might potentially be better off. (You can see that it might be worth thinking a little more about the newspaper selling books.)

Focus on the consumer's experience should in itself work to keep most projects to the left (i.e., to say, the right side) of the dissynergy line (point C in Figures 13.1 and 13.2). The obesity crisis in America marches on unabated, despite the significant growth in health and fitness magazines and web sites as well as special sections in general-purpose newspapers and magazines. Perhaps consumers do not only need to be "informed," but need experiences that integrate other help and support to achieve their health and fitness objectives. Into this fray steps *Self* magazine and its "Workouts in the Park" series, a veritable cornucopia of advertiser-media synergy. Each summer, *Self* uses its brand to endorse beauty and fitness classes sponsored by major advertisers. You can attend "Buff Yoga," sponsored by Kashi, "Awesome 80s Dances" by Yoplait, or "Stunts" by Seiko. *Self* brings its competence in knowing the classes that will appeal to this audience. *Self* recruits advertisers whose products not only seek access to high-value eyeballs but whose brands receive a boost from the context and the consumer's level of engagement. Further, consumers benefit from in-context exposure to (and free samples of) products and services that can help them achieve their self-improvement objectives. The clear focus on consumer value virtually assures that this is on the left side of the line.

One useful practical guideline is for media companies to seek out and coordinate with advertisers who actually reinforce the media brand. For example, fans of CNN's Glen Beck view him as the somewhat cantankerous voice of caring Americans. Having Glen promote your product on his show has proven to be far more effective than traditional ads. But, when faced with the choice of advertising a dubious financial product for much higher CPM than for promoting Chevy trucks, Glen wisely chose Chevy, sacrificing a few pennies today in favor of the better value for consumers (and ultimately a stronger Glen Beck brand).

## THE FORK IN THE ROAD

We think advertising and media companies are fast coming to a fork in the road and, unlike Yogi, cannot just take it. There are three paths. One is pretty much the traditional status quo option: media companies maintain the Walls, keeping advertisers' paws off their information and entertainment content. We just cannot trust ourselves to stop at B, where consumers are best off; we'll fly down the slippery slope to C and beyond. Stick to your knitting and let creatives and journalists do their thing. As a result, these firms will end up contributing less to consumer value and make less money to boot.

The cost of this approach is lost opportunity. The *Friends*/Starbucks phenomenon illustrates the point. Conventional wisdom holds that the coffee shop scenes on *Friends* effectively helped fuel the Starbuckification of America. Back in 1993, before *Friends* and its coffeehouse hangout became a cultural icon, there were 272 Starbucks. By the time the first runs of *Friends* signed off, Starbucks had surpassed 8,000 locations. Both Howard Schultz of Starbucks and social scientists like Ray Oldenburg preached in the 1990s of the need for a "third place." The coffee shop on *Friends* glorified such a "third place" on the tube, while Starbucks provided the "third place" in real life, on virtually every street corner. *Friends* gave us the fantasy and Starbucks the reality. Of course, Starbucks didn't have to pay a penny for this privilege. In fact, Starbucks has been a notoriously minimal advertiser, spending just $25mm in 2002, less than 1 percent of revenue, compared to around 6 percent for McDonald's. In other words, *Friends* gave Starbucks a free ride. Not that they need the money, but hypothetically NBC could have anticipated the coffee-house effect and approached Starbucks or Caribou with a proposal.

A second path is for more and more advertisers to go it alone. For example, Kraft's longstanding reputation for comfort and easy-to-prepare foods has spawned wildly popular Kraft Foods web sites and magazines, where time-constrained cooks can quickly find tasty recipes to fit any occasion, chock full of an assortment of Kraft products. In this case, synergy abounds, as Kraft Kitchens is perceived to be a credible source of cooking information and recipes, an ideal context for promoting products.

In a similar vein, the American Girl is the synergistic hybrid child of a media and merchandiser marriage. Born as the Anti-Barbie, each $80 doll was accompanied by a book, followed by a magazine subscription, filled with how-to advice to keep her busy and happy, and advertising for more American Girl merchandise. With a profound understanding of the social connection between a nine-year-old girl and her favorite doll (collection), the product spawned new entertainment venues, such as Teas, and American Girl Place, with its musical revue and doll infirmary, all encased in a retail shell of tempting dolls, matching dresses, and assorted doll paraphernalia.

A downside of this second path, however, is that advertisers may have an incentive to waste money on less than desirable media content. For example, recent research clearly demonstrates that consumers would prefer to get their health advice from general purpose and ailment-specific web sites, rather than pharmaceutical industry ads and sites. Nevertheless, the pharmaceutical industry continues to pour money into synergy-free, warning-laden web sites. The result: confusion and over-prescription. Perhaps a little coordination with more credible information and entertainment sources might be of more value to health-concerned consumers.

Finally, there is the path we have proposed. To us, collaboration is the ideal situation where advertisers and media players cooperate to generate the greatest consumer value and share in the greatest profit. There is a line, but The Wall is gone. Media content providers and advertisers coordinate at each stage of the content generation process. They discuss the selection of content subject matter that offers the greatest value through consumer experience. In producing a new animated feature, Disney considers merchandising potential. Is this another symbol of the fall of Western Civilization with sinister commercialism trumping artist expression? Or, is this making the choice to bring even more joy to the tots of Mudville, able now to relive the joy of Snow White with seven pint-sized plastic elves? If you think toys cross the line, how about selling vegetables (which Disney is)? By excluding advertisers from programming and editorial decisions, are media companies doing consumers a disservice? Of course, this will often require a new mindset, where the purpose becomes to help consumers achieve their objectives, not simply receive the information or entertainment deemed worthy by the media.

In an ideal world, for most companies the partnership option would appear to be the clear winner. In reality, many powerful and successful media companies will continue to see collaboration as taboo. And too many advertisers may accordingly be led down the do-it-yourself path to very uneven results. Even the collaboration path will have its potholes, however. The Wall might be gone, but we still have to find the line. We need more research and a better understanding of both the benefits and costs of collaboration—for consumers, for advertisers, and for media companies. Our hope is to convince a new generation of media and advertising executives to open up the lines of communication.

## NOTES

1. Of course media content-advertising synergies are multidimensional, taking many forms, some offering more consumer value and others more advertiser value. For simplicity, we have chosen to represent synergy as one-dimensional, assuming that media companies and advertisers start with the synergies that are most beneficial to consumers.

2. Please note that we have chosen to simplify this discussion by ignoring the costs of collaboration and by assuming that consumer value is directly proportional to content value to media companies ($I \times P$).

3. Further, there is a chance the B might lie in the dissynergy zone, beyond C.

## REFERENCES

Baldasty, Gerald. 1992. *The commercialization of news in the nineteenth century.* Madison: University of Wisconsin Press.

Klinenberg, Eric. 2007. *Fighting for air: The battle to control America's media.* New York: Metropolitan Books.

Neff, Jack. 2003. Procter & Gamble Company. In *The advertising age encyclopedia of advertising.* Vol. III, ed. John McDonough and Karen Egolf, 1270–1279. New York: Fitzroy Dearborn.

Rosen, Jay. 1999. *What are journalists for?* New Haven: Yale University Press.

Starr, Paul. 2004. *The creation of the media.* New York: Basic Books.

Williams, Carol. 2001. Guiding Light. In *The guide to United States popular culture*, ed. Ray Browne and Pat Browne, 351. Madison, WI: Popular Press.

# About the Contributors

**S**cott Berg is the Director of Worldwide Media at Hewlett Packard. His role is strategic and tactical leadership for the company's global media investment. Berg has a wide marketing background including: brand, direct response, database marketing, media, advertising, and emerging technology. Berg holds a BBA in Finance/Economics and an MBA from Wichita State University and is a frequent contributor to numerous media, marketing, and business publications.

**Bobby J. Calder** is the Charles H. Kellstadt Distinguished Professor of Marketing and Professor of Psychology at the Kellogg School of Management, Northwestern University. He is also a Professor of Journalism in the Medill School of Journalism. His work is primarily in the areas of marketing strategy, advertising, media, and the psychology of consumer behavior.

**Clarke L. Caywood** is Professor of Integrated Marketing Communications and Director of the Graduate Program in Public Relations in the Medill Graduate School at Northwestern University. He is the editor of the *Handbook of Strategic Relations and Integrated Communications*. In 1999, he was named by *PRWeek* as one of the 100 most influential public relations practitioners of the twentieth century, and in 2000 one of the top 10 outstanding educators. He was also named Educator of the Year by the Public Relations Society of America in 2002–2003. He is publisher of the *Journal of Integrated Marketing Communications*.

**Daniel Diermeier** is the IBM Distinguished Professor of Regulation and Competitive Practice and Director of the Ford Motor Company Center for Global Citizenship at the Kellogg School of Management, Northwestern University. He is also a Professor of Political Science in the Weinberg College of Arts and Science. His work is primarily in the areas of corporate reputation and crisis management, stakeholder management, business and politics, and strategic aspects of corporate social responsibility.

**Richard I. Kolsky** is Senior Lecturer of Management at the Kellogg School of Management, Northwestern University, and President of Kolsky & Co., a management consultancy dedicated to helping companies take marketing to the bottom line. His research and consulting work is primarily in the areas of marketing strategy, distribution channel management, and innovation.

**David le Brocquy** is a Director of VISION Consulting, a Dublin-based consultancy. He is a thought leader and leading practitioner of commitment-based design. He works globally with 1,000 clients, mainly in financial services and utilities. He regularly guest lectures at the London Business School. The designs le Brocquy develops with clients provide them with authentic communication with customers that significantly enhances brand promises and top- and bottom-line returns.

**Angela Y. Lee** is the Mechthild Esser Nemmers Professor of Marketing at the Kellogg School of Management, Northwestern University. Lee's research interests include consumer learning, conscious and unconscious influences of memory on judgment and choice, motivation and goals, affect and emotions, and cross-cultural consumer psychology.

**Edward C. Malthouse** is the Theodore R. and Annie Laurie Sills Associate Professor of Integrated Marketing Communications at the Medill School of Journalism, Northwestern University. His work is primarily in the area of database marketing, media marketing, and advertising. He is an editor of the *Journal of Interactive Marketing*.

**Claudio Marcus** is Executive Vice President of Market Development at Visible World, an award-winning technology firm at the forefront of video advertising innovation. His prior experience includes work with world-renowned brands as an industry analyst, marketing director, database marketing consultant, and advertising agency executive. Marcus is also a graduate of the Kellogg School of Management at Northwestern University.

**James Newcomb** is a Senior Manager in the Brand Management and Advertising Department at the Boeing Company, where he leads the company's global corporate identity program. He is also a graduate of the Kellogg School of Management.

**Julie A. Roehm** is an expert in marketing and media with a special interest in emerging media and progressive marketing platforms. She has an MBA from the University of Chicago and a Civil Engineering degree from Purdue University. She has led the marketing and communications functions at Ford, Chrysler, and Wal-Mart and is currently a marketing consultant for several media, new technology, agency, and telecommunications companies. She has been much lauded for her work including being named a Marketing All-Star 2004 by *Automotive News,* and Automotive Marketer of the Year by *Brandweek.*

**Michelle Roehm** is an Associate Professor and the Board of Visitors Fellow in Marketing at the Babcock Graduate School of Management, Wake Forest University. Her research and teaching interests include branding, marketing communications, and consumer behavior. She is a graduate of the Kellogg School of Management.

**Michael Schreiber** is the Director of Business Development for NBC Universal's Digital Distribution Division. He manages the wireless, online, and emerging platforms efforts for NBC Universal with a focus on developing new content businesses and partnerships. He holds an MBA from the Kellogg School of Management at Northwestern University, and an undergraduate degree from the McIntire School of Commerce of the University of Virginia.

**Charles Spinosa** is a Group Director at VISION Consulting, a Dublin-based, international consultancy. He leads VISION's marketing practice and delivers innovations in service, customer understanding, and communication with customers. He helps clients bring their brand promises to life and drive financial value through loyalty and word-of-mouth growth. His clients are mostly global 1,000 clients in financial services, manufacturing, telecommunications, media, and life science industries.

**Alice M. Tybout** is Harold T. Martin Professor of Marketing at the Kellogg School of Management, Northwestern University. She also is Director of the Consumer Marketing Strategy Program and Co-Director of the Kellogg on Branding program at Northwestern University's executive education center, the James L. Allen Center. Her work focuses on issues related to consumer psychology and brand positioning and strategy.

**James G. Webster** is a Professor of Communication Studies and former Senior Associate Dean at Northwestern University's School of Communication. His work is primarily in the areas of audience measurement and audience behavior. He has been on the Editorial Board of the *Journal of Broadcasting and Electronic Media* since 1985.

# INDEX

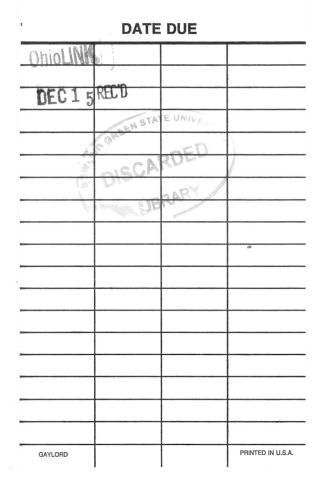